We've Only Just Begun

Van Pelt Seminar Workshops available:
The Compleat Marriage
The Compleat Parent
The Compleat Courtship

For further information contact the author by writing to:
Better Living Programs, Inc.
P.O. Box 1119
Hagerstown, MD 21741

The exercises and projects used in this book on pages 28, 43, 48, 57, 60, 65, 77, 79, 89, 96, 97, 109, 119, 134, 141, 157, 165, 168, 182, 187, 208, 211, and 216 have been adapted from *The Compleat Courtship Workbook* and are copyrighted © 1984 by Nancy Van Pelt and are used with permission.

Library of Congress Cataloging in Publication Data
Van Pelt, Nancy L.
    We've only just begun.

    Bibliography: p. 223
    1. Courtship—United States. 2. Dating (social customs) 3. Marriage—United States. I. Title.
HQ801.V32   1985   646.7'7   85-11981

We've Only Just Begun

A Guide to Successful Courtship

Nancy Van Pelt

Published jointly by
REVIEW AND HERALD® PUBLISHING ASSOCIATION
Washington, DC 20039-0555 / Hagerstown, MD 21740

PACIFIC PRESS PUBLISHING ASSOCIATION
Boise, ID 83707 / Oshawa, Ontario, Canada

Dedication

To my sons Rodney and Mark, who yet have the opportunity to make that final choice. And to Cheryl, Pam, Susan, Karen, Sherry, JoAnn, Lois, Amy, Helen, Barbara, Joan, Ann, Cathy, Debbie, Linda, Jean, Carol, Judy, Diane, Esther, Chris, Mary Lou, Lisa, Ana, Cindy, Lorraine, Connie, Beth, Jackie, Marilyn, Beverly, Jane, Denise, Norma, Pearl, Stacy, Gigi, Jennifer, Lizzie, Bill, Tom, Richard, Tim, Larry, Frank, Dan, Scott, Herb, Tony, George, Michael, Harry, Jeffrey, Fred, Paul, Charlie, Jim, David, Norm, Bruce, Randy, Marvin, Brian, Jerry, Matthew, John, Bob, Ed, Phillip, Bert, Al, Steven, Art, Keith, Neal, Walter, Ron, Skip. And to all young people who wish to make their marriages better than ours—and you have a long way to go!

Text copyright © 1982 by
Nancy Van Pelt
Illustrations copyright © 1985
by Review and Herald Publishing Association
ISBN 0-8280-0306-8

Printed in U.S.A.

Foreword

It has only been in the past fifteen years that we have had several significant books and related material written for couples who are serious in preparing for their marriage relationships. I am delighted to say that *We've Only Just Begun*, by Nancy Van Pelt, is going to be a very welcome addition to the resources that are already available. This particular material combines a sense of realism with practical suggestions and applications for the couple who will be working through these issues together.

The style in which it is written, as well as the author's sensitivity to the issues of life and marriage, makes it a book that should strike a responsive chord in couples who are reading it on their own, as well as for teachers who would like to use it as a text in their classes.

Careful thought and consideration has been put into the content. I believe that couples reading *We've Only Just Begun* will find themselves much better prepared for their marriage and will probably want to refer to the material following the wedding ceremony.

H. Norman Wright

Acknowledgments

Although this book springs from my own knowledge regarding interpersonal relationships and a vast amount of research into the subjects presented, I am particularly indebted to:

Judy S. Coulston, an inimitable friend whose joy in Jesus, profound perceptions and creative ideas have made her an indispensable source. In all her endeavors she is a precious servant of the happiest magnitude.

Diane DeVries, home economist, teacher, and friend, who evaluated the manuscript and gave valuable suggestions from an educator's point of view.

Jo Ann Hobbs, my close friend, who read the manuscript and shared with me insights from a parent's perspective.

Paul R. Madsen, M.D., associate clinical professor at the University of California, San Francisco, department of obstetrics and gynecology, who provided technical advice.

All the colleges and students who were brave enough to risk anonymous participation in the survey so that I might have candid, firsthand information.

Preface for Young People

This past week Harry and I presented a Compleat Courtship Seminar for high school students. During our four days on campus, we talked with many troubled teenagers: a young woman who wanted help in deciding which of two young men she was in love with; a black fellow who was concerned about a serious dating relationship he had with a white girl; a 17-year-old who showed extreme jealousy when her boyfriend talked with other young ladies; both partners in a steady relationship of two years who wondered if they should date others before marrying; a 17-year-old girl two weeks out of an abortion clinic who realized that she is a prime candidate for repeated abortions. A multitude of other teens had questions about dating, breaking up, and how to recognize true love.

Questions, questions, questions. Thousands of questions. Every response must be individualized for each relationship. Dating is more complicated now than ever before. Every couple must make complicated decisions dependent on many factors. Where can young people turn for answers? While shopping in Fresno Bible House recently, I overheard a woman ask the clerk for any books dealing with dating. She needed a gift for a friend's son. The clerk shook his head and apologized because there wasn't much of a choice.

Before attempting to write this book, I decided I'd better find out what questions you were asking and what areas of dating and courtship troubled you the most. Consequently I designed and administered an anonymous survey to hundreds of teenagers. I didn't want to answer questions you aren't interested in! This book, then, addresses these issues in a very open and practical way.

As a marriage specialist, I deal with marriage problems each day. On every side I see couples suffering from heartache, hurt, and disappointment. Their dreams for a happy marriage have not materialized. Every year the divorce rate rises. Meanwhile few people are making any serious attempt to help young people sort out all the decisions that should be made during courtship. Society centers its efforts on helping save marriages already on the brink of disintegration. We seem to forget that while we are saving one group from disaster, another is rapidly progressing toward it!

I wish to raise my voice in protest against the foolish way marriage is approached in the world today. In this book I propose a plan to help you avoid the mistakes repeated by thousands before you. Drawing on my personal knowledge of what contributes to marital success, as well as the experience of other authorities, I cover every subject I feel is vital to your dating and courting future.

It is my desire to present the information in an open and forthright manner so that you will be able to make intelligent choices throughout your dating years. And as your field of choice narrows down to the one person you are considering seriously, I want you to be able to recognize any danger signals early so that you can avoid disaster. Today we are intelligent enough to put men on the moon and fly a space shuttle, launching and retrieving spaceships while anticipating and averting all hazards that might destroy the venture. Surely it should not be beyond our ability to devise a plan for courtship that will significantly reduce the level of risk as a couple advances toward marriage.

My plan has two phases. *We've Only Just Begun* offers information on the various aspects of dating, love, sex, mate selection, and engagement. It provides a unique opportunity to find this much vital information within one book. You might be tempted, however, to read the information superficially. Consequently, the second phase is necessary—that of helping you evaluate yourself, your partner, and your relationship. This second phase will help you dispel any distorted romantic notions you may have about your current relationship. You must be able to evaluate whether you possess the degree of emotional maturity necessary to meet the thousands of minor and major crises you might encounter in the future.

As many of the dating and marriage guidelines as possible have been incorporated into this book. The evaluation will take place as you thoughtfully complete the exercises and projects in the companion workbook. I urge you to share copies of these books with every young person possible. Even then it will be up to each person to carefully and prayerfully read the books and evaluate what it is that he or she wants from each dating relationship.

In a very real way many marriage failures are really courtship failures. I don't want this to happen to you. It is my prayer that with the help of this book you will be able to face reality before you marry.

Preface for Significant Others

A preface allows the author to explain how a book came to be and the purpose for writing it. The Preface for Young People has partially fulfilled this design. However, I feel that many parents, teachers, pastors, and other adults will also read a book of this nature. They will attempt to "check out" the material before allowing or encouraging their young people to read it. Therefore, I must separately address this audience.

The incompetent way that we adults have allowed our young people to drift toward marriage through their dating years overwhelms me. We take to the sidelines as our young people move closer and closer to their life commitment. We tend to view it all though rose-colored glasses. With tear-filled eyes we watch as our precious young people float down the aisle to make solemn commitments to each other in the presence of God. We give hearty send-offs that often involve vast sums of money. *Yet we make no serious attempts to enlighten the couple about the life-changing commitment they are making.* We spend thousands of dollars and invest months of planning for a wedding ceremony that ends in a couple of hours, but we leave the outcome of the marriage to chance!

This book is an attempt to end such a foolish way of allowing young people to enter marriage. In it I openly and realistically address some very threatening subjects. I have not wanted to preach or moralize. Instead, the book presents information and facts in an open discussion of the pros and cons of the subject at hand.

I request any adult reader who may have grave concerns about the morality of young people to read with an open mind—open to the possibility that more good may be accomplished by informing young people of the facts than by keeping them ignorant. While young people read this book, we should not stand by, preaching and moralizing but praying that the Holy Spirit will guide and direct them during the decision-making process.

We may have our values firmly entrenched and defined regarding moral issues, but young adults are in the throes of searching for their values. It is one of the objectives of parenthood to train and instill proper dating and moral values. But logic, preaching, and moralizing carry little weight with young people and may turn them off. The best ways to teach during this critical period is through "modeling" appropriate behavior and providing teenagers with opportunities to grow.

Young people are searching for answers—for answers to many of the subjects discussed in this book. As you read you may dispute my motives, disagree with my logic, and question my openness. At times you may even wish to hide certain sections from your teenagers. But to deny them the opportunity to receive the vital pros and cons of these subjects will not ensure purity. It may, however, ensure that they will go to less reliable sources for their information. It may force them to seek counsel from those whose moral values are not solid or based on Biblical principles. It may force them to approach decisions ill-prepared. It may bring them to the point of decision without helping them think through the consequences of their choices.

So very humbly I ask you to pray with me that when our young people read this book they will be eager to acquire the information given and that the Holy Spirit will provide them with the wisdom to make proper decisions.

From Cover to Cover

THE
FIRST WORD

You come to
adulthood searching
for ways of building
successful relationships
with members of the
opposite sex. Remember,
half the fun
is getting there.
Ready,
Set,
Go!

Chapter 1

The Launching Pad

The young couple in the counselor's office had not yet celebrated their first wedding anniversary, and already they found themselves quarreling frequently. Just eight months earlier 19-year-old Sharon had made a stunning bride. Now, she fought back the tears, but they spilled anyway. "Marriage is so different than I thought it would be," she sobbed.

Roger, her husband, was equally disturbed and resentful as he spoke. "Sharon began to change right after the wedding," he began with evident bewilderment. "Before marriage we agreed on everything and could talk about anything. But that came to a rapid halt the minute we got back from our honeymoon. I've tried to bring up our problems for discussion, but she fights all my suggestions, cries a lot, and refuses to talk about changes that need to be made. Our relationship isn't at all what I had hoped it might be. Where do we go from here?"

What shattered the dreams of this young couple? Before the wedding each envisioned what married life would be like. Roger pictured himself in the starring role of strong husband. He fantasized about the many love scenes he would stage. He dreamed of the pleasure and satisfaction his marriage would give him. He had visualized the scenes many times in his mind. From the moment he said, "I do," he began to

---

Chapter at a Glance

I. **People's Expectations Differ**
   A. The husband's expectations
   B. The wife's expectations

II. **When Expectations Differ**
   A. Misunderstandings arise
   B. Disappointments come
   C. Incompatibility surfaces

III. **Prospects for Marital Success**
   A. The prospects get weaker year by year
   B. Divorce statistics are astounding

   C. Marital satisfaction declines

IV. **Why Marriages Fail**
   A. There are many reasons
   B. Lack of preparation is a key factor

V. **Marriage Is Demanding**
   A. It calls for knowledge
   B. It calls for effort
   C. It calls for maturity
   D. It calls for patience
   E. It calls for outside guidance
   F. It calls for outside support

play the part for which he had been rehearsing.

His script had included a wife in the plot, and he had chosen Sharon to play the part. But Sharon had never seen Roger's script. Therefore she never learned the part he expected her to fill. She had studied to play another character—quite different from the one Roger expected. Naturally her script read differently because someone other than Roger had written it. Her script comprised all the memories and happenings from her childhood to the present.

Roger's father was from the old school, and he ran a tight ship. Roger's mother willingly took a back seat and was totally dominated by a world of men. Roger and his brother quickly learned that when their mother disciplined them, they could go to Father for a strong defense. He usually sided with them against Mother, and if she dared to utter any rebuttal he would say, "We'll not discuss this any further," and give a look that silenced her for hours.

This was how Roger's script read, the script he'd been rehearsing for twenty years. He had carefully observed how a husband acts, and that's just the character type he'd play after he married. Now he had stepped onto the stage, but things were not going well.

Other factors also influenced Roger's

performance. He had picked up additional ideas for his script from television, books, uncles, teachers, church, and other sources. All his life he had been unconsciously collecting and storing information about how a husband acts. In addition, he had constructed a picture of how his wife would act. But Sharon resembled his ideal in looks only. She was tall and willowy. Infatuation had glossed over the noticeable differences.

Sharon had always wanted to play the part of a wife, but not the type Roger's mother played! Sharon had not been raised in that kind of home. Her mother was hardly the timid junior partner who obeyed orders from a dictator. Instead she was an efficient homemaker who had a part-time business career of her own. Sharon's father left the management of the home and children to his wife while he busied himself earning a living, enjoying sports, and participating in service projects. Sharon had been a good understudy. Now that she had a home of her own, she knew exactly how a good wife acts and what was required of her. Prior to marriage she hadn't entertained the slightest doubt about her ability to star in her role as queen of the home. She'd prove her ability as soon as she had her chance.

But now that the opportunity had come, the production was proceeding with difficulty. Roger's refusal to act the part that everyone knows a good husband is supposed to act complicated matters. "Everything I do seems to irritate him," Sharon mused as she dabbed at her tears again. "He tries to boss me around. He wasn't like that before we were married."

Of course Roger wasn't like that before marriage, because he wasn't yet acting the part of husband. He was still playing the role of sweetheart. He stopped playing sweetheart and began playing husband the day he marched Sharon down the aisle of the church. Now he was desperately trying to play the character for which he'd prepared but which he'd never had a chance to play except in his imagination.

Within eight months Roger and Sharon sought professional counseling to solve what they termed "incompatibility."

Incompatibility! Any couple might be incompatible when they don't know what they are doing. And this happens far too often with young people today. They are not being prepared for dating, courtship, or marriage. The little preparation they do get will never suffice. So young people do the best they can—stumbling along—hoping, dreaming, and praying that somehow everything will turn out all right.

But this isn't good enough. It wasn't good enough for Roger and Sharon. They were not incompatible. They were ignorant! They had proceeded toward marriage with romantic notions about what it takes to live together as husband and wife. All the while they made no serious attempt to find out what it would take on their part to achieve a compleat marriage.

The prospects for success in marriage get weaker every year. One out of three Americans who marry will get divorced in less than a dozen years. At the time of this writing the national divorce rate for first marriages is nearly 41 percent, and the trend toward higher divorce rates sweeps the globe. The United States has the dubious distinction of leading the world in broken marriages. Yes, the U.S. is number one in something! And the picture is no better for second marriages. More than 60 percent of those end in divorce.

In addition to today's high divorce rate, many marriage partners, as the years pass, find less happiness in marriage rather than more. The curve of satisfaction in marriage shoots downward rather than upward over the span of married years.

Presenting such information may seem like a strange way to begin a book about dating, courtship, and marriage. However, we must face the facts. During the past twelve years, I have spent many hours with couples in distress. I am well aware of the many pitfalls in marriage, but this awareness of marital problems does not embitter me against marriage. God forbid! It has, however, impelled me to write this book and get it into the hands of serious-minded young people who wish to avoid such pitfalls. The magnificent institution of marriage offers tremendous rewards if we enter

"Do you, Bill and Sherry, solemnly vow—genuinely promise, Boy Scout's honor, really truly promise without having your fingers crossed—that you will put up with each other and not run off to Mexico for a quick divorce the first time you shout at each other? Say 'I do.' "

into it wisely.

Why do so many marriages fail? There are many reasons, but the main reason is a lack of preparation. As I deal with couples in the throes of marital distress two feelings engulf me—compassion and anger. I feel compassion because they have not discovered their dreams for a mutually satisfying relationship. I feel anger because of their ignorance regarding the complexity of the task. And when I think of society's complacency, which allows such ignorance to burgeon, the waste of human resources that

it breeds appalls me. These families could be using their time and talents for the betterment of society.

Our educational system provides adequate input regarding the responsibilities of citizenship and choosing a vocation, so we are well prepared there. We learn about values, standards, and ideals in our homes. Our churches prepare us for a purposeful life, but we allow our young people to remain unprepared for marriage and parenthood.

Every couple needs to see marriage as a

task—difficult to attain, but not unattainable. If you drift into marriage, thinking that marriage will provide your lifelong quest for lasting bliss, you are being unrealistic. If you feel that "our love will take care of everything that stands in our way," you have a dangerous philosophy. And if you say, "Hold it! I'm not thinking of marriage—only dating and a little fun," you have not matured sufficiently to realize that your dating patterns set the stage for marriage. *You will not marry someone you have not dated.*

Marriage is demanding. It calls for knowledge, combined with effort and maturity and patience, in order to achieve the rewards it offers. It also requires outside guidance and support.

An educator, Dr. R. R. Bietz, checked a college bulletin and found an abundance of courses listed from which a young person could choose. They ranged in scope from topology to mammology. Of the 844 courses listed, however, only ten had anything to do with the family, and none of these were compulsory. Dr. Bietz asked: "How many of our youth go through college studying about the behavior of rats and lizards, but fail to learn about the behavior of two people called husband and wife?"

Someone else has noted that we send children to school for ten to fifteen years so they can learn a vocation. Yet we teach them practically nothing about marriage, which is far more important than any profession.

No one should enter marriage without a series of effective studies on marriage and the interpersonal relationships that lead to marriage. Even this will probably not turn the tide of divorce sweeping the world, but at least it is a start in the right direction. A six-to-eight-week period of premarital guidance by the couple's pastor would prove very helpful. Those who have taken such preparation have much lower divorce rates.

In reviewing other materials on the market about dating and courtship, I found that many authors are largely out of touch with what young people want to know. I remember, too, what I read during my teens on the subject. It gave a few facts—barely. In order to find out what I really wanted to know, I had to sift through a lot of dull and boring reading. This was, and is, particularly true about books that deal with sex for young people. How I wanted to know the facts about this important subject! If I could find such a book, it either dealt with the subject in such clinical terms that I could only vaguely understand it or was so vague it didn't answer my questions.

Books are often like that. Maybe that's why young people have almost given up reading books about dating, courtship, and sex. I hope this book will indeed answer the questions the present generation is asking. To make sure I could and would do that, I have surveyed several high schools and colleges with a questionnaire on the subject. I will refer often to the results of the survey. And many times I will let the young people say it themselves in their own words, because they do it so "straight" and so well.

You can never experience
a true love relationship
with someone else
unless you first take care
of any self-accepting
problems within you.

Chapter at a Glance

I. **Life's Three Greatest Decisions**
  A. The role of religion
  B. Choice of an occupation
    1. Vitally important
    2. Brings rewards or frustrations
  C. Selection of a marital partner
    1. Most people marry
    2. A poor choice spells disaster

II. **Self-image Is Important**
  A. Do you hate yourself?
  B. What does it mean to like yourself?

C. Self-respect frees you
  1. to be tolerant of others' weaknesses
  2. to appreciate others' differences
  3. to accept God's acceptance
D. What happens when you dislike yourself?
  1. You erect false fronts
  2. You become oversensitive
  3. You daydream a lot
  4. You are less efficient
  5. You rehash the past
  6. You criticize others

Chapter 2

Making Friends With Yourself

Buford loved to swim. Luckily, his home had a built-in swimming pool. In fact, his home was one large swimming pool—a pond. Buford, you see, was a pudgy, bulgy-eyed frog.

Buford recognized that he wasn't much to look at, so he spent most of his time hiding among the slippery weeds that thrived along the edges of his pond. Usually only the tip of his nose and his big round eyes protruded from the water. And whenever anyone neared the pond, Buford would croak in alarm and plunge out of sight into the deeper water. He really was quite bashful. Maybe he felt self-conscious because of the brown birthmarks that

mottled his green skin.

The other frogs would have little to do with Buford. They had their own circle of froggy friends, but Buford was never included. How he hated his lonely existence! He felt homely, mucky, creepy, sluggish, and dull. Sometimes he even felt like a retard. As a result, he spent his time sitting in the shallows, where he could watch the other frogs having a fun time as they leaped from pad to pad. Buford, the friendless frog. As a frog he was a washout!

On certain days when the sun's rays would drench the area with radiant heat, Buford would rivet his courage together and sunbathe high and dry on an exposed

III. **Consequences of a Poor Self-concept**
   A. It limits your capacity to love
   B. It influences your choice of a mate
   C. It influences the future of your children
   D. It affects your sex life
   E. It may cause you to resist authority
   F. It hinders genuine friendship
   G. It diverts your attention to false goals
   H. It hinders spiritual growth

IV. **Mechanisms People Hide Behind**
   A. Cover-ups
   B. Denial of reality
   C. Conformity
   D. Withdrawal
   E. Fighting

V. **Learn to Like Yourself**
   A. Make an inventory
   B. Rebuild your thought patterns
   C. Compensate for weaknesses
   D. Develop admirable qualities
   E. Don't compare self with others
   F. Give yourself to others
   G. Seek God's help

surface. He couldn't laze around for long, of course, or else he would quickly dry up and turn hard and brittle. And too much sun caused his birthmarks to darken. But still it felt mighty nice to loll in the sunshine once in a while, even if he had to do it all by himself.

One warm summer day Buford lazily stretched himself out on a large lily pad. As the heat washed over his cold, slimy body, the lounging Buford drowsed into a lackadaisical mood.

Suddenly Buford heard footsteps on the bank. Lethargically he rolled his eyes toward the sound, and Buford's little heart started thumping inside his chest. He caught a glimpse of a beautiful young woman. Never had those frog eyes of his focused on such an enchanting person. Her beauty absolutely captivated him.

"Hi, there," this beauteous vision said. "What's your name?"

Buford couldn't even find a raspy croak with which to respond.

"Let's be friends," this charmer invited as she splashed her way into the water toward little Buford. Her beauty so transfixed him that he forgot how to jump! She scooped

him into her hand and lifted him up to eye level. Buford could tell that she was a princess—no doubt about it.

"Want a kiss?" she asked. And without waiting for Buford to respond, she pressed her lips to the very tip of his nose. Buford felt ecstatic.

But when she gently lowered him to the water, his old reflexes took over, and he vaulted from her hand. With a plop he splashed into the pond and disappeared. With powerful strokes of his hind legs Buford swam to the surface. When he poked his head out of the water, he heard her promise in musical tones, "I'm coming back to see you tomorrow. I like you."

At first Buford felt so excited he didn't think he could wait for tomorrow to arrive. But then his cynicism took over. Why should such an exquisite young woman show an interest in *him*—a homely old frog?

But true to her word, the enchantress returned the next day. In fact, she came daily with a kiss and kind words for Buford, who felt flattered with all the attention.

Buford didn't realize it, but the affections of this lovely person caused a metamorphosis to take place in his life. No longer did he relish living in the murky pond waters. No longer did he hop about on all fours. No longer did those large brown blotches blemish his complexion. Buford left his froggy feeling behind and turned into a handsome prince!

Perhaps you remember from childhood days a variation of this tale. Many versions exist. Most emphasize the transforming power of love as symbolized by the kisses of the beautiful maiden.

I suppose one could draw many morals from such a parable. Some of the lessons could be spiritual, some social. It is important for us to recognize that we do have the capacity to build up each other and put each other back together again. But I want to take this one step further.

Life's Three Greatest Decisions

Every young person must face three big decisions. Likely you are facing one or more of them right now. They are: What place will religion have in my life? What vocation shall

I choose? and Whom will I eventually marry? We have to make these serious decisions at a relatively early age, usually between the ages of 18 and 22. These decisions weigh heavily on you, because their consequences will follow you the rest of your life. Let's take a look at these issues one by one.

What place will religion have in my life? Whether you realize it or not, you have already begun to choose the central point around which your life will rotate. Since you cannot serve two masters, you will have to choose between God or Satan. If you have absorbed spiritual values in your childhood, you will probably make God your major focus. If you have had negative input and have been brought up by hypocritical or legalistic parents, you might be fighting what you know is right. If you have chosen pleasure as your major thrust, then your life will be far different from the one committed to value and purpose. This first decision, then, determines the other two choices in life.

What vocation shall I choose? The choice of an occupation, whether it be as an engineer or a homemaker, is of vital importance because we spend so many hours a day engaged in the chosen vocation. If your lifework fails to challenge you and bring you the rewards you hoped for, you will find yourself sentenced to years of boredom, frustration, and unhappiness.

Whom shall I marry? Studies indicate that 9.5 out of every ten Americans marry. The consequences of this decision dictate with whom you will spend your entire adult years in the most intimate relationship known to men and women. This person will become your partner in rearing your children and will share every level of your life. A poor decision here could spell disaster not only for you, but also for your spouse, your family, and your friends. It can be even more tragic if you enlarge your family with children.

One thing seems clear, then. A poor choice on any one of these three major decisions will lessen your chances for happiness and self-fulfillment.

Have you been daydreaming about finding your "prince" or "princess" in the near future so that you can drop out of school and stop worrying about your problems, or so you can settle down in your own private world? Many people expect marriage to resolve all life's problems. After all we feel alone in a big world. We can go about in a depersonalized world only for so long without identifying a personal niche in the scheme of life. By finding a partner to love and to share life with, we escape for a time from grappling with life's problems. At least we matter to one other person! We grasp—blindly at times—for such a relationship because it seems to provide the obvious answer to the dilemma we find ourselves in. Falling in love holds tremendous attraction for millions. Thousands wait in anxious anticipation for love to hit so they can escape from their problems.

But don't count on your dreams and expectations to take care of the future. Instead, carefully look at the present, especially at your own feelings of worth before you oversell the future. What kind of person are you realistically? What makes up the whole of you? What goals, values, and beliefs do you hold? Where are you going? Are you in control of your life, or do others control it? Can you be responsible for your own actions? Can you trust your own feelings? Do you resist taking a good hard look at your life to see if you need to make some changes? Is something or someone preventing you from being the person you'd like to be?

Who and what you are predetermines your search for the answers to these questions. If you feel like a frog, you will make froggy decisions. If you feel like a prince or princess, then you will much more likely make intelligent choices regarding life's three greatest decisions. You see, being ready for dating and courtship begins, first of all, with you. If you have never learned to like yourself, your chances for love are very slim. Every young person needs, then, a healthy perspective on him/herself. Unless you like yourself, you are neither capable of making intelligent decisions nor ready to form a romantic relationship with another.

Self-esteem Evaluation

A positive self-esteem is essential to forming solid friendships with members of the opposite sex. By determining your current degree of self-esteem, you can then determine what time and effort will be needed to improve it. In order to obtain an indication of your current feelings of worth, score the following statements as follows:

"0" If not true   "2" If largely true
"1" If somewhat true   "3" If true

SCORE STATEMENT OF PRESENT CONDITION OR ACTION

_____ 1. I usually feel inferior to others.
_____ 2. I normally feel warm and happy toward myself.
_____ 3. I often feel inadequate to handle new situations.
_____ 4. I usually feel warm and friendly toward all I contact.
_____ 5. I habitually condemn myself for my mistakes and shortcomings.
_____ 6. I am free of shame, blame, guilt, and remorse.
_____ 7. I have a driving need to prove my worth and excellence.
_____ 8. I have great enjoyment and zest for living.
_____ 9. I am much concerned about what others think and say of me.
_____ 10. I can let others be "wrong" without attempting to correct them.
_____ 11. I have a strong need for recognition and approval.
_____ 12. I am usually free of emotional turmoil, conflict, and frustration.
_____ 13. Losing normally causes me to feel resentful and "less than."
_____ 14. I usually anticipate new endeavors with quiet confidence.
_____ 15. I am prone to condemn others and often wish them punished.
_____ 16. I normally do my own thinking and make my own decisions.
_____ 17. I often defer to others on account of their wealth or prestige.
_____ 18. I willingly take responsibility for the consequences of my actions.
_____ 19. I am inclined to exaggerate and lie to maintain a self-image.
_____ 20. I am free to give precedence to my own needs and desires.
_____ 21. I tend to belittle my own talents, possessions, and achievements.
_____ 22. I am free to speak up for my own opinions and convictions.
_____ 23. I habitually deny, alibi, justify, or rationalize my mistakes and defeats.
_____ 24. I am usually poised and comfortable among strangers.
_____ 25. I am very often critical and belittling of others.
_____ 26. I am free to express love, anger, hostility, resentment, joy, et cetera.
_____ 27. I feel very vulnerable to other's opinions, comments, and attitudes.
_____ 28. I rarely experience jealousy, envy, or suspicion.
_____ 29. I am a "professional people pleaser."
_____ 30. I am not prejudiced toward racial, ethnic, or religious groups.

_____ 31. I am fearful of exposing my "real self."
_____ 32. I am normally friendly, considerate, and generous with others.
_____ 33. I often blame others for my handicaps, problems, and mistakes.
_____ 34. I rarely feel uncomfortable, lonely, and isolated when alone.
_____ 35. I am a compulsive "perfectionist."
_____ 36. I accept compliments and gifts without embarrassment or obligation.
_____ 37. I am often compulsive about eating, smoking, talking, or drinking.
_____ 38. I am appreciative of others' achievements and ideas.
_____ 39. I often shun new endeavors because of fear of mistakes or failure.
_____ 40. I make and keep friends without trying.
_____ 41. I am often embarrassed by the actions of my family or friends.
_____ 42. I readily admit my mistakes, shortcomings, and defeats.
_____ 43. I experience a strong need to defend my acts, opinions, and beliefs.
_____ 44. I take disagreement and refusal without feeling "put down" or rejected.
_____ 45. I have an intense need for confirmation and agreement.
_____ 46. I am eagerly open to new ideas and proposals.
_____ 47. I customarily judge my self-worth by comparison with others.
_____ 48. I am free to think any thoughts that come into my mind.
_____ 49. I frequently boast about myself, my possessions and achievements.
_____ 50. I accept my own authority and do as I, myself, see fit.
SELF-ESTEEM INDEX. Turn to page 224 for scoring instructions.

Do You Ever Hate Yourself?

Have you ever felt like Buford? Just about as slow, low, ugly, puffy, drooped, and pooped as Buford?

Judi feels that way about herself, although you would never know it. She has a lovely figure and beautiful clothes. She is attractive and talented in music. Last week she told me how totally inadequate and ugly she feels.

Tall, handsome, blond Tom is outgoing, fun-loving, and intelligent. But he flunked out of college. Why? He has such an inferiority complex he didn't think he could succeed.

Joan has a nice personality, and her many friends like her very much. She is good at sports and active in intramurals. Basically, she dislikes herself because she is racially different and has never learned to accept it.

Kurt, better than average scholastically, is a student body officer, and he frequently participates in religious activities at church. He has real leadership capabilities, but he feels inadequate and useless. Therefore Kurt is not accomplishing what he could in life.

Another graphic case in point. Written on a restaurant washroom wall were these words: "I have taken the pill, hoisted my hemline above my thighs, and dropped it to my ankle . . . I've rebelled against the university, skied at Aspen, loved two men, married one; earned my keep, kept my identity, and frankly, I'M LOST!"

If you have ever felt like one of these young people, you can sit on a lily pad and wait for a prince or princess to change things for you with a magic kiss. But a better way would be to improve your feelings of worth. Learn to like yourself.

What Does It Mean to Like Yourself?

We all have a mental picture of ourselves. It reflects our concept of the sort of person we think we are. If you have a healthy "self-like," it simply means that you have accepted yourself. It does not mean that you are puffed up with self-importance. You make no false claims. Rather, you accept yourself with your faults as well as your strengths, and you feel you deserve the respect of others. You realize that you goof from time to time, but you feel secure in what you can do. You have learned to build on your strengths and to compensate for your weaknesses. What you have been unable to change, you have learned to live with. You are sincere and open. You accept yourself as a worthwhile individual.

Such a healthy type of self-respect frees you to turn your attention to others. You can then be as tolerant of other people's weaknesses as you are of your own. You can appreciate the differentness of others instead of resenting or fearing it. You realize that this differentness makes each human being unique. Such an attribute also frees you spiritually, for you can more fully appreciate God's acceptance of you as you are and the potential for good within you. If God accepts you as you are, why should you reject yourself?

What Happens When You Don't Like Yourself?

Each of us could probably find a long list of reasons to dislike ourselves. On occasion we may even hate ourselves! Times may come when we feel that no other human has ever experienced what we are going through. So we attempt to hide our insecurities behind false fronts, all the while trying to fool ourselves as we try to fool others.

If you feel inferior, it may affect you in a number of ways. You may feel extremely self-conscious when you walk into a room. You think that everyone is staring at you. You wonder if you look OK. "Did I zip up my pants?" "Button my dress?" "What shall I do with my hands?" "Where can I hide?" "If only the floor would open and swallow me!"

Self-dislike tends to make people highly sensitive to blame and praise. How do you respond when someone compliments you on your clothes? Do you get all flustered and finally stammer, "Oh, this stupid outfit? It's as old as the hills!" If you respond in such a manner, you deny the other person's taste in clothing, as well as the compliment. How should you respond? A simple "Thank you" will do. The way you accept compliments indicates how much respect you have for yourself.

Feelings of inferiority also evidence themselves in daydreaming. Daydreaming is an effort to escape reality. The more you daydream, the poorer you feel about yourself. Everyone daydreams occasionally, but the person with deep feelings of inferiority will spend a great deal of time spinning fantasies. In an effort to escape the reality of how poorly he feels about himself, the daydreamer lives in a make-believe paradise that is supposed to be better than life.

Feelings of inferiority also decrease efficiency at work and school. Your grades and job performance will be affected in direct proportion to how secure or how insecure you feel about yourself. If you have a low self-concept and constantly berate yourself, you will not be able to give your whole attention or energy to the task before you. You will be too busy jabbing yourself, running yourself down, and ridiculing your performance. Because of their low opinion of themselves many people drop out of school or accept jobs far below their training and capacity. They also tend to leave projects partly completed, jumping from one task to the next. They lack confidence in themselves and cannot conceive of finishing anything successfully.

Feelings of worthlessness will also cause

you to rehash the past and imagine ways in which you could or should have done things differently. Do you tend to relive your mistakes and shortcomings over and over and squirm with embarrassment every time you do?

Such feelings will make you critical of others. Barbara is always bragging about her home, pool, car, parents, and clothes, all the while cutting everyone else's things down. Why does she act this way? She is scared that no one will accept her for what she is. Her bragging is an attempt to convince herself and others that she really is worthwhile. By criticizing others she can make herself look better.

Criticism isn't easy to take. But how you accept constructive criticism also indicates how you feel about yourself. Can you accept it gracefully? Or do you nurse hurt feelings and withdraw? Can you thank the person and evaluate the criticism objectively? Or do you get mad and defensive?

After reading this section you should have a pretty good picture of how you feel about yourself. But don't be too hard on yourself. Remember: *We all struggle with feelings of inferiority at one time or another!* Even the most "together" person has probably disliked himself at times. Such feelings particularly haunt young people. It is part of the maturing process and has very little to do with genuine self-worth.

The Consequences of a Poor Self-concept

The consequences of a poor self-concept are far-reaching. Not only does self-hatred warp the person's feelings about himself, but it also reaches out and entwines everyone the individual contacts.

A poor self-concept will limit your capacity to love and accept others. Modern psychology has discovered that people cannot love anyone else unless they have a healthy self-like. We can genuinely love and receive love from others in direct proportion to how we feel about ourselves. If we cannot like ourselves, then we cannot like others. If we do not feel secure and worthwhile at the very core of our beings, we cannot like or respect others.

Although your low self-concept most directly affects you yourself, almost everyone with whom you come in contact will feel a backlash from your inner turmoil. Those close to you—your parents, your relatives, your boyfriend/girlfriend, your circle of friends—will become disturbed over your distress. Eventually your marital partner and your children will suffer as innocent victims of your attitudes unless you conquer them before you marry.

A poor self-concept will influence your choice of a marital partner. The person who lacks self-respect often picks a partner who will devaluate, criticize, or put him down. Why? To recreate the feelings to which he has become accustomed. Others will choose a partner who is a model of virtue and achievement. Then he will constantly compare himself unfavorably with the accomplishments and positions he wished he held. This, too, is an effort to recreate the past in which this person continually compared himself to others and never measured up.

A poor self-concept will influence the future of your children. Parents can pass a low self-concept on to their children. You may think you can hide it so well that no one will ever find out. But they will see in your every attitude toward yourself and life that you do not respect yourself, and they will not respect you either. They will unconsciously pick up tendencies toward a low self-concept. It is impossible for a person with a low self-concept to pass on to his children a healthy self-concept unless someone or something else compensates for that low self-esteem.

A low self-concept will affect your sex life in marriage. Society has taught us that in order to win a mate we must become preoccupied with our physical appearance. It has become a consuming passion for both sexes to be made slicker, sleeker, and more captivating to the eye. Therefore, if we feel

we don't have the perfect body size, it tends to make us dissatisfied with the body we have. If you don't like your body—if you aren't tall enough or your breasts are too small or your legs are too thin or you have no hair on your chest—you will find it difficult to understand how anyone else could find your body appealing. It could cause you to undress in the bathroom and to dread sexual relations.

A low self-concept may cause you to resist authority. Whenever we don't like the way we are made or the way we act, we begin thinking that life has somehow

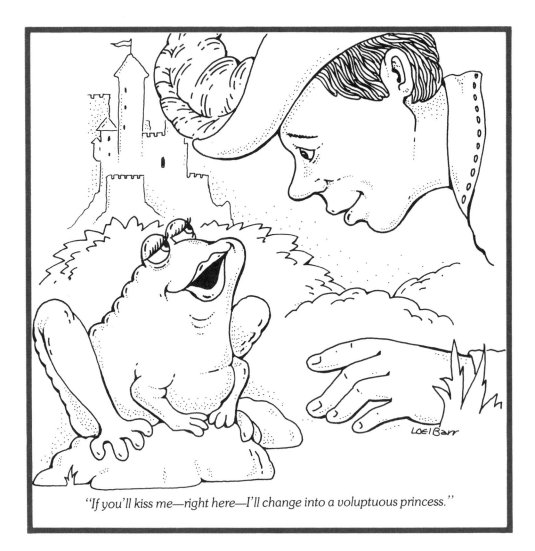

"If you'll kiss me—right here—I'll change into a voluptuous princess."

cheated us. Consciously or unconsciously we develop the attitude that the world owes us something. This attitude produces a bitterness against parents, school authorities, police, employers, our country. Whenever an authority figure comes along and lays down further restrictions that we feel will hinder our chances of happiness, we resent it.

A low self-concept is a hindrance to forming genuine friendships. Hating ourselves not only hinders our response to others but also hinders others' responses to us. If you are oversensitive about your appearance or what others think of you, you become unable to focus on the other person's needs. You are too wrapped up in worrying about their response to you! The only way to build genuine friendships is to forget self and concentrate on the needs of others.

A low self-concept will divert your attention to false goals. If you truly feel you are worthless in certain areas, you may try to gain acceptance by achieving goals that will bring the acceptance and approval of others. For instance, some people buy expensive clothes, drive foreign cars, and live in elegantly furnished homes in an effort to cover up feelings of inadequacy. Accumulating material possessions has diverted their attention from more important goals. As a result, their search for self-acceptance goes on and on, because things cannot cover up an unstable self-concept. Real achievement involves the developing of good character traits. As you develop inward qualities, they will show up in your actions.

A low self-concept will hinder spiritual growth. Young people frequently feel troubled about their inability to trust God. Try as they will, they feel they lack faith. This inability to trust God can often be traced to a deep rejection of self. One young woman reasoned this way: "God created everything, didn't He? He is supposed to be wise and everlastingly loving. If what I see in the mirror is an example of His creation and His love, then I'm not interested in that kind of God."

Such feelings are usually not conscious. More often than not, they are unconscious murmurings that we have never knowingly voiced or explored. But they are widespread among young people whose self-rejection hinders their relationship with God.

Where Can I Hide?

A person can suffer more from a lack of self-respect than from physical pain. Inferiority gnaws on the soul through the conscious mind by day and haunts dreams by night. So painful is the lack of self-respect that our entire emotional system is designed to protect us from its oppression. A great proportion of our lives is devoted to protecting us from the inner pain of inferiority. If you wish to understand yourself, your friendships with others, and your progression toward marriage, you must investigate the ways people use to cope with personal inadequacies.

Cover-ups. People have invented a number of cover-ups to hide themselves from the world. One is "the clown act." The clown deals with inferiority by laughing it off. He conceals his self-doubt and makes an enormous joke of everything. Many famous comedians have amassed fortunes by poking fun at their own physical appearance—Phyllis Diller, Jimmy Durante, Woody Allen, Carol Burnett. Sarcasm, tough talk, superior attitudes, and highly rational and logical arguments may all be cover-ups so that others might always come out on the short end of the stick.

Denial of reality. A person who cannot seem to erect a good defense to hide behind might choose a more psychotic approach—that of denying reality. Such a person pulls down a mental shade and creates his own dream world. He copes with problems by refusing to believe they are there. Experimentation with drugs is one method of denying reality. That's why drugs are so popular with youth. Alcoholics use a similar approach.

The conformist. The conformist is a social doormat who is afraid to express his own opinions. He seeks the approval of others without regarding the expense to his own convictions and beliefs. For nearly ten years most adolescents find themselves caught in the press to conform to their peers in dress, music, and activities. Conformity also plays a big part in the drug-abuse problem among teenagers.

Withdrawal. The person who chooses this route surrenders completely and totally. He has measured himself against others and has concluded that he is worthless. Having decided that he is unworthy, he tries to protect himself from further hurt. He withdraws into a shell of silence and loneliness, choosing to take no chances or to assume unnecessary emotional risks. He fears to initiate a conversation, speak up in a group, enter a contest, run for election, or even to defend his thoughts and ideas. He proceeds through life, coping with inferiority by withdrawing. He has learned that the best way to face life is to button his lip.

The fighter. Sometime in life the fighter learned that it hurts less to fight back than to withdraw, so instead of surrendering, when he feels rejected, he gets mad. He carries a chip on his shoulder and dares others to knock it off. Insignificant issues can trigger his temper, and he lashes out cruelly at others. He is a mean, temperamental, bitter person who always looks for a hassle with anybody. Pity the person who marries this defense mechanism!

Learn to Like Yourself

Have you had to struggle with any of the traits just mentioned? If so, isn't it about time you made friends with yourself? Doesn't life present you with enough headaches already without your beating your head against a wall of inferiority? If you are carrying a heavy burden of remembered humiliations, failures, embarrassments, and rejections, free yourself of it now. You need not carry this load for a lifetime. And the sooner you can accept the worth of your own humanness, the sooner you will be able to construct solid friendships with members of the opposite sex.

No one has any easy answers for the deep problems of inferiority, but there is constructive help. Everyone feels inferior and insecure at times. This knowledge alone should help you through some of

your struggles. You have lots of company.

Even I have gross feelings of inferiority at times (although to observe me you probably wouldn't pick up on it, because I, too, have learned to hide these feelings very carefully). I usually feel the least adequate when I grant radio and television interviews to defend the virtues of a Christ-centered home. My "Gethsemane" experience occured when I was asked to debate the president of the local chapter of NOW (National Organization for Women). I kept saying to myself, "What am I doing here? How did I get here? What can I possibly say to match her rhetoric?" If you could have observed my internal conflict, you would have felt very tall in comparison!

So everybody has inferiority feelings. Where do we go from here? Let's look at some ways to improve the self-concept.

Make an inventory of your strengths and weaknesses. Take a sheet of paper and draw a line down the middle. Label the left column "Weaknesses" and the right hand column "Strengths." In the Weaknesses column write down all the things you do not like about yourself. Take your time, making sure you get everything down. When you finish with your list, put a check by the thing that bothers you most. Now go over the list again. This time write down what you can do to change the things you have checked. If you feel shy, list some ideas about how you might overcome shyness and what you are willing to do.

Next write down your strengths, good qualities, abilities, and talents that others have admired in you. You may find this difficult. It seems easier to list our negative qualities than our positive attributes. But take your time. Do you have some special skill? Are a good listener? Do you know how to be a friend to someone? What hobbies do you have? Write down your thoughts about yourself under the following headings: Physical attributes, strong character traits, personality traits, achievements, talents, skills, abilities, husband/wife attributes to offer, father/mother attributes to offer, job skills (mechanical, intellectual), artistic or musical abilities (decorating, singing, playing an instrument), and sports/hobbies (skiing, macramé, football).

You may not accomplish this project in one sitting, but it should give you more value as a person when you realize the potential you have to offer. You are a person of worth, a person with unlimited potential, a unique individual who cannot be duplicated anywhere.

Rebuild your thought patterns. A researcher conducted an experiment with three groups of students who were instructed to sink basketball free throws. One group practiced daily for twenty days. The second group did not practice at all. The third group threw no balls, but spent twenty minutes a day visualizing that they were sinking free throws. If in their imagination they missed the hoop and failed to make the free throw correctly, they were to correct their aim accordingly. The researcher tested the three groups on the first and last days of the experiment. The first group, who actually practiced every day, improved in scoring 24 percent. The group with no practice showed no improvement. The third group, who practiced only in their minds, improved in scoring 23 percent! Rebuilding your thought patterns and imagining yourself to be successful really works!

Your greatest battle will be in controlling your thinking from this point on. You will still be tempted to think that you are not worth much. And before you know it, once again you'll be feeling worthless inside. So plan in advance for times when you will feel negatively about yourself. Don't give in.

I often suggest to those who wish to reprogram their mind that they carry little cards on which they have written scriptural or inspirational verses. You can keep such cards in your Bible or in your wallet. You can paste them on mirrors, dashboards, or by a light switch. Here are some Bible verses that will help you meditate on the worth that God places on you: Romans 8:31-39; Psalm 56:9 (last part); 100:3; 139:14; Isaiah 40:11, 28-31; 41:10; 43:1, 2. If you set your will in the right direction, your emotion and feelings will follow.

Learn to compensate. When you substitute something for an attribute you cannot change, you have compensated. If you have a bad knee and will never be good in active sports, you can compensate by developing an interest in something else—photography, oil painting, or interior design. Or perhaps you are overweight, but this does not mean you are an inferior person. People come in all shapes and sizes. God did not create one human being and insist that we all look like this perfect ideal. Be fair to yourself. Don't exaggerate your poor qualities just because others remind you of them. Instead, call attention to another attribute—beautiful eyes, broad shoulders, naturally curly hair, or some other feature.

When compensating make sure you know your limitations. Don't stake everything on trying to overcome one handicap. If you were born with one leg shorter than the other, don't expect to take first place in a track meet. Or if you are plain in appearance, don't expect to win a beauty contest. Some things you just cannot change—being tall, small-framed, large-framed, short, blind, deaf, racially different, cross-eyed or bowlegged.

Be honest with yourself about your limitations. Then you will not need to dislike or resent others if they remind you of them. You are already aware of your limitations. They no longer hurt you, because you can compensate for them. This, then, frees you from having to invent cover-ups to protect yourself. It frees you to develop genuine friendships. You no longer have to do a lot of worrying about yourself. You are free to give, to love, to accept, to respect, and share with others. Your limitations cannot ruin your life unless you allow yourself to be defeated.

Develop admirable qualities. Develop an outlook open to new experiences, and develop those inner qualities that help nurture a sense of self-like. Begin to learn the things you need to know so you can use to the best advantage the abilities you possess. Take any one talent listed on your sheet, any hobby, or any attribute, and begin to develop it. You'll have to practice, of course, for no one learns a skill without practice. And you must invest the time necessary for such practice.

If you are shy and want to learn how to speak to people confidently, then join a club that will force you to do just that. If you are plain in appearance, learn what you can about posture, social graces, clothes, and conversation. The world's most charming people are not necessarily beautiful. If you have to wear thick glasses or cannot make the gymnastics team but you have some ability to write short stories, then take a class that will help you develop your talent. If you can't make the grade as "most popular" don't weep over it. Instead learn racquetball or macramé, but do something!

As you practice some new skill you will gain confidence in yourself. Gradually you will emerge from behind your cover-ups to become a more genuine person. But don't expect miracles overnight. Give yourself time to change. You can rid yourself of fear and thoughts of failure only by replacing them with confidence, so be kind to yourself while waiting for old attitudes to slough off.

Never compare yourself with others. The biggest single cause of low self-esteem is comparing yourself with someone else. We tend to judge ourselves and measure ourselves not by our own standard but against someone else's standard. When we do this, we will always come out second best. The end result of such reasoning is that we believe we are not worthy, that we don't deserve happiness or success, that it would be out of place for us to express our own abilities or talents.

You do not have to look or act like anyone else. You are not in competition with any other person on earth. The truth is, you are not inferior; you are not superior. You are simply you, *equal to others.* And that you is unique. So stop comparing yourself with others.

Give of yourself to others. Our own needs and problems seem less threatening when we help someone else handle his problems. You will not have time to wallow in self-pity if you are actively seeking a solution to someone else's problems. For every one of you who feels rejected, unloved, and unworthy, there is someone else who is worse off than you.

Bake something for a friend, surprise an elderly person with a small gift, visit the sick, sign up for volunteer work with an agency that needs help, use your car for someone without transportation, or listen to someone with a problem. The world is crammed with lonely, discouraged people who need you to empathize with them. And while you are doing all this, your own sense of inadequacy won't seem so important. The best medicine for self-pity is to give of yourself to others.

Ask God to make something beautiful out of your life. Ask God to forgive you for your past attitudes—resentment of your appearance, lack of abilities, parentage, or anything else. Ask God to forgive you for any bitterness you have had toward His creation—you.

When you are over this hump, thank God for creating you *just the way you are.* This will not be an easy step. You may feel that you cannot thank God for creating you tall when you *hate* being tall. You may think that this would make you a hypocrite, that you can't thank God when you don't *feel* thankful yet. But you can do it even if you don't feel like it. *Giving* thanks is an act of the will. *Being* thankful is a feeling emotion. You can discipline your feelings of thankfulness and give thanks even though you don't feel like it. Do not let your emotions control. Set your will in the right direction, and in time your emotions will follow.

When you know that God accepts you and loves you *just the way you are,* you don't have to feel as though you must change in order to have God love you. You don't have to act sanctimonious. You don't have to become a religious fanatic—or even act pious. He wants you *as you are.* The only things God dislikes are the things that would destroy you. He is interested only in helping you leave destructive attitudes behind.

If you take God at His word, believing that you are loved and worthwhile, then you have a solid base from which to operate. You will have a firm center to your life. You will be free to put the same kind of love and respect you have for yourself to work in your relationships with others— even with the opposite sex. Remember, you can never experience a true love relationship with someone else unless you first take care of any self-acceptance problems within you. This does not mean that you have no room for improvement. There will always be room for improvement. You don't think of yourself as perfect, only as acceptable to God and others. A beautiful sense of peace and relief should come over you at this point. Not only does God count you as acceptable, but He stands ready to work miracles in you, to change your worst failures into successes.

Once upon a time there was a frog. But he wasn't really a frog. He was a prince who looked and felt like a frog. There he sat—too frightened and disgusted and froggish to budge as he floated on his lily pad down the great river of life. Only the kiss of a beautiful young maiden could save him. But since when do cute chicks kiss frogs? So there sat the unkissed prince in frog form. But miracles still happen. One day a beautiful maiden grabbed him and gave him a big smack. CRASH! BOOM! ZAP! There he was, a handsome prince. And you know the rest of the story. They lived happily ever after . . .

You, too, can change any "froggy" feelings you have about yourself. But not as long as you sit on your lily pad and do nothing. Muster your courage and ask God to take over in your life as you hop to the edge of the pond. God will take care of the mud and muck that has been holding you back from becoming the prince or princess you ought to be. God wants to uncover your worth, but you must give Him permission to prepare the way for this adventure. Give Him a try.

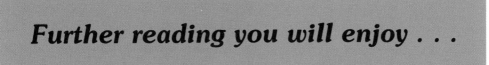

Further reading you will enjoy . . .

Kirby, Scott.   DATING: GUIDELINES FROM THE BIBLE.
Trobisch, Walter.   LOVE YOURSELF: SELF-ACCEPTANCE AND DEPRESSION.
Wright, H. Norman.   IMPROVING YOUR SELF-IMAGE.

Dating refers not so much to
going out on a "date"
as to the relationship
between a certain guy
and a certain gal.

Chapter at a Glance

Chapter 3

The Most Popular Game on Earth— The Dating Game

Dating poses one of the greatest problems that face young adults today. Frequently, they experience frustration, discouragement, and depression over this important aspect of their lives. Some feel guilt-ridden because of their sexual involvements. Others suffer depression because they have no one to date or because they care for someone who fails to return their affection.

Today's market is glutted with courses and books on marriage but is nearly devoid of information on how to improve one's love life prior to marriage. High school teachers of marriage and family living classes try to assist young people in clari-

fying standards already held, but they offer little or no information to help a young person discern right from wrong. Meanwhile, television and radio programs, movies, billboards, magazines, novels, and a myriad of other sources provide an almost constant diet of misinformation about love, sex, and marriage. What should a young person believe in the face of such teachings?

Perhaps this chapter will provide some of the answers you have been looking for. It contains a straightforward combination of practical information meshed with Biblical concepts. I hope that those of you who seriously want to bring your lives into harmony with God's will can find acceptance, assurance, and happiness during your years of dating.

The Stages of Dating

When I asked one young lady to define the word *date,* she told me that she thinks of a date as a special experience when a guy calls up a gal and they set up the time, date, and place to go out together. They dress according to the occasion. Then he stops by her home and rings the doorbell . . . and so on. Yes, that certainly is a date, but the term *dating* here refers not so much to going out on a date as to the relationship between a certain guy and a certain gal.

What is a date, then? Dating is a special kind of friendship between two persons of the opposite sex that may lead to love, courtship, and marriage. Please note that dating begins with friendship—a special kind of friendship. Love and all the romantic stuff follows the developing friendship. Too often couples get things backward. They become lovers before becoming friends.

Dating progresses through five stages, the first of which is friendship. Yes, dating springs from a friendship between two members of the opposite sex. The better a young person is at developing good friendships, the more successful he or she will be at the dating game. If you want successful dating relationships, then you must begin by learning how to develop positive friendships.

In the second stage, friendship moves into dating itself. But there are three phases of dating—casual, special, and steady dating.

Casual dating involves no special emotional involvement. You date for the pleasure of having something to do and someplace to go with a member of the opposite sex. This necessary and positive step gives you the chance before you become emotionally involved to get acquainted with members of the opposite sex and understand somewhat how they react to life.

Special dating requires a limited degree of emotional involvement. Let's say that a very special event will soon come up at school. Sue has had her eye on a special someone for several weeks and has hoped he would ask her. She can hardly believe it one night when she answers the phone and hears his voice. Butterflies flit around in the pit of her stomach as they enjoy small talk for a few minutes. When he finally gets around to asking her if she will go with him, she casually says she'd like to go. The minute he hangs up, she calls twenty of her friends to break the news. Sue buys a new dress and waits not-so-patiently for the big day. When it finally arrives, she spends hours preparing her nails, hair, and face.

Steady dating means that two young people commit themselves to date only each other (or that's the way it is supposed to be—and is—as far as you know). The depth of emotional commitment will vary with the couple. Some teenagers take steady dating seriously and form long-lasting relationships. Others use the relationship as a means of security so they will never have to attend a function alone or appear dateless.

The third stage—the engaged-to-be-engaged stage—is a relatively new term applied to the period between going steady and becoming officially engaged. A couple who has gone steady for some time begins to talk in terms of a permanent relationship and makes *tentative* plans toward marriage. The understanding is private and personal and not final or binding. They make no formal announcement, set no wedding date, and prepare no wedding plans. They do, however, plan to get married and talk of a future time "someday" when they will get married.

During this period the couple tests and retests their values, goals, and future plans. Much of what engaged couples usually discuss they now open up to scrutiny. This approach offers several advantages to the couple and should reduce the number of broken engagements, thereby making the engagement period more meaningful. It also can take the pressure off couples who are only going steady by not forcing them into a premature relationship. It allows a more casual time period when a couple can

How Good Are You at Making Friends?

Score in the following manner:

1. Definitely yes	3. Unsure	5. Definitely not
2. Probably yes	4. Probably not	

1 2 3 4 5   1. When I am conversing with others, I frequently engage in one-upmanship, trying to show myself better, more clever, or more experienced than they.

1 2 3 4 5   2. I am inclined to criticize my friends, feeling it my duty to point out their mistakes so they may be corrected.

1 2 3 4 5   3. When I do something for someone, I usually want everyone to know about it.

1 2 3 4 5   4. I frequently demand help from others even when it comes to small jobs or assignments.

1 2 3 4 5   5. I find it difficult to praise the successes and good qualities in my friends since I harbor secret feelings of jealousy.

1 2 3 4 5   6. I tend to be moody around others, giving friends the "hot and cold" treatment.

1 2 3 4 5   7. I enjoy being in the limelight when others are around.

1 2 3 4 5   8. When a friend confides a personal or secret matter to me, I have trouble keeping the information to myself.

1 2 3 4 5   9. I frequently make promises to others that I do not follow through with.

1 2 3 4 5   10. I belong to a clique of friends who exclude others from joining our fun and activity.

1 2 3 4 5   11. I frequently drop in on my friends unannounced whether or not I have been invited, and sometimes I get the feeling I don't know when to leave.

1 2 3 4 5   12. I appreciate having my friends help me out of a jam, but have difficulty doing the same for them when they need me.

Turn to page 224 for scoring instructions.

43

take an in-depth look at whether their total life styles and personalities might be compatible for marriage.

Fourth, following the engaged-to-be-engaged level comes formal engagement. In engagement the couple commit themselves to marriage by exchanging some symbol that binds their commitment to each other. They also publicly announce their intention to marry, conclude their exploration of personalities, and establish a time for planning the wedding.

The fifth and final stage, of course, is marriage. Marriage is supposed to follow the engagement stage. I say "supposed to" because 40 to 50 percent of all engagements are broken.

Many authors have written numerous books concerning the failure of marriage in today's society. But we hear next to nothing regarding dating failure. Yet in a very real way, marriage failure is in reality dating failure. Generally speaking, the couple failed to allow sufficient time to become acquainted, failed to make intelligent decisions, failed to correlate values with behavior, and failed to make wise choices. The opportunity to check the other person out occurs *prior* to marriage, but the results become apparent only *after* the wedding.

Why Date?

Why do you date? If you haven't begun dating yet, why do you wish to date? It is your purpose in dating that will determine the eventual outcome of the relationship you establish. It isn't enough to date just because your friends do, or because you are old enough, or because someone asked you out, or because you want something to do. It is important for you to think through your reasons for dating.

There are a number of positive reasons for dating.

For Personality Development. We all have areas of our personality and character that need development and improvement. When by dating you interact with a member of the opposite sex, you will get to know yourself better. Various strengths and weaknesses will surface during a romance. The knowledge you gain will become valuable in helping you learn how you can relate to others. From every person you date you should learn something about yourself and how your personality affects the opposite sex.

To Learn to Know and Understand the Opposite Sex. Dating paves the way to understanding a variety of personalities, attitudes, and problems of the opposite sex that you might never be exposed to otherwise. One authority has suggested that a young person should have dated twelve persons by age 19. From such exposure to the opposite sex you will begin to understand certain differences and how to relate yourself to these differences.

To Fill the Human Need for Love. Every human being longs to form an intimate relationship in which love can be given and received freely. Dating helps mature these skills. (These needs can be filled in ways other than dating or marriage, to which many a well-adjusted single person can testify.)

To Fill Social Needs for Fun and Recreation. All work and no play makes for a dull personality. A creative date life opens up opportunities for good times with someone you care about. It fills the need during a time in life when young people need to be together, to relax, to have fun, and to play.

To Find a Future Marriage Partner. There is a 100 percent chance that you will marry someone you have dated. Although the statement may not be profound, it is true. Every date should help sharpen your reasoning skills so that when you make the final decision to marry, you can make an intelligent one regarding the traits you want in a future partner. Paul Meier, a Christian psychiatrist, advises young people to date as many members of the opposite sex as possible in order to evaluate what type of mate suits him/her best.

To Develop Spiritual Growth. A dating relationship should help you grow spiritually. As you get closer and closer to the person you date, you should also be drawing closer and closer to God. You see, dating is a forerunner of marriage, and marriage is a miniature replica of the relationship that should exist between us and God. So if your date life does not help you grow spiritually, something is wrong.

Think of dating as a workshop in which you can develop the skills needed to achieve a positive intimate relationship in marriage. This will make your date life a healthy activity in which you can grow as an individual.

Shaky Reasons for Dating

Just as there are good reasons for dating, so are there bad reasons. Most of the bad reasons involve selfish motives.

Fran, a popular gal on campus, makes the honor roll and has a nice figure and attractive clothes. She is president of the girls' club and a reporter for the school newspaper. Leo, a mediocre character, is only average in sports, and he barely squeaks through when it comes to grades. He is definitely middle-of-the-road all the way. Leo wants more social acceptance and decides he could get it by dating Fran. Fran wouldn't consider Leo except that he drives a customized van. Fran and Leo are exploiting each other because each has something the other wants.

"That's not what I had in mind when I asked for a perfect match."

Carl thinks Ellen is a cute little number and eagerly tries to date her. Ellen refuses because he asks so frequently and seems too eager. So Carl devises a plan to ask Donna out in order to make Ellen jealous. He knows he can date Donna because she has flirted with him frequently. But Carl is using Donna as a means to an end. He doesn't care about her as a person.

Frank and Mary were going steady. After six months Frank tired of Mary and broke it off. Mary felt terribly hurt but began dating Herb within a week. She not only went out with Herb, but in front of friends put on quite a display of public affection, hugging and kissing him so that friends would notice and word would get back to Frank. Mary had no real feelings of affection for Herb. She pretended such emotion in order to get revenge on Frank.

David loved Melinda's figure. She was a sharp-looking gal, and heads turned whenever she walked by. She looked so good that David couldn't wait to get his hands on her—on as much of her as he could manage. He dated her with only one thing in mind—to use her for the maximum amount of physical involvement she would permit.

Each of these dating situations has a common denominator—exploitation. Each person was using the other as a means to a desired end. The individual who dates for prestige is exploiting the other person's popularity in order to gain status in the group. The one who dates to make someone else jealous or to get revenge is exploiting the new date to get back at the other. The guy who dates for sex is exploiting the body of another to satisfy his selfish sexual desires.

What Do Fellows Like in Girls?

When Harry and I were talking with a group of young people one evening, a young woman asked a very interesting question: "What do fellows age 13 to 18 really want from girls? Do they like old-fashioned girls or forward girls, or what? I'd really like to know what goes on in their heads about us and what they expect from us."

Jane had posed a good question because young ladies understand very little about young men and vice versa. Before I answer her question directly, let's consider some of the social and psychological feelings of a fellow between the ages of 13 and 18. A boy reaches puberty between the ages of 13 and 14. At this time his reproductive system begins to produce sperm cells. Typically, his height will spurt up and his attitudes will change. Cars become very important to him, and yet he cannot drive. He cannot vote or drink until he turns 18. He often feels suspended. He can't marry, enlist, borrow money, drink, make his own decisions, or vote, but he must continue in school whether he wants to or not. And this state lasts as long as he remains financially dependent upon his parents. During this time he has neither the privileges of childhood nor the freedom of adulthood.

Uncertain about himself, he lacks self-confidence—although he would never admit this and may work hard to cover up his true feelings. But nevertheless they are there. In addition, he feels unsure of

himself, of his sexual desires, and about girls. He is also unsure of life and is searching for identity and purpose.

Boys should not be ashamed of puberty. Instead they should be happy, proud, and challenged with the fact that they stand at the entrance to manhood. What they are experiencing is normal and natural. Girls and parents should try to understand fellows when they are going through this period of uncertainty.

Now that we understand this much, let's look at what guys like and want from gals. Let's establish one thing: boys do like girls! During the earliteen years they will enjoy boy-girl gatherings, but they will tend to stay together in groups because of their inexperience with the opposite sex. For the most part, they hesitate to show their interest in boy-girl relationships. About age 14 boys tend to lose interest in girls for a while. Some do not show interest in females again until they are about 17 or 18 years of age. Others embark on a series of romances that changes with the seasons. Breakups appear to bother them little, if at all.

Other fellows at ages 15 and 16 like group boy-girl gatherings. They feel more secure when they do not have to depend entirely on their own abilities for entertain-

47

ment, conversation, and social skills. Still others feel most comfortable in "brother-sister" relationships. Our son Mark had several of these during his midteen years, and they were good for him. He learned about girls and formed solid friendships that did not commit him prematurely to a love relationship. Boys enjoy such companion-

ship but will drop the "sister" immediately if she begins to get serious.

A few boys will rush into going steady and heavy relationships. In most cases those who choose this route are insecure and do not wish to make the effort to know many other young women. They lack confidence in their abilities to meet others, carry on a

Dating

1. Strongly agree
2. Mildly agree
3. Not sure
4. Mildly disagree
5. Strongly disagree

Read each of the following statements carefully. Respond to each statement according to the scale of 1 to 5 as shown at the left. Circle the appropriate number for each statement. Your responses should represent your personal opinion at the present time.

1 2 3 4 5   1. When to start dating is a matter of maturity, not a matter of age.

1 2 3 4 5   2. Dating is more important for women than it is for men.

1 2 3 4 5   3. Young people should be able to date whomever they wish, regardless of what their parents say.

1 2 3 4 5   4. The best marriage partner is the person who has dated many different persons over a long period of time.

1 2 3 4 5   5. When I marry it will be my only marriage.

BEFORE I MARRY, I WOULD LIKE TO ACCOMPLISH THE FOLLOWING (list five accomplishments):

1. _____

2. _____

3. _____

4. _____

5. _____

conversation, and interact, so they choose a steady relationship, thereby sheltering themselves from new circumstances that might underscore their feelings of inadequacy and self-consciousness.

Although most midteen fellows enjoy associating with young women, the majority are not ready for serious relationships as the girls often wish they were. At 18 Mark began going with a girl of the same age who really was pushing him for marriage. He stayed her off well, and they continued their rocky relationship for two more years. When we were discussing the status of their relationship, I asked if Sally still pushed him for marriage at age 20 as she did at 18. "Oh, no," Mark responded. "She hardly even mentions it now." How much their values and interests had changed in two years! They were both beginning to find themselves and no longer needed to look to marriage as the solution for all their problems.

What Do Girls Like in Fellows?

Just as young ladies want to know what the fellows want in them, so young men want to know what girls look for in them. What do girls 13 to 18 want out of boys? Do they like decent guys, fast guys, forward guys, or old-fashioned guys? Do they like to be around fellows at all?

Let's consider the development of a girl during puberty, which she reaches at about 12½ years of age. Her monthly menstrual cycle begins, and she undergoes a major change in height and attitudes. Life will begin to mean something different to her. She now becomes openly interested in boys.

Some girls reach puberty at age 11 or even earlier. These girls will become interested in the opposite sex two years before the fellows show any interest in them. This often places a girl in an uncomfortable and embarrassing social and emotional situation. Her parents and peers may call her "boy crazy" when she is merely responding to the changes taking place inside her. She is leaving the little girl behind and entering young womanhood. Her parents should be proud of her

development rather than making it more difficult for her.

Girls do like boys, and they will make it known in a multitude of subtle and not so subtle ways. But basically girls like fellows who are neat, clean, and well-groomed. They like young men who are honest and do what they say they plan to do. They want a guy to come by at the time he said he would and not an hour early or late. They like individuals who contribute to interesting conversation, not leaving it entirely to them. They do not enjoy young men who only talk or brag about themselves or who get jealous or possessive when they talk to other fellows.

They also like decent, "old-fashioned" young men who respect them as persons. They prefer men who respect their moral code and do not persistently push for more. They relish fun-loving guys who can tease but know when to stop. They like fellows who can give honest compliments, who appreciate their attractiveness but who also appreciate their inner qualities. They want to date courteous guys who know their manners. They prefer nonsmokers, nondrinkers, and nondrug users. They very much dislike guys who swear, are crude and brash, or who tell dirty jokes in their presence.

At What Age Should Dating Begin?

There are two kinds of age: physical and emotional. Your emotional age reveals how mature you are. It is far more important than your physical age when it comes to dating. Differences in emotional age vary greatly among young people. Some 13-year-olds are as emotionally stable as some 18-year-olds. Some 18-year-olds act more like 13-year-olds. So it is difficult to answer this question in terms of how many years you have lived.

Dr. Thomas Poffenberger conducted a survey and found that 13 percent of both junior and senior high school students had dated by age 13. He also learned that 5 percent had gone steady at age 12, and 9 percent had gone steady at age 13.[1] When you take into consideration that the average

that dating should not begin until 17-18 or after.

Parents who allow their children to date before puberty or in some cases even push their children into dating are behaving irresponsibly. On the other hand, parents who arbitrarily refuse to allow their sons or daughters to date until they have turned 16 or 18 are expecting the absurd.

Fifty years ago the acceptable age for first dates was 16, but now young people begin to date earlier. This is due largely to the increased affluence of our society, along with movies, television, and the media. Many parents have become alarmed over this new trend. Some well-meaning individuals have suggested that Congress pass a law that would forbid youth to date until after age 15! Early dating creates some personality and emotional problems, but a national law is not the answer!

If you are a girl between the ages of 12 and 14, you probably are overanxious to date. Most 13-year-old girls feel that they are more mature than the average and therefore should have dating privileges. If this description fits you, and your parents are holding back, it isn't that they wish to deprive you of pleasure or that they are old fogies, but because they know what lies ahead. Data indicates that the earlier you begin dating, the earlier you will marry. One other fact: the earlier you marry, the greater your chances of becoming a divorce statistic.

It is normal and natural for boys and girls during the early-to-midteen years to show an interest in the opposite sex. If they have no interest, parents might really have something to worry about! But if a national law to prevent dating isn't the answer, what is? The solution to this dilemma is actually quite simple. Every religious organization and school should provide regular recreational activities for early-to-midteens in order to accommodate their desires to mingle with the opposite sex. These gatherings can allow for some pairing off, but there should be no official, individual dating. The emphasis should be on being together in a relaxed and healthy atmosphere that a few adults can properly supervise.

girl reaches puberty at 12½ and the average boy at 13½, a considerable number in this study were dating and going steady before puberty!

The study I conducted revealed the same trend. A slight 2 percent stated that they began dating at age 10-12, but one quarter had by 13-14. When asked, "At what age do you think single dating should begin?" 11 percent suggested 13-14 and 67 percent agreed on 15-16. The remaining believed

Parents should support such plans to provide this kind of social opportunity. And parents can go one step further. If a teenager shows an interest in a member of the opposite sex, parents can invite the other teenager and his/her family on an outing, a water-skiing party, a picnic, a trip to the mountains, or whatever.

Conversing With the Opposite Sex

If you want to survive in the world of dating, you must learn how to talk to members of the opposite sex. Two main problems often crop up here. First, when males talk to one another, their conversation usually centers on cars, sports, work, and women. Their manner often tends to be coarse if not crude. When females talk to one another, they tend to discuss clothes, other people, their relationships with men, recipes, and sewing. They are often cliquish. Obviously, if the sexes attempt to talk to each other about such things, in most cases each would bore the other. Second, nervousness and self-consciousness when talking to the opposite sex sometimes produces foolish behavior.

Your attitude toward the opposite sex is actually more important than tips on what to say, because your attitude will determine your behavior. If a fellow is concerned about a girl's feelings, he won't talk or joke with her in a coarse manner. He will ask questions designed to find out what she is like and what her interests are. A man who rambles on about the medals he has won in track and field and how much money he made in a recent deal hardly appears interested in his date. No one would consider him a good conversationalist. Likewise a young woman who is preoccupied with her hair, dress, confiding in a girlfriend, or making catty remarks about other girls would make her date feel ill-at-ease. She, too, must put away some of her own interests and desires in order to sound him out.

When initiating a conversation, ask open-ended questions. For instance, if you ask, "Do you like pizza?" you will likely get only a yes or no answer. An open-ended question would be phrased, "Tell me about your favorite foods." You can follow up with an invitation to say more: "Tell me more"; "I'd be interested in your point of view"; "It sounds to me like you have more to say on this subject." These responses open the door for the other person to expand on his or her interests. Disk jockeys and newspaper reporters have developed skill in asking such questions. That's how they obtain interesting information for their audiences. You can learn these skills too!

It will take actual concentration and focused attention to show interest in the activities of the other person. But if you concentrate on the other individual, you will eliminate your feelings of self-consciousness because you can't be thinking of yourself right then. The less self-conscious you are, the less likely you are to make social blunders. Self-consciousness contributes to talking too much, talking too loudly, and only about one's self.

If you are one of those individuals who gets painfully nervous when talking with the opposite sex, try to forget yourself and think about the other person. This one hint can make an amazing difference as you relate to and are accepted by others.

How to Ask for a Date (for Guys)

After you understand the basics of conversation in relating to the opposite sex, the next most important thing is to know how to ask a girl out. There are certain things to remember and a sequence of events that should take place.

Step 1: Decide which young lady you wish to date. She will probably be someone you find physically appealing—someone you know but not well enough. In choosing this girl, hopefully you will take into consideration more than just her looks and personality. Think also of her moral characteristics and her relationship to God. If she is lacking in both, sharply question your motives for dating her.

Step 2: What would you like to do on your first date? A first date should be an activity that is easily acceptable to someone whose likes and dislikes are unfamiliar to you and that allows you to talk and become better acquainted. The easiest date in the world is to attend a movie, but watching a film leaves little opportunity to discuss topics that will help you get to know each other.

Step 3: Where will the date take place? If you want to have dinner at a restaurant, you will have to choose the place as well as the time. If you attend a sports event, the location and time have been selected for you.

Step 4: Get the facts. Get the time, date, and place down pat so that there will be no misunderstandings. Now devise plan B. In other words, if she should turn you down, choose another girl, activity, or place. Be prepared in advance. If the activity requires reservations, now is the time to purchase your tickets. If you do not have your own car, you must also arrange for transportation.

Step 5: Ask her. This is the trickiest part of the process, because most of us fear rejection. Look for an opportunity to find her alone and when there will be no interruptions. Many guys find it easier to ask over the phone than in person.

When asking her, avoid such questions as "What are your plans for Sunday night?" or "Do you like roller-skating?" Her personal habits and schedule are none of your business at this point. By all means don't say, "Hey, Judy, how about bumming around with me Saturday night?" And don't be negative: "You wouldn't want to go out with me Saturday night, would you?"

Perhaps the best way to ask would go something like this: "Judy, I'd really like to get together with you so we could get better acquainted. There's a new Mexican restaurant I've just heard about that serves great enchiladas, and I thought maybe you'd like to go with me." Act and sound as though you expect her to accept the invitation, and she will be more likely to.

You need not be afraid of her. She is just another human being like yourself. The big difference is that she's female. Avoid talking too fast or being too pushy. Otherwise she will likely back off. If you mumble and act as though you don't know what you are doing, you will turn her off, and she won't want to

date someone like that.

Ask for the date several days in advance of the event. If it is an annual banquet that occurs on Sunday night, better not wait until Saturday to ask someone. If you planned only to drive down Christmas Tree Lane, there would be no need to invite her three weeks in advance. The more formal the occasion, the earlier you should ask. You can set up more casual dates only one to five days prior to the occasion.

Step 6: If she answers affirmatively, you have it made. But avoid acting overly grateful, lest she wonder why you are so overjoyed about dating her. It will make her think that you have never had a date before! After she accepts the date with you, gather your wits together and make sure you give the necessary details she needs to know. If you plan to pick her up in a convertible, she'll need a scarf for her hair. The dress required for a banquet differs from what she would wear for miniature golf.

If she turns you down, try not to fall apart. Analyze what kind of No she gave. Did her tone and approach say, "No, and that's final"? or did they say, "Due to circumstances beyond my control, I can't go with you this time, but please ask me again"?

"No, and that's final" will sound something like this: "Sorry about that, but I'm busy," or "I just can't work it into my schedule." These responses mean that she doesn't have time and isn't interested in making the time.

Examples of "Due to circumstances beyond my control . . ." include: "I'm busy Thursday night, but I'd enjoy it some other time," or "I'd enjoy going to that with you, but I'm committed to something else that night. How about another time?" If a gal suggests an alternative date, you know that she wants to go out with you.

By the way, if a gal turns you down with no explanation, forget about asking why. You have no right to that information just because you asked her for a date, and she does not have to respond. It would be out of place.

Step 7: If your self-esteem is still intact and you would still enjoy going out with someone, ask another girl. But never let the word slip that she is second choice! Openness and honesty are good to a point, but this would hurt her feelings and likely leave you dateless *again*.

How to Accept a Date

First dates are just as nerve-racking for girls as they are for guys. I heard of one young lady who on the day of her first date made everyone in her family cater to her wishes, refused to help around the house because she had to get ready for her date, shouted at everyone to let her alone so she could have perfect peace, and tied up the bathroom for hours. This is overdoing it a little!

Scene 1: The phone rings. Your mom answers it and says it's for you. She has a funny look on her face and sports a mischievous smile. "It's a b-o-y," she whispers in mock horror.

Scene 2: Your mind races, your heart gets stuck in your throat, and your pulse pounds. In spite of all this activity, you listen closely because you have to know who it is and what he wants.

Scene 3: You hear his voice, and instantly you know who it is. You have been dying for him to pay some attention to you. While he is still asking, you will have a few split seconds to decide whether you want to date him. (There seems to be only one way out of making this decision on the spot. Make an agreement with your parents that you will never accept a date without checking with them first. This might sound a bit childish, but it will give you the time you need to investigate the fellow, think about it, and get input from others as well as your parents. What do you really know about him—his reputation, character, and morals? Why does he want to date you?)

Scene 3: Evaluate the activity before you give him an answer. Is it something you wish to participate in? If he has suggested going to a rock concert and you have chosen not to attend such entertainment, you will need to respond in such a way that he understands that it is rock concerts you are opposed to and not him. If it is a healthy, fun-filled activity about which you have no

himself, you remember him from a class you took last semester. Big problem: *He is not someone you want to date.*

When turning down a date, honesty is always the best policy even if it hurts the guy a little. Avoid making excuses in order to put him off. It rarely solves the problem. One fellow kept calling a girl trying to get a date with her. She invented one excuse after another. One night he called her again, and she said she had to wash her hair. He said, "You told me that a couple of days ago." She said, "Well, I decided to do it tonight since you called." He got the message.

Avoid saying, "My parents won't let me go," unless they won't. He might see you going to the same event with someone else. Or don't say "I'm busy that night," as he might ask again. Or don't reply "I'm going steady with Charlie Brown," unless you really are. Don't respond with "Let's make it some other time," unless you want him to take you literally. Avoid any sarcastic remarks that would put him down: "What? Go out with you!" or "You must be kidding!" Just because you do not care to date him does not make him an unworthy person. He thought enough of you to ask you out. You can think enough of him to leave his self-respect intact.

One other no-no. Don't say, "I've got a date with Skip that night, but Lori would love to go out with you." Don't try to pass off a friend of yours in your place. It is in very bad taste to do so, and it puts him in an uncomfortable position. He may not be the least interested in dating Lori.

Keep your response simple, and as courteously as possible tell him why you choose not to go out with him. It might go something like this: "Thanks for asking me, Ron, but at the present time I'm not ready for a dating relationship with you." Or if it is someone you have known fairly well you might even say, "We've been good friends, and I've appreciated our friendship. I hope you won't take this wrong, but I'm not ready for anything more right now. My decision has nothing to do with liking you as a person."

Regardless of how tactful you attempt to be, your refusal may hurt his feelings. It may

questions, let him know how much you would enjoy going with him.

Scene 4: Check your calendar for any conflicting events. If you can't go at the suggested time, it is perfectly all right for you to let him know you would enjoy going with him another time if it could be worked out.

Scene 5: If you have no objections to the fellow, his character, or the activity, then accept. And accept with enthusiasm (without overdoing it). If you act too nonchalant, he may assume that you don't really care whether or not you go out with him.

Scene 6: The phone rings. Your mom answers it and says it's for you. She has a funny look on her face. She hands you the phone as she says, "It's a boy who wants to talk to you." Your heart does flip-flops as you take the phone. This time you do not recognize the voice. After he introduces be uncomfortable for a while if you have to be around him, but it is kinder to turn him down than to string him along. Rejection is never fun; it always hurts. But it is harder on him and you to tell "little white lies," make up excuses, or give insincere answers filled with uncertainty. A simple, courteous response with a reason why is the best way to handle it.

If it is someone who doesn't share your religious convictions you should not say, "I'm sorry, but I'm a Christian, and I can't date you because you aren't one." Such an attitude would imply that you somehow feel superior to others. When you turn down a date with such a person, do so in a way that doesn't give the impression that you feel self-righteous or sanctimonious. If it is appropriate, you can tell him that you have chosen your personal values and decided not to date those who are not members of your own faith. Or you might say that you have made a pact with your parents that you won't date those who hold differing spiritual values. If you don't know the person well enough to know what his spiritual inclinations are, say so: "I don't know where you stand on this, but if you would like to discuss it with me sometime I'd be happy to get together with you." This could set the stage for you to share your religious ideals in a positive way. If the person is someone you would never care to date, then you need not bring religion into the picture at all.

One more thing. When dating, both sexes try to date the most desirable persons—obviously! This is only good and natural. But may I suggest that many persons would make really fine dates despite the fact that they wear glasses or are short, underweight, overweight, have acne, or are shy, not a part of the "in" crowd, and not a star athlete or a beauty queen. Sometimes the best "finds" just haven't blossomed yet. You might be overlooking someone with great potential just because you want so badly to date some good-looking, popular person you've had your eye on. Avoid such shallowness. You might find some very interesting people inside some rather plain packages. Look around.

Where Should We Go? What Should We Do?

Peter: My first date with Petunia. A spaghetti dinner and a Christian music concert. I can't wait. Petunia is some chick. What a night!

At dinner:

Petunia: (to herself) Boy, he sure has lousy table manners. And he isn't much of a conversationalist, either.

Peter: (to himself) Petunia isn't nearly as much fun as I thought she'd be. She sure ordered a lot of food, and at these prices she'd better finish every bite. (Out loud) "Pass the bread."

Petunia: "Here."

At the concert:

Peter: "Good music, huh?"

Petunia: "Yeah, real good."

On the drive home:

Peter: "I really enjoyed that music tonight."

Petunia: "Me too."

Peter: "G'night."

Petunia: "G'night."

Later:

Peter: (to himself) That will be the last time I take Petunia out. She's a dud.

Petunia: (to herself) I wouldn't go out with Peter again if he begged me.

Have you ever experienced a date similar to that of Peter and Petunia? We probably all have. We looked forward to it with great anticipation, spent a good deal of money, and had a rotten time. And afterward we couldn't figure out why. The combination of personalities certainly has a lot to do with it, but so does where you go and what you do.

Basically there are two kinds of dates: (1) the spectator date, during which you sit while watching and listening to entertainment, and (2) participation dates, in which you are actively involved in recreation that is provided for you or is created by yourselves.

Spectator dates include movies, plays, concerts, sports events, watching TV, and listening to records. Spectator dates are common, popular, and fun. Usually everyone is eager to attend spectator entertainment. They are popular on first dates because they reduce the stress and tension

55

involved in keeping up your end of the conversation. Furthermore, literally everyone already knows how to do it—sit and watch. That's another plus.

On the other hand, spectator events are expensive. And watching someone else perform allows little time for conversation. This actually defeats one of the main purposes in dating—getting to know each other better. In addition, we all do too much sitting and watching already. Spectating does very little to raise feelings of self-worth, requires very little creativity, and will likely make you tired of each other faster than during other kinds of activity.

Participation dates include playing miniature golf or tennis; canoeing, sailing; visiting museums, art galleries, and zoos; planning and cooking a meal together. Participation dates seldom turn out boring. They allow an outlet for your creative abilities, and they also provide fewer opportunities for petting or sexual temptations. These kinds of dates will reaffirm your feelings of worth, because you will be developing skills and abilities, as well as insights about yourself and your date. Usually participation dates cost less and allow you to get to know each other better than do spectator dates.

But participation dates call for an investment from both parties. Many young people are lazy and uncreative. They would rather take the easy way out—sitting and watching something rather than planning an activity. Would you prefer a picnic or a hike in the mountains rather than sitting at home and watching a TV special? Of course, some people feel they aren't good at bowling, canoeing, or sailing. They tend to resist competing with someone who can paddle, bowl, or sail circles around them.

Since participation dates offer far more advantages than do spectator amusements, they should make up the larger portion of your dates. Even on a first date, if you can manage it without getting questioning looks from your would-be partner, go for it!

You are already well-acquainted with spectator dates and what they include, so I'll not include any suggestions. But sometimes young people need a little help in thinking up some creative participation dates. Here are some ideas.

Cross-country skiing
Go jogging
Take tennis, golf, or swimming lessons
Hike in the mountains
Play ping-pong, croquet, or horse shoes
Buy a bus pass and ride all over town
Read a book together
Throw Frisbees
Go roller-skating or ice-skating
Ride bikes
Look through each other's family albums
Window shop in some antique stores
Make some craft projects together
Visit a museum or a zoo
Make homemade ice cream
Walk through a cemetery and read markers
Explore a new town
Cook a meal together
Go on a picnic
Take your parents out
Go picture-taking
Borrow a BB gun and in a safe place shoot at cans
Wash your car together and have a water fight afterward
Go to the beach or a shopping mall and pass out religious literature
Refinish a piece of furniture together
Visit a nursing home or call on a lonely person

Our son Rodney has always been able to think of creative ways to date young ladies. One time he invited a girlfriend for a motorcycle ride and a picnic in the woods. It rained that day, but they went anyway, built themselves a small fire in an enclosure, and ate as they huddled by the fire. (I checked with him to see what he served when he asked a girl out on this kind of date—fruit Jell-O that he made himself in the dorm, chips, apples, and cookies.) They had a fun time and got to know each other better despite the adverse circumstances.

Participation dates not only are fun, but they also stimulate creativity, are educational, tend to be more helpful to others, are more relaxing, are less selfish in nature, and provide unique and unhurried ways for a

Viewpoint

1. Strongly agree
2. Mildly agree
3. Not sure
4. Mildly disagree
5. Strongly disagree

Read each of the following statements carefully. Respond to each statement according to the scale of 1 to 5 as shown at the left. Circle the appropriate number for each statement. Your responses should represent your personal opinion at the present time.

1 2 3 4 5   1. If I had the opportunity I would date a non-Christian.

1 2 3 4 5   2. I have gone steady with a non-Christian.

1 2 3 4 5   3. My parents don't care if I marry a non-Christian.

1 2 3 4 5   4. Religion doesn't matter in a relationship, but love does.

WHAT DO YOUR RESPONSES TELL YOU ABOUT YOUR ATTITUDES IN DATING NON-CHRISTIANS? _____

_____

_____

_____

_____

couple to get to know each other better. Most of them are inexpensive or free. Some people may be too inhibited to try a participation date, and for such a person they may not make good first-date situations. But many persons will welcome the change of pace, and this type of involvement and interaction with another person will certainly perk up a relationship between individuals who date regularly.

I have not mentioned the big social events—banquets and the like. These often constitute first dates for many. Such a date gives security by requiring an escort. It provides the time and opportunity to talk with your date. Likely you will be among friends who can contribute to the conversation and make you feel more comfortable. However, these dates can be expensive and often encourage attempts to impress the other one. Another disadvantage comes from being around those who know you well. They might say, "Well, look who's dating whom!"

To Kiss or Not to Kiss

Sam walked Susie to the door after their first date. He had enjoyed going out with her and reached for her hand. She's a nice gal, he thought. We had a good time together. I'd like to kiss her goodnight.

Susie's heart skipped a few beats when

Sam took her hand. She anticipated what was coming next and let him kiss her. After she was inside she threw herself on her bed, her mind racing. L-O-V-E! At long last she was really in love, and he loved her, too!

On the way home Sam thought, I enjoyed Susie. Dating is a great activity, and I must do more of it. Sure glad I'm not tied down to anybody.

Demonstrations of affection can mean different things to different people. The significance of handholding and kissing will vary from person to person. But overall, girls tend to see more meaning in a kiss than fellows do. In this case, Susie had kissed only one other fellow in her whole life—her first steady boyfriend. Sam, on the other hand, had dated quite a number of gals, and a first-date peck meant little more to him than affectionate friendship. He didn't mean to lead Susie on.

Imagine what might happen next in the case of Susie and Sam. If she thinks she has found true love, Sam will withdraw when she tries to latch onto him. Then she will think he didn't like her at all and might conclude that all that men want out of women is sex!

In actuality, neither perception would be accurate. Generally speaking, fellows seek demonstrations of affection because they consider it fun. Girls, however, interpret affection as love. Both sexes need to recognize the other's perspective and not attach more significance to certain acts than the person intended.

If a couple has just begun dating and they begin making out too soon in their relationship, several problems will surface immediately. One of the main purposes of dating is to get to know each other better. Obviously, if you spend a good deal of your time necking and petting, you can hardly engage in much verbal communication (although a lot of nonverbal communication is going on). Your relationship will tend to remain at a very shallow level. I do not mean that a couple should never hold hands or kiss on their first date, but holding off a little will tend to help a couple develop a more balanced relationship. Many a perfectly good dating relationship has been ruined

prematurely because the couple was preoccupied with making out.

How to Get a Date

Whether you are a guy or a gal, choose someone who is at the same or about the same stage of dating as you are. A college freshman who tries to snag a popular senior is generally getting out of his league. When you choose someone who is approximately where you are along the dating road, both of you can learn and grow together with as little pain and embarrassment as possible.

Establish friendships before you begin dating. You must know what it means to be a friend, how to treat a friend, help a friend, and meet a friend's needs. After you learn how to be a friend, you are ready for dating a member of the opposite sex.

Fellows, most young women have their own ideas about how they would like you to approach them for a date. A girl would rather not have you move in with no advance warning and—boom—ask her out. In most cases she would rather have you pay a little attention to her first. Greet her several times, and single her out for a little small talk. In other words, a girl would rather have you be friendly first and work up to asking her out.

Many girls nowadays think it is all right to call a fellow and arrange for a date, but most fellows still prefer to do the asking. Though dating today is not nearly as structured and formal as it used to be, in a recent *Seventeen* magazine survey of 1,005 girls, 64 percent said they had never asked a young man out. (Nearly 71 percent of the girls were currently dating.) Only a tiny 2 percent frequently asked a fellow for a date. Even college girls, who are expected to behave in a more liberated fashion, are traditional. More than half have never asked for a date, and only 10 percent said they do sometimes.[2]

Girls who become too aggressive in dealing with guys scare them off. (Guys are already a little bit scared of girls as it is! This is the reason some fellows don't date at all. Young ladies often forget that every time a guy asks someone out he puts his masculinity on the line and risks being rejected. It

58

hurts to be rejected, and consequently many guys will not take the risk unless they have good reason to believe that the girl will accept.)

But times are changing, and a girl has many options today that she didn't have a few years ago. Some schools initiate a "reverse weekend," or a "slave day" or "Sadie Hawkins Day," in which everything is backwards. The gals invite the guys, pay the bills, help them with their coats, carry their books, and open car doors for them. This can be a lot of fun and a real opportunity for a girl to date a fellow she's had her eye on. Usually, however, when a girl makes the first move, she has to be very subtle or find a way to make the guy think it was all his idea.

But a girl can use some subtle ways to show a fellow that she is interested in him. You can arrange to sit near him or across from him. Try to catch his eye, and smile. Your eyes can convey a lot. (Caution: Don't overdo it!) He'll get the message. One fellow actually had his best friend sit next to him and poke him every time the girl across from him looked at him!

If you are having a conversation with him, pay close attention when he speaks to you. Act interested in what he says. This impresses a man. Sometimes a friend can pass on information in the right manner. Make sure this person can drop hints tactfully, or you might be worse off than when you started.

Join the same club or engage in the same activities that he participates in. Ask for help with homework or a project you are working on. Plan a party that includes some couples along with some nondaters so that people do not have to "couple up." Participate in group dates, and go where young people meet each other—parties, sporting events, or church activities. Get together with a couple of friends and plan an afternoon picnic. Invite four or five guys to join you. (Hint: keep the numbers uneven to avoid the tension of having to pair up.)

Women are freer than ever before to initiate friendships in the dating process. When kept in the balance, this can be healthy. Some women even want to share in the expense of dating activities. Even some very "macho" men no longer hold this as taboo. Both males and females are less role-conscious today than ever before. In dating relationships, it is more important to be supportive of one another than to be overly conscientious about which sex is supposed to do what.

The Makings of a Good Date

One interesting study revealed that 90 percent of the students polled felt they were "good" dates. However, when the same males and females rated each other, they were quite critical of each other's dating abilities! A lack of respect and courtesy, along with rudeness and inconsiderate behavior, turned off the girls, as did heavy drinking, swearing, drugs, and smoking; failure to plan for the date with attempts to get the girl to decide; aggressive attempts to neck, especially on first dates; and too much bragging and self-centeredness.

Fellows complained that the girls were difficult to please, conceited, self-centered, and artificial; acted like "gold diggers";

Many teenagers encounter problems with their parents when they begin to date. Teenagers find that their parents are constantly worried about their choice of companions, their activities, and curfews. You could probably eliminate much of this kind of trouble by drawing up your own "dating agreement" and presenting it to your parents. Listed below are the topics you might wish to mention in your agreement.

My Dating Agreement

I,_____, do hereby agree to abide by the following standards in my dating life:

1. State how many times per week you feel you should be permitted to date. Make it reasonable for your age and grade level.

2. State what hours you think are reasonable curfews for both weeknights and weekends. Also state what you would do if circumstances forced you to miss meeting a curfew, such as a car breakdown.

3. State your standards for dating Christians versus non-Christians.

4. State your standards regarding blind dates or pickups.

5. Dating is a PRIVILEGE, not a RIGHT. This privilege should be granted you by your parents on the condition that you are carrying your load of responsibility—that your homework, grades, and duties are completed satisfactorily. State your intentions toward such responsibilities.

6. There are acceptable and unacceptable dating activities. State the forms of entertainment that you consider acceptable and unacceptable.

7. State your standards for limiting physical affection.

8. Since parents are often anxious about who it is you are dating, how will you go about introducing your dating partners to them?

9. Read the following Bible verses and write out a brief statement on how you will allow these texts to influence your dating life (read them in the Phillips translation):

Romans 12:1, 2	Ephesians 5:3-5
2 Timothy 2:22	Colossians 3:5, 17
1 Corinthians 6:15-20	1 Thessalonians 5:22
1 Corinthians 7:1	1 Timothy 5:2
Matthew 5:27, 28	1 Corinthians 13

placed too much emphasis on "rating" in choice of dates; insisted on being asked too far in advance for dates; and were habitually late for dates.

When the researcher asked the students what qualities and values were the most important in both casual and serious dating, the following seven traits appeared (I list them according to rank):

1. physical and mental fitness
2. dependability
3. pride in personal appearance and manner
4. clean speech and action
5. pleasant disposition and sense of humor
6. consideration and thoughtfulness
7. acting own age and not being childish

Success in dating depends largely on your personality, your behavior, and your appearance. However, please note that these things are determined by your self-concept. All the dos and don'ts for a great dating future won't do you any good if you cherish negative feelings about yourself. Who wants to be around someone who is always running himself or others down, or feeling sorry for himself, or lacking confidence in his ability to do things? A person with positive feelings of self-worth can make a much better dating partner.

Self-examination prior to the time you begin dating is essential, but if you are already dating you can still evaluate yourself. Look at yourself; listen to yourself, especially when you are around friends. Would you like to be with you? The information you gather about yourself will indicate your readiness for a great dating future.

Curfews

Dear Van Pelts: My parents are impossible! They never allow me to stay out past midnight. This is ridiculous nowadays. Frequently, I have to leave a party just as things get going. It is so embarrassing. My dad says he doesn't want me to get into trouble. I can do so just as easily before midnight as after. I know I'm supposed to obey my parents, but do I have to when they are so unreasonable?

How should young people react when they feel their parents take an unrealistic position on curfews and dating regulations? Most likely when your parents made the rules regarding curfews they were thinking back to their own dating days and what they did after midnight! Those thoughts haunt them, and they wish to protect their own child from some of the same mistakes they made—whether or not their young people want such protection.

Sometimes a simple rule like "You must be in by midnight" can save you a lot of grief. Parties that just get going by midnight bother me. What goes on at a party that just begins at midnight? Whatever the activity, couldn't it begin earlier? And many intimate moments get started after midnight. Obviously, if you are alone with a member of the opposite sex for long periods of time after midnight, all the resolves about how far to go could easily get lost in the excitement.

Undeniably there is more to do after midnight than just making out. If you really feel your parents are being unfair when it comes to curfews, ask them to discuss the rule with you. Explain to them exactly what you would like to do after midnight, why you can't return home before that time, how it makes you feel when you must excuse yourself and leave before the others, and exactly what time you would be home.

If you haven't proved yourself trustworthy in the past—if you have come in late repeatedly after your curfew and have gone places you said you wouldn't go and done things you said you wouldn't do—don't expect your pleas for leniency to impress your parents. If you want to prove that you are trustworthy, then you will have to be trustworthy. Your parents might listen more openly to your point of view if you were to draw up a dating agreement. (The workbook gives a sample.)

Remember, the parents who gave birth to you and raised you may know you better than you know yourself.

Interracial Dating

About one quarter of the 1,005 girls surveyed by *Seventeen* magazine had dated someone of another race. Nearly 50 percent of nonwhites have crossed the color line as opposed to 20 percent of the whites. Girls who live away from home and those over 20 years of age date interracially the most frequently. Forty-seven percent of the young women polled said they would not even consider interracial dating.[3]

The Bible does not address the issue of interracial dating and interracial marriage. It is explicit only on the fact that "believers" should not marry "unbelievers." However, interracial dating presents some problems. Interracial couples will probably get static from both sets of parents—and parental approval rates very high when it comes to marital success. And if you say, "Hold it! I'm only dating the person, not marrying the person!" you have not matured sufficiently to realize that your dating patterns set the stage for marriage. If you engage in interracial dating, you will have a lot of pressures to fight, stresses to bear, and barriers to break down.

When parents disapprove of the relationship, reject the idea of dating on the sly. Dating in opposition to your parents' wishes will increase your guilt feelings and create more problems. If you have the urge to flaunt the fact that you love a person of another race, you had better take a second look at the relationship. If you are out to prove something, you are likely heading for disaster.

Does Religion Really Matter?

While ministers, marriage counselors, and parents continue to debate the pros and cons of marrying out of one's religious faith, the trend to do so is growing. Current estimates indicate that one out of four Jews marry a non-Jew, and one out of two Catholics and Protestants marry outside their faith.[4]

When *Seventeen* asked 200 teenaged girls throughout the country about their opinions on dating and religion, 97 percent responded that they felt religion played no part in determining whom they dated. Not all these teenagers wanted their interfaith relationship to end in marriage, but even then more than 75 percent said they would

not object to marrying someone from a different religious background.[5]

Take Shelly. She says, "Yes, I'm dating Jeff. I know he's not a Christian, but I'm only dating him, not marrying him. There's no one else to date right now. He's the only one around, and if I want to date, it has to be with him."

Because there is no Bible verse that states, "Thou shalt not date a non-Christian," we must look for scriptural principles to help us draw proper conclusions on this subject. However, some Bible passages do teach that a "believer" should not marry a "nonbeliever." Look at 2 Corinthians 6:14, for instance. It reads, "Do not be bound together with unbelievers; for what partnership have righteousness and lawlessness, or what fellowship has light with darkness?" (N.A.S.B.).* The expression "Do not be bound together" is translated "Be ye not unequally yoked" in the King James Version.

If you hitched a donkey and a horse together to pull a wagon, they would probably fight or be pulling in different directions—anything to get away from each other. Or since the horse's legs are longer than the donkey's legs, they might go around in circles. Whatever the outcome, one thing is certain: it makes for a poor team.

Similarly, dating someone who does not

share your religious perspective poses problems. You resist for a while, but then the rationalizing processes of your mind win the battle and you begin spending a little time with this person. Then you wonder why it took you so long! It may be the greatest relationship you have enjoyed yet. And before you know it you deeply love each other.

Once you are in love, you have problems. You will find yourself being pulled in opposite directions. Finally comes a time when you must make a choice. Either consciously or unconsciously you must choose between God and your friend. If you choose God, you will hurt emotionally because you will lose the affection of someone you love dearly. But if you choose your friend over God, you will hurt spiritually because you have put your relationship with another human being above that with your Maker. If you choose the latter course, you may find that you rapidly lose interest in spiritual things, and soon you grow hard and cold toward spiritual matters of any kind. You try to convince yourself that you are happy in the choice you have made, but underneath you know that when you are not right spiritually, you can't be right in any other area of life.

Marriage must be a relationship based on emotional, physical, and spiritual oneness. Once you get married, all kinds of forces will work against you, and you'll need all your resources to fight against them. Young people often reject this idea. One girl said, "If I loved a man, his faith wouldn't matter. Religion doesn't count—love does!" Another young man said, "The marital relationship is between you and your partner, and the religious relationship is between you and your God. The two are different!"

If you wish to establish a home where you think you can rely on your own strength during times of stress, you are free to try. But all the evidence and statistics are stacked against you. Currently almost one out of every two marriages ends in divorce. But, according to Billy Graham, in marriages where prayer and family devotions form a regular part of life, only one in 400

marriages breaks up. You may be well-matched emotionally and physically, but without spiritual oneness the chances for success are slim. How foolish, then, to take such a chance!

Josh McDowell, popular author and lecturer among young people, tells the story of an attractive young woman who was one of the most popular students on campus. Many fellows wanted to date her. She was very interested in the social aspects of Christianity, so she began attending meetings of the Black Nationalist Movement. During these meetings she spoke up frequently, relating all issues to God. The groups listened to her because she made sense and because she lived what she spoke about.

After one of the meetings a real "big wheel" on the campus who was used to dating whomever he wished whenever he wished, asked her for a date. She turned him down. He was astounded and asked why she refused. As simply and nonreproachfully as she could she told him, "I'm committed to Jesus Christ, and I don't want to date anyone who isn't committed to Christ also. You're not committed to Christ."

Her response didn't turn him off. It only increased his desire to date her, so he began trying to break her down. For three weeks he persisted in his efforts to make her change her mind. Finally she replied, "OK, there's college life [a religious meeting] tonight. You can take me to that."

The fellow wanted to go out with her so badly that he took her to college life. The next week he asked her out again. She said she would go if they went to college life. In four weeks she led this fellow to Christ, and today they are missionaries.

She sorted out her standards for dating and then trusted God with her date life. If you want to see God do great things through you, then you must be careful about dating those who do not share your own religious convictions.

Social Security for the Young—Going Steady

Everyone has favorite foods, favorite

friends, favorite teachers, favorite clothes. And after dating around enough, a young person comes to realize that one person stands out above all others. So begins the pairing up and exclusive dating. Others end up going steady simply because no one else will give them a second look or because they enjoy the security it offers.

The rules of the dating game change during steady dating. Usually in casual dating you like each other but are not in love, and both of you are free to date others. In steady dating you have exclusive rights to each other's time and attention. Neither partner can accept or initiate a date with someone else. Exchange of gifts on special days such as birthdays, Valentine's Day, and Christmas is usually expected.

Steady dating offers several advantages. Neither person wonders who will take him/her to a party or function. It is a foregone conclusion—and without any formal invitation—that they will attend together as a couple. Going steady offers security for both sexes. It protects both from being dateless or stuck with an undesirable date.

It also offers emotional security. The years of youth provide many crises when it seems that parents, teachers, brothers and sisters, friends, and even the church stand in the way of everything you want to do. Sometimes it seems that the whole world is crashing down on your head and that no one understands what you are going through. A steady partner, one who knows how to listen and understands how you feel, can be a great emotional asset.

In a steady relationship, it is meaningful to receive someone's special attention and affection. It symbolizes trust, attraction, and a degree of commitment that makes you feel cared about in a special way. This in turn builds up your feelings of self-worth. Perhaps you never had the opportunity of counting on anyone in a special way before. But now that you are going steady you find that your confidence in other areas of your life is increasing. You feel more likable and worthwhile. You begin reaching out to others and speaking up in groups—something you never would have dared to do

previously. Feeling loved and cared for can work wonders for feelings of personal worth.

A steady relationship also can save money. The longer a couple dates steadily, the more casual the dates become. You no longer have to go out on costly formal dates. Now you plan times of just being together—watching television at each other's home, shopping, or studying together. No longer do you try to impress each other, so you can begin to enjoy togetherness and sharing.

Lastly, a steady relationship can teach you about human relationships. The closer you get to someone, the better you know and understand that person. This closeness will demand that you become less selfish and more giving. As a result, you will learn how to get along with members of the opposite sex in the wider circles of your social life.

On the other hand, going steady is not all roses. Too much togetherness can be a burden, especially if you move too quickly too soon. Going steady at a young age or too soon in the development of a relationship presents certain temptations that can inhibit personal and spiritual growth. The greatest drawback to a premature steady relationship arises from the arrest of personal, emotional, and social growth.

Steady dating can cause identity problems for some young people. Paula likes classical music, onion rings, and antique cars because her steady date loves these things. She has become a carbon copy of the likes and dislikes of her current flame. In chameleon like fashion she changes personality and values along with boyfriends. She has never let her own personality develop, and someday she likely will wake up and find that she is bored and frustrated.

Another disadvantage to going steady is the increased opportunities to get "hot and heavy." It is difficult to pace a steady relationship, especially if you are years away from marriage. Many times even young persons with high ideals fall into premarital sex as a result of going steady. Often such young people get caught by pregnancy because they think of them-

The Most Popular Game

1. On the following scale the six stages of dating are listed as they move toward marriage. Circle where you are now.

Friendship	Casual Dating	Special Dating	Steady Dating	Engaged-to-be-engaged	Formal Engagement	Marriage
1	**2**	**3**	**4**	**5**	**6**	**7**

This gives you an idea of how close you are to marriage.

2. There are six major reasons for dating. Rank from 1 to 6 the reasons why you wish to date with one being the MOST important.

_____ To develop my personality

_____ To better understand the opposite sex

_____ To fill my need for love and intimacy

_____ To fill my needs for fun and recreation

_____ To find a future marriage partner

_____ To help me grow spiritually

3. What qualities are most important to you in a dating partner? List six qualities you value most.

1. _____

2. _____

3. _____

4. _____

5. _____

6. _____

4. If you are currently dating one person steadily, put a check mark after each quality your dating partner possesses.

5. If your dating partner possesses only a couple of the qualities you desire, why do you continue to date this person?

selves as nice kids who would never go too far. They get caught by the emotion of the moment, take no precautions, and the girl ends up pregnant because to have taken precautions beforehand would have meant they planned to disobey God.

Another major hazard of going steady is that it gets to be a habit. Many couples continue to go together long after a good thing is over because neither knows how or has the courage to end it. One fellow put it like this: "At first I liked Connie a lot. I eventually talked her into doing some things I'm not too proud of now. I have lost interest in her. I feel like a rat, but I don't know how to ditch her without hurting her."

What happens after you have gone steady? Do you assume that someday you will break up, or do you plan someday to go into the next stage—the engaged-to-be-engaged phase? How can you build a relationship with someone without thought of marriage?

A couple who are years away from marriage and yet desire a workable relationship must face many problems. They don't want to break up. They are not ready for marriage. And they don't want to wait for sex. This causes a couple to continue in a relationship for social reasons, but it offers no basic purpose or direction. A dangerous state!

Going steady in itself is neither right nor wrong. It is an important and essential level of the courtship experience. It is a serious trial period during which a couple thoroughly studies each other's emotional, moral, spiritual, and social characteristics while analyzing whether they will make a safe marriage risk.

Time is your friend when trying to evaluate your compatibility. No one can play a part forever. Sooner or later the mask will slip. During the evaluating process, avoid artificial conditions that do not allow both of you to observe one another under various conditions. Too often dates are on their best behavior, which makes it difficult to learn what they are really like.

The teen years are precious years, so use them to your full advantage. They are carefree years with few obligations. It is the time for developing honorable values, worthwhile goals, and standards of behavior. Get involved. Meet new people. Date a lot. You shortchange yourself if you limit your opportunities during the early years.

Everyone who comes in contact with your life will leave a part of himself with you. You can learn lessons even from a complete bore, braggart, or gossip—lessons like tolerance! Give yourself a real basis for comparison. Don't be like the fly in the bottle of vinegar who thinks it is the sweetest place in the world because it is the only place he has ever been!

A Word to Nondaters

Charlie Brown, of the "Peanuts" comic strip, has become a favorite of mine because he puts his finger on so many basic issues in life. I was watching one of the Charlie Brown Valentine Specials that depicted another episode in the lonely life of Charlie Brown. All the students in Charlie's class brought valentines to school and put them in a brightly decorated box. When the time for the party came, the box was shaken and then "teacher's pet" passed out the valentines. Everyone in the room began to receive valentines—everyone, that is, except Charlie Brown. There he sat with all his friends, but entirely forgotten. In coloring books he parks himself outside his mailbox on Valentine's Day and tells Snoopy: "I'm going to stay right here until I hear from someone." He never hears. He's the loneliest guy in town. And hence comes the popularity of Charlie Brown. Many people identify with the episodes in his life.

How hard it is to sit on the sidelines and watch others having a good time in a round of dates with friends! A young person left out of this activity can cry out in loneliness to God, "Please, God, if You are there, why can't You provide a special friend for me now?"

Oh, how it hurts to be left out! The emptiness and sadness of not being loved when others seem to have it all. What despair! It might be the most discouraging emotion that a young person can have. A survey by the Purdue Public Opinion Poll confirmed that loneliness is the biggest problem confronting teenagers today.

But sitting on the sidelines and begging God to "send somebody—anybody" is hardly the right way to respond to loneliness. If you are not dating yet, relax. Remember that in six months you may be seeing someone on a steady basis, and the popular person you envy so much now may be sitting on the sidelines. And just because the popular kids are dating does not mean that you have to. Each group has many different subgroups. If the "in group" isn't your speed, then seek out a more informal subgroup you can relate to more informally. Share something of yourself with the group—a common interest, time, activity. Develop some new interests and goals. Then you will not as often measure yourself by other people's standards, and you will find it easier to form relationships you really value.

One of the worst things you can do is to live your life from day to day as if you are waiting for something or someone to happen. Don't act as if you are in limbo waiting to come to life when "Mr. Right" or "Miss Perfect" enters the scene. Without goals and a sense of direction, you will be a poor specimen of humanity, and no one will want to date you. And if you finally do get into the swing of dating, you will find that you still have not discovered the key to

happiness. You have never developed the qualities you feel you need to make a success of your life. Chances are you will still feel lonely and frustrated.

Learn to accept loneliness for what it is—an emotion. Our emotions are not permanent but change according to our moods. In the meantime form some solid friendships with both sexes so you will be ready for a one-to-one relationship when it comes. Join a group, take up a hobby, and stay active. The loneliness you are experiencing can develop attributes of caring for others that you might not develop otherwise. Perhaps God wants you to search out other lonely persons and minister to their needs. You might also begin to forget your own misery and be a real blessing to others. God may also be allowing you to experience loneliness so He can draw you closer to Himself. He may want your full attention and allegiance.

---

* From the *New American Standard Bible,* © The Lockman Foundation, 1960, 1962, 1963, 1968, 1971, 1972, 1973, 1975. Used by permission.
[1] Herbert J. Miles, *The Dating Game* (Grand Rapids: Zondervan, 1975), p. 32.
[2] Jody Gaylin, "What Girls Really Look For in Boys," *Seventeen,* March, 1979, pp. 131-137.
[3] *Ibid.*
[4] Janice Kaplan, "Can Interfaith Romance Work for You?" *Seventeen,* January, 1981, pp. 104, 105, 120.
[5] *Ibid.*

Further reading you will enjoy . . .

Butler, John.   CHRISTIAN WAYS TO DATE, GO STEADY, AND BREAK UP, chapters 1-4.

Miles, Herbert J.   THE DATING GAME.

Scalf, Cherie, and Kenneth Waters.   DATING AND RELATING.

Dating forms a cycle—
dating around, going steady, breaking up.
With the exception of the person
you eventually marry,
you will break up every time
you go steady.

Chapter at a Glance

I. **Danger Signals to Look for**
   A. Extreme arguing and fighting
   B. Extreme physical involvement
   C. Conflicting goals and values
   D. Abuse
   E. Withdrawal
   F. Separation

II. **Breaking Up Without a Heart**
   A. Avoid the guilt trip
   B. Don't appear in public with your new love before you have broken up

C. Don't give your date the silent treatment
D. Don't purposefully avoid your dating partner
E. Avoid the hot-and-cold treatment
F. Avoid sending ambiguous "signals"

III. **Breaking Up With a Heart**
   A. Seek counsel
   B. Pray
   C. End the relationship once you've decided
   D. Warn the other person

Chapter 4

Breaking Up Is Hard to Do

He's been treating you differently. You can't quite put your finger on what it is, but things just aren't the same. Last night after the game he dropped you off at the house and didn't even come in for a visit. Said he had to get right home. You heard from a girlfriend that he spent some time with another group of kids after that. The last time he kissed you goodnight you got the impression that he did it because you expected him to do it. Lately you phone him more than he calls you.

He doesn't seem to be as happy as he used to be. He doesn't laugh and joke and share as much as he once did. When you ask him if there is anything wrong, he always gives the same negative response. Nagging doubts plague you. Then panic begins to rise. You don't hear from him for several days, and you don't call him either. When you finally see him again, you ask in a whisper, "What's the matter between us?"

You're afraid to hear the answer. He looks away. His shoulders droop. You know what he will say before he speaks: "I guess it's time for us to begin dating others."

It's over. Your dating partner wants to date someone else. What happens now? Dating forms a cycle—dating around, going steady, breaking up; dating around, going steady, breaking up, et cetera. With the exception of the person you eventually

---

E. Spare the other's feelings of self-worth
F. Admit your own failures
G. Be truthful
H. Choose the proper time and place
I. Afterward, keep quiet about problems
J. Let your emotions heal

IV. **How to Fall Apart After a Breakup**
   A. Beg him to take you back
   B. Make wild promises
   C. Look sorrowful and shed a few tears
   D. Threaten to jump off the World Trade Center
   E. Be gracious—and fall apart in private

V. **Surviving a Breakup**
   A. Bow out gracefully
   B. Don't be ashamed to feel sad
   C. Know the stages of grief recovery
   D. Don't immediately begin a new relationship
   E. Keep busy
   F. Pray

marry, you will break up every time you go steady. But how you handle it when the time comes is crucial. Let's learn to do it right.

Spotting Danger Signals

Occasions arise when it is healthier to break off a relationship than to keep it going. Some couples become so wrapped up in each other that they fail to see the danger signals that could wreck their future. Here are a few signs that should help you realize when emotional dependence has overwhelmed common sense.

Extreme Arguing and Fighting. Some arguing and fighting during a steady or ongoing relationship is normal. If a couple never disagrees or argues, they are not really being themselves, neither have they learned to interact with one another. But there is such a thing as too many disagreements, especially if they are loud, long, or continuous. Even well-matched couples may have a series of misunderstandings, but, overall, if your fights outnumber your periods of peace, then you have something to worry about.

Extreme Physical Involvement. Fred and Claudia can hardly wait for a few minutes alone together so they can make out. The sum total of their relationship revolves around the physical thrills they receive from each other. They spend most of their time together enjoying each other's physical attractions, but they engage in few participation activities and little or no verbal communication. When a couple gets this involved physically, the other areas of their relationship fail to grow. If physical intimacies dominate your relationship with someone, then you should break up and begin fresh with someone else so you can balance the emotional, physical, and spiritual involvement.

Conflicting Goals and Values. Phillip and Penny think they are compatible. They both enjoy basketball, country music, hamsters, and pizza. But this only tells what they like to do in their spare time. Goals and values make up what you are, who you are, and what you will be in the years to come. If one of you has dropped out of high school

and the other wishes to pursue a Ph.D. in chemistry, your goals in life differ so drastically that even compromise will likely not solve the problem. The college students who answered the dating questionnaire I designed listed values and philosophy of life as the most common sources of disagreement in their present or most recent love affair.

Abuse. To tolerate mental or physical abuse while suffering in silence and hoping the other person will change his or her behavior only encourages such behavior. If a fellow twists a girl's arm and roughhouses with her until she is black and blue but all the while insists that "it's only in fun," she had better take another look at their relationship. Individuals can also play any number of "mind games" that relegate others to the land of the stupid. Intentional public embarrassment that makes you look like a fool in front of others might be termed mental abuse. It indicates that the person needs more help than you can possibly give.

Withdrawal. Christy spends so much time with Dave that her friends hardly see her anymore. She just doesn't have time for them. Her grades have dropped, and she seems to have lost interest in sports, school, friends, and church activities. Love should expand Christy's interests, not close her off. Love is a constructive force that helps you develop into the best kind of person you can be. It releases energies within you that should help you produce your best, not drop out from life. Relationships that crowd out friends, school, sports, and church should be terminated.

Separation. When distance separates a couple, two factors should be considered as to whether they should break up—their age and the distance between them. If a couple is 14 or 15 years of age, ten miles might suffice to cool their heels after a while. However, an older couple might be able to keep things going even though a thousand miles separate them. If you are in your midteens and your special friend moves away, don't try to prolong the agony by swearing faithfulness to one another "forever and forever." All the long-distance phone calls, love letters, and promises won't stall the mortality rate. Young love can survive only in a here-and-now environment.

Poor Combination of Personalities. Whenever you begin dating someone, you link your personality with his or hers. Sometimes these personalities blend into a dynamic duet, and sometimes they bring out the very worst in each other. If two likable, well-adjusted, and outgoing individuals become selfish and bitter when combined as a couple, they should not date each other. Every person involved in a love relationship really needs to ask him/herself: "Am I a better or a worse person when I am with my special friend?"

Breaking Up Without a Heart

Breaking up is painful, so we refuse to think much about it and consequently never learn the procedures for correctly handling this aspect of life. Much of the pain associated with breaking up could be avoided if couples used a little tact during the process. Here are some things *not to do* when breaking up.

Avoid the guilt trip. Georgette has grown

"My boyfriend said he wanted to be like AT&T—break up and diversify his interests."

73

tired of Lance and knows she should break up with him, but she feels guilty about hurting him. So she magnifies his every negative trait in her mind until she can justify telling him off. After Georgette unloads on Lance, he hurts badly. Not only has Georgette dumped him, but she has also made him feel like an unworthy and unlikable person.

If you become interested in someone else and don't know how to break the news to your present steady date, the meanest way to do it is to appear in public with your new love. Especially ditch the idea of expressing public affection in front of your old flame in order to help that person get the message quicker.

To give your date the silent treatment or to avoid showing up when and where you usually do is not the way either. Such treatment transmits varying questions to the other person's mind: "What did I do wrong? Did I say something to hurt his/her feelings last night? Maybe he/she has been trying to ditch me for weeks and I've been too stupid to realize it. I never catch on!"

74

Avoid the hot-and-cold treatment. Bruce is seriously thinking about breaking up with Lori. Yet he hates to lose the security of what they had going. She is good-looking, and many of the guys envy his relationship with her. He vacillates in his treatment of her according to his present mood—sometimes he is thoughtful and attentive, but other times he forgets to call her. The truth is Bruce has tired of Lori. By treating her attentively he is trying to convince himself that they can still make a go of it, and by ignoring her he is sending the signal that it is all over. Such treatment only confuses the other person. Don't indulge in it while you try to make up your mind.

Avoid sending messages that your date could misinterpret. On a conscious level you may not even understand what is going on inside of you; yet you may say things you don't really mean.

If you say:
"I'm not ready to settle down yet."
The other person might interpret it as:
"I've met somebody else I like better than you. Get lost."
"We seem to be growing apart."
"You've changed, and I don't like the change in you."
"We don't have the same interests anymore."
"I used to find you interesting, but now you bore me."
"We don't communicate on the same level anymore."
"We used to be on the same wavelength, but now we have nothing to say to each other."
"I'll be leaving for college next month, and we won't be able to see much of each other from now on."
"When I get to college, I want to look over the whole field."
"I'm so involved with my studies and my job that I hardly have time for a social life anymore."
"You aren't as important to me as you used to be."

If you feel the time has come to break your relationship, examine your reasons carefully and then state them openly, clearly, and honestly.

An immature person may end a relationship just because the other individual no longer meets his needs. But surely it is selfish to view a relationship only in terms of having one's own personal needs met. Such an immature individual has failed to see that he too has a responsibility for certain aspects of the relationship. But he finds it easier to blame the other person rather than accept his share of the guilt; consequently the immature person often chooses the easy way out of ending a relationship. Rather than facing difficulties within himself, he will move on to a new partner and leave the other one wondering and hurting.

Mature persons will face the inadequacies in a relationship and evaluate whether they can overcome the unfulfilled expectations or whether they should separate. Those who do not have high ethical standards can sever the relationship and never see one another again. But such an unfeeling, uncaring way of ending a steady relationship will not do for those who cherish high ideals. Such individuals try to end a relationship without encouraging bitterness to develop between them.

It is possible to break up in a spirit of thankfulness for what the two of you have shared, for the pleasant memories of good times, and for the personal growth that resulted from your friendship. In the last few years Rodney has had seven or eight romances; yet he remains on friendly terms with each of these young women. It can be done.

Breaking Up With a Heart
I know of no gentle way to break up. Whenever two people who have cared for each other part, they will suffer. But you can do something to soften the blow and prevent more serious problems during this difficult time.

Seek counsel. If you have doubts about your decision to call it quits, seek advice from someone you trust and respect. When we are emotionally upset, we often say and do things we regret later. Many couples who have broken up during the heat of an argument later wish they hadn't. Unburden

75

yourself, if necessary, to a trusted friend, a minister, a counselor, or a teacher. Explaining the whole situation in detail will help clear your mind, and the objective opinion of someone not emotionally involved in the situation often proves helpful.

Pray about it. Seek divine guidance. Ask the Lord to make it clear that you have chosen the right course of action. Also request His help in carrying out your decision with kindness. Pray that the person you are breaking off with will get over the breakup without suffering serious emotional or physical problems.

End the relationship as soon as you decide to do so. Rather than leading the other person on, take steps to end things after you have reasonable doubt. Don't pretend to care about someone whom you have lost interest in. Once you have made the decision, stick with it. Don't be conned by promises to change, compromise, or do things differently.

If possible, give the other person a warning. An abrupt break can have the same kind of impact as the sudden death of a close relative. Most people find it easier to accept the death of a terminally ill person than to face an unexpected highway fatality. They have had an opportunity to prepare themselves emotionally. When your dissatisfaction with a relationship reaches the breaking point, you might drop hints about how you feel. For instance, you might say that you think you are depending on one another too much. Explain that you feel it might be better if you both dated others with the possibility of picking up the threads later after each of you has had the opportunity to make comparisons.

Spare the other person's feelings of self-worth. It is a major loss to the self-image when the person you have loved rejects you. Avoid dragging up all the negatives about the other person. Instead, emphasize all the good times you have had. Talk about what the other person has contributed to your friendship during your time together. Spell out your appreciation for his or her finer qualities.

Admit your own failures in making a go of

the relationship. Perhaps the person you've been going with did not possess the character traits you first saw in him/her. Admit your own lack of insight. (Admit this to yourself if you can't bring yourself to admit it to the other person!) This will help you learn to accept responsibility for your own actions and prove your maturity. Sort out why things went wrong and the part you played in it.

Be truthful regarding your reasons for breaking up. You have a responsibility to tell the other person why you want to break up. All the young people I've talked with regarding this point agree that they want to know the reason even though it might hurt to find out. In the long run it will prove beneficial. Mature persons want to learn from their mistakes. Even though it hurts a lot, it is better to be told why than to continue wondering what was said or done to cause it. Proceed in the following manner: (1) Admit your own failures in making the relationship work; (2) point out some facet of the other person's personality that you have appreciated; and (3) then honestly and openly state the problem area *without being brutally frank.* Do not deliver negative information unless you can do it kindly.

Choose the right time and the right place for the breakup. Don't drop the bomb on the way to a big event or the night before a heavy exam or in front of others. Breaking up in private hurts enough as it is, but to deliver such a jolt publicly or just before an important event is cruel and inhuman.

After the break, keep to yourself any personal problems the two of you have had. Avoid the desire to broadcast information and gossip to your friends. The nicest thing you can say (for yourself and the other person) is: "We used to go together, and he/she is a fine person. We'll always be friends." If you circulate damaging information, you do yourself a serious disservice. If the other person was such a jerk, why did you go with him/her anyway? Don't advertise your own poor judgment.

Let your emotions heal a little before trying to see the other person again. When you do see each other, keep your conversa-

You, the Counselor

You, as the counselor, must decide if the following relationships should be broken. Read each case study and place a check in the appropriate column.

yes	no	

Kathy and Sam are deeply in love. They have been going together for five months and have hit it off well. Kathy is a deeply committed Christian and Sam is not, but Kathy is sure he will become one after they are married. Sam has some other faults that worry Kathy. Every now and then he really blows his top. Kathy is sure her love will change this, too.

Jack and Jean are engaged. They have had several serious misunderstandings that they are always able to patch up. Most of these misunderstandings are over Jack's mother, who disapproves of Jean. Jack has been engaged three times before to other girls.

John and Dorothy have been "engaged-to-be-engaged" for several months. John is trying to break off the relationship. Dorothy threatens to do something drastic if he does. She has attempted suicide before.

Bob is Catholic and Joan is Protestant. During the early stages of their relationship they discussed their religion and neither would change. They avoid the subject entirely now, and the wedding is three months away.

A week before the wedding Susan meets, quite accidentally, the former wife of Frank, her fiancé. She learns details of his first marriage that he never told her. Susan's family tries to assure her that everything will be all right. Frank was only 18 and infatuated. This time it will be different.

Janice and Herb have known each other for two years and been engaged for six months. Wedding plans are in progress. They live five hundred miles apart and see each other two times a month. Janice has met a fellow at work who is very attentive to her and has asked her out. She hasn't accepted yet, but is tempted.

Betty is 21 and has her own apartment. She is a deeply committed Christian and believes, after much prayer, that it is God's will for her to marry Les, a young man she has been dating for a year. Les too has a strong faith in God. Betty's parents strongly oppose the marriage. Betty's parents are not Christians. Betty and Les are convinced their marriage will work.

tion light and short. Don't try to sound overly friendly too soon lest the other individual misconstrue it as an attempt to get back together.

How to Fall Apart After a Breakup

It's over. Your steady wants to date someone else. What will you do? Check one:

1. Fall on your knees and beg him/her to take you back.
2. Make wild promises to become exactly what the person wants you to be. You *promise* to change.
3. Look sorrowful and shed a few tears so he/she will feel sorry for you. If that doesn't work, resort to open crying and let the sobs rack your body.
4. Threaten to climb to the top of the World Trade Center and jump off.
5. Thank him/her for the good times you have shared and part with your head up and your step light. Then fall apart in the privacy of your room.

If you have never yet been through the experience of a broken romance, chances are very good that someday you will. How will you cope with it when someone you care about deeply indicates that he/she no longer wants a romantic relationship? There are dignified ways to survive. If you can handle a breakup with a little class, it will do wonders for your self-esteem and help you save face. Or breaking up can be messy and create ugly scenes that will embarrass both parties. The choice is up to you.

Often the person who has just been dumped feels so hurt that he/she angrily lashes out at the other person. The individual usually does this to justify the hurt. You, too, might be tempted to rant and rave about how stupid he was in the first place and how you should have broken up with him ages ago. But refuse to mend your broken ego by slandering the other person. Try not to defend yourself by intimating, "He is the undesirable one, not me. I'm still very desirable." Or, "When word gets around about what you're really like, buddy, no one will want you either! I'll see to it that justice will be carried out!" Don't indulge in the luxury of saying to yourself:

78

Parting Friends

If you have never been forced to break off with someone you care for, chances are you will have to do it sometime. In order to help you be prepared for this event, write here what you might say. But before you do, remember to:

1. Admit your own shortcomings in making the relationship work.

2. Point out something about the other person that you have appreciated.

3. Then honestly and openly state the problem without being brutally frank.

"Since I can't have you, I will personally see to it that no one else will want you either." Few of us actually verbalize these thoughts, but they are ever-present thoughts and subconscious responses for some.

Other times revenge takes form in a more direct attack. When Matt breaks off with Sue, she lashes out at him. "This is exactly what I always knew you would do. I never should have gone with you in the first place. You really enjoy hurting people, don't you? You've hurt me so many times I've lost count. This time you will really finish me off. I've given you everything, done everything for you, and look at the way you treat me. I should have known better. You never were good enough for me in the first place!" Sue wants to make Matt feel as terrible for dropping her as she does for getting dropped.

Sometimes when the emotional dependence on the relationship has been great, the reaction against the person initiating the break takes the form of threats, blackmail, or even violence. Threats to tell personal secrets, to get high or drunk, to commit suicide, or other wild statements usually are only desperate attempts to hold onto someone. Occasionally the rejected person

will rush into a short but intense physical relationship with someone new, partly for revenge and partly to compensate for the lost love.

Beware of all romances after one has just ended. If you cry on Ron's shoulder because you and Fred have broken up, it is all right to accept Ron's sympathy, but don't get carried away. Remember that you are very vulnerable to any attention right now and will probably leap at any chance to fill the void. Rebound romances are phony to the core and will likely burn out quickly.

Surviving a Breakup

If you still care for the person who initiates the breakup, how much better it would be to leave him/her wondering if he/she has made a terrible mistake in breaking up rather than creating a scene and removing all doubt from his/her mind. Try to leave the other person thinking, "He/she is really something," rather than, "Whew! Am I ever glad I'm rid of that one!"

Bow out gracefully with your self-esteem intact. Tell the other person that knowing him/her has been good for you. You don't understand why it is over, but if it has to be this way, then you hope the person will be happy. Assure the other person that you always want to be a friend. You may also say, if you care to, that you find it difficult to stop loving someone overnight and that he/she will likely be a part of you for a while. You may also ask why. Talk it over if you can. But when all has been said and done, accept the situation and use it to your advantage rather than detriment. Instead of looking and acting like your world has fallen apart, carry your self-respect away with you.

Don't be ashamed to feel sad. It is a normal reaction during a time of hurt. If you feel like crying about it, go ahead—and this advice goes for males as well as for females. Crying is a natural release for stressful situations and relieves the pressures that build up. But do your weeping privately.

You'll probably find it helpful to take a look at the psychological response to a deep loss. Psychologists have discovered that people go through fixed stages following intense grief. This process applies regardless of the kind of loss—the death of a loved one, divorce, or a serious breakup. First comes *denial*—an unwillingness to accept what has happened. Then follows *anger* turned outward—toward others, at those who have caused the hurt, as well as anger directed toward God. The third stage is *anger and guilt turned inward*—a process of blaming oneself for what has happened. The fourth and last stage is *genuine grief*. During this stage the impact of the loss hits the grieved person with full force. Weeping characterizes this final stage—the resolution phase. Now the grieved person can finally deal with the grief and resolve it.

Knowledge concerning the four stages of grief cannot prevent you from going through the emotional turmoil, but it might help you pass through the stages more easily. And, in effect, the individual on the receiving end of a broken relationship is going through the process of grief. The longer the couple have gone together and the more intimate the relationship, the deeper the grief will be. Passage through each of these stages is a normal reaction. After one good cry over it all, you can probably rest assured that the worst lies behind you. Try to avoid becoming trapped in any one phase, for it could lead to depression.

Remember, too, that your ex probably had no more fun breaking off with you than you have had in receiving the news. Anger, hurt, and resentment may have constituted your first reaction, but through it all try to be understanding of what he/she is going through also. The other person's explanation (as painful as it may have been for you to hear it) may contribute to your personal growth and future development. Just because this person has broken off with you does not mean that no one in the world wants you or that you are not a worthy person.

So now that the relationship has ended, where do you go from here? Your entire life seems out of whack. You may feel like dropping out of school, running away, quitting your job, getting drunk, jumping off a cliff, or pursuing some other drastic course of action. You may feel low, lower than ever before.

However you feel, do not immediately seek another relationship. Give yourself a chance to heal. Time is a wonderful healer, although some people take longer to recuperate than others. The time involved in bouncing back from a breakup will be in direct proportion to the intensity of the severed relationship. While you are recovering take time to look at yourself and evaluate your progress in personal growth.

Yes, give yourself time to hurt and grieve and adjust to the loss. But after you have sorted out your responsibility for what has happened and talked it over with a friend, it is time to get on with life. You may be tempted from time to time to bask in your own misery and pain while trying to enlist the sympathy of friends. But learn how to put the past behind you and keep it there.

Keep yourself busy. Don't hibernate in your room and brood over all your failures. Enter group activities that will help distract your mind from your problems. Get involved with helping others. This way you will be more inclined to forget your own troubles as you think of others who just might have bigger problems than you.

And pray about it. God knows and cares about what has happened to you. Tell Him how you hurt, and ask Him to help you heal. Claim the promise that ''all things work together for good to them that love God'' (Romans 8:28). God has a purpose in allowing hurt to touch our lives. It teaches us how to respond more sensitively to the needs of others. We also have a tendency when hurting to seek a closer walk with God. But whatever the reason hurt enters the life, we must trust God.

Andrae Crouch, the gospel singer, loved a young woman ardently. Then one day they broke up. Andrae Crouch hurt deeply, but he turned his thoughts to God, and out of the depths of his grief he wrote the beautiful gospel song ''Through It All.'' * Through it all Andrae Crouch came to depend on God's Word. Through it all he learned that God could indeed solve his problems.

You are attending a football game with a friend, and suddenly you see him enter the stadium. A redhead clings to his arm. You don't know her, but you've seen her around. You wait for the inevitable hurt to engulf you, but only a twinge of pain comes and goes. It surprises you. Then you take another look at the redhead and wonder what she's got that you don't have. Naturally you wonder if he already feels the same toward her as he once said he felt toward you. You reflect for just a moment. Your home team scores a touchdown. You cheer along with the others and heave a big sigh of relief. It doesn't hurt the way it used to. ''At last,'' you whisper under your breath, ''I've finally put myself back together again!''

---

* Andrae Crouch and Nina Ball. *Through It All.* (Waco, TX:Word, 1974), pp. 93-95.

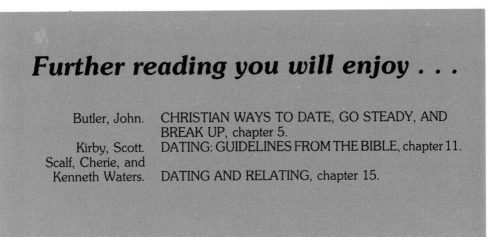

Further reading you will enjoy . . .

Butler, John.   CHRISTIAN WAYS TO DATE, GO STEADY, AND BREAK UP, chapter 5.

Kirby, Scott.   DATING: GUIDELINES FROM THE BIBLE, chapter 11.

Scalf, Cherie, and Kenneth Waters.   DATING AND RELATING, chapter 15.

Almost no studies have been conducted
to determine the components, effects,
or results of infatuation,
although volumes have been
devoted to love.

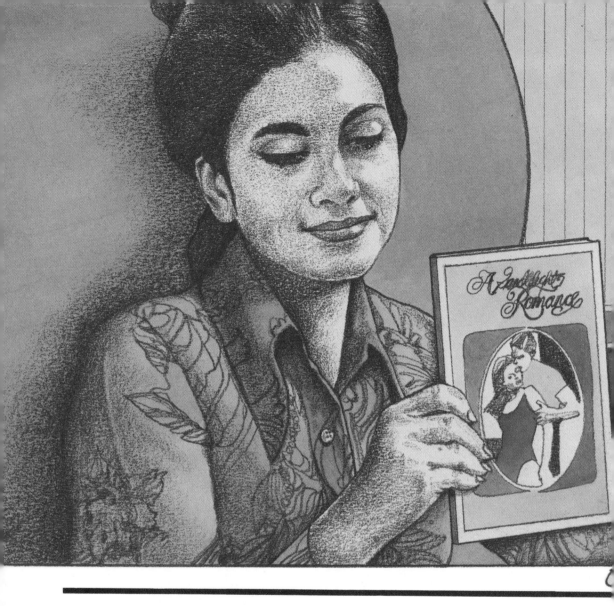

Chapter at a Glance

The Young Person's Number 1 Dilemma— How to Tell if You Are Really in Love

According to recent studies, most people will have from seven to ten romances in a lifetime. One survey found that the average college student will have experienced infatuation six to seven times and love once or twice.[1] You may already have experienced a portion of your allotment of romance. But the big question is, How can you tell for sure if you are really in love or if it is just infatuation?

The following What-Do-You-Know-About-Love Test for Young Lovers will help you understand what you really think about love. This love test will help you determine how well informed you are about the subject. It consists of a series of true and false statements. Circle T for true and F for false. Take the test before reading the rest of this chapter.

The What-Do-You-Know-About-Love Test for Young Lovers[2]

T F 1. Love at first sight is possible between some people.

T F 2. Premarital sex is acceptable when a couple cares a lot about each other.

T F 3. When real love hits, you will know it.

T F 4. When a couple truly loves each other, they will not fight.

---

    5. Love recognizes compatibility
    6. Love recognizes faults
    7. Love survives separation
    8. Love limits physical contact
    9. Love is selfless
    10. Love brings family approval
    11. Love produces security
    12. Love recognizes realities
  D. Infatuation isn't all bad

V. **Looking Through the Keyhole at Love and Infatuation**

VI. **The Truth About "Falling in Love"**
  A. The word love has many meanings
  B. It is better to grow in love
  C. The longer one loves, the harder it is to stop loving
  D. Falling in love is not enough

T F 5. It is easy to tell the difference between real love and infatuation.

T F 6. It is quite normal for someone to be in love with several persons at the same time.

T F 7. When you are really in love, you lose interest in other people, things, and activities.

T F 8. When you fall head-over-heels-in-love with someone, you will know by your feelings if it is the real thing.

T F 9. Once a couple find true love they should marry as soon as possible.

T F 10. The average young person, before becoming a mature adult, will have been in love several times with several different persons.

T F 11. Love is something you cannot study or prepare for, since it is an emotional response.

T F 12. When you are really in love, you will see only the good in the other person.

T F 13. It isn't very important whether family and friends approve of your love relationship—it is of concern only to the two of you.

T F 14. Absence makes the heart grow fonder.

T F 15. Frequent quarrels, arguments, and misunderstandings will not be present when you are really in love.

T F 16. It is better to marry the wrong person than to remain single.

T F 17. When you are in love, you can overcome all obstacles regardless of the differences between you.

T F 18. When you are in love, you will spend a good bit of time daydreaming.

T F 19. When you are in love, you will work harder, produce more, plan better, and function at a higher level than ever before.

T F 20. God has created and chosen one special person for me, and through prayer and searching I will be guided to this person.

Turn to the end of the chapter (p. 99) for scoring and evaluation instructions.

Help! I Think I'm in Love!

If you are a typical young person, chances are you think you are in love—right now! One researcher asked 500 young women at nineteen American colleges if

they felt they were in love right at that moment. Seventy-two percent said they thought to some degree they were. Only 27 percent said they probably or certainly were not.[3]

While most youth think they are in love, many express real doubts about it. Nearly a third of the young women in this study only "guessed" about the probability, and another 23 percent thought they were "pretty much" in love. In other words, more than half felt unsure. And we can reasonably assume that many of those who reported they were in love were actually experiencing infatuation.

Another researcher asked a group of college students if they felt they knew what love really was. That question turned up the following results:

	Males	Females
I'm sure I know what love is.	25%	36%
I think I know what love is.	59%	54%
I don't think I know what love is.	12%	8%
I'm sure I don't know what love is.	4%	2%

This means that three quarters of the men and about two thirds of the women were not sure they understood what love is. The study also found that students thought of their current romantic involvements as love, but rated past romances as infatuations. Undoubtedly, many of these past romances might have been described as love if the interview had been conducted while they were in progress.

Furthermore, few love affairs, in spite of their intensity, lead down the aisle. One study found that only a scant 15 percent lead to marriage. Another study on the courtship patterns of 400 college students discovered that almost three fourths of the 582 love affairs reported broke up before marriage.

Such information helps us understand that there is tremendous confusion when it comes to ascertaining true love feelings. It all leads back to the original question, "How can you tell if you are really in love?" Before answering this question directly, let's take a look at the stages of love.

How Love Develops

The average person progresses through five stages of love. If you wish to learn how the capacity to love develops, you will need to understand these five stages.

Infantile Stage. A baby receives love just because he has been born. He cannot love others, and no one expects him to. The infant thinks only of himself. He is concerned only about getting what he wants and satisfying his own desires. He doesn't care how he puts others out as long as he gets what he wants. His parents need sleep, but he doesn't worry about their needs. He'll wake them up at 2:00 A.M. just to get a drink! A baby loves only himself.

Hal seems stalled at the infantile stage, because he thinks only of himself. He is old enough to vote, but he often behaves like a 6-month-old infant who demands what he wants when he wants it.

Parent Love Stage. The child's first love—other than himself—revolves around his parents, particularly his mother. Probably this is because she spends the most time with him and does the most things for him. Soon she means more to him than anyone else does. He wants his mamma to stay with him, and he dogs his dad's footsteps when he's around. Now the child loves himself and his parents.

Meet Jennie, who has never progressed beyond the parent love stage. She wants to live in a dream world and never wake up. She expects Lloyd to spend his whole time making a fuss over her, planning little surprises for her, sympathizing with her, and arranging picnics and parties at which she is the center of attention. In short, Jennie wants another parent to cater to her every whim.

Buddy Love Stage. A few years later the child ventures out of the home and begins to take an interest in children his own age—particularly those of his or her own sex. He now adopts the standards of his buddies rather than the standards of his parents. He is becoming socialized and learning to deal with his equals. Parents take second place in his thoughts now as he begins breaking away from dependence upon the home. He now loves himself, his buddies, and his parents—in that order.

At the buddy level is Les, who hangs out with the guys. He has little to do with the girls. Although he belongs to several clubs, he lacks confidence in himself and his abilities when separated from his friends. Unless Les advances from the buddy stage, he may always fear women, even his wife. He may never want to take her anywhere, preferring to stay home and have her cater functions for his men friends. He may release his energies through clubs, church, work, and the like—to the tune of three or four nights a week!

Adolescent Stage. During adolescence, the horizon expands once more. Now the individual takes an interest in the opposite sex. At this level a girl finds boys worthy of more serious study, and vice versa. But the tendency is still to consider love in much the same way as a baby does—in terms of what it can do for oneself rather than what can one do for others.

George, who is as intoxicated with sex now as when he was in college, has gotten stuck at the adolescent level. During his college years, sexy pinups decorated his room, and he was constantly on the make. Now that George has married, he continually criticizes his wife because she does not dress, make up, or do her hair the way some other woman does. He continually tries to cover up his own feelings of insecurity by making jokes at her expense and by sneering at marriage as a form of slavery. When they go out together, he makes a fool of himself by paying too much attention to other women. When they get home, they quarrel bitterly. His defense is, "Well, I'm only human!" Yes, at an adolescent level!

The adolescent level is a trial-and-error period when attention focuses on one person for longer and longer periods of time. At first one guy is as interesting to Evie as another. She goes out with a different fellow each time. Later in high school she dates Bill for a whole semester before she makes a change. Then she goes steady with Ted for a whole year, only to begin with someone new in the fall. In her senior year she actually becomes engaged to Stuart, but this falls through after graduation. Little by little, Evie is learning what men are like and what she is like in relation to men. At last her interest becomes specialized and she marries Ben. Her love feelings finally have matured.

During the early teen years particularly, a girl may dream about older, handsome men—a movie star, a television idol, a musician, an outstanding singer, or someone in the public eye. As she becomes older she becomes more realistic. Instead of dreaming about a distant television idol, she may dream about the handsomest boy in school, the star athlete, or the student body president. Again, though, she doesn't think of what she could do for her dream love, but only what he might do for her. She daydreams that if she can make one of these good catches, all the other girls would envy her. They would have to admit that she really had something if she could catch him!

So love begins with the idea of what you can get, not what you can give to a relationship. And if you have nothing to give, it can't last long. You will probably learn (if you haven't already) that your dating partner may expect you to do much, to make sacrifices, to satisfy needs, and to cater to whims. You finally realize that your partner does not want to spend the entire evening praising you, whispering sweet nothings in your ears, seconding your suggestions, or agreeing with your views. You recognize that your date wants recognition and appreciation just as much as you do.

Bit by bit, after many experiences that start out with the appearance of love but fail to grow into anything meaningful, you begin to understand that love consists of much more than the feelings involved in romance during the early stages of dating.

Mature Love Stage. When you reach this level, physical attraction becomes less and less significant, and emotional and psychological factors become more important. You move from thinking about what you can get out of the relationship to what you can give to it. You shift your thinking from

There are five progressive stages of love:

INFANTILE STAGE—the one who is busy filling his or her own needs only

PARENT LOVE STAGE—the one who expects his or her parents to make him or her the center of constant attention

BUDDY LOVE STAGE—the one who likes the security of hanging around with friends constantly

ADOLESCENT STAGE—the trial-and-error period during which you go with a series of different partners while you are searching for the real thing

GENUINE LOVE STAGE—the time in which you are more concerned over what you can give to the relationship rather than what you can get out of it

Place a check where you are now. At which stage is your partner?

yourself to your partner. If you are truly in love, in a spirit of unselfishness you try to do what is best for your partner. And if your sweetheart really loves you, he or she will think about your best interests in an unselfish way. So while you are giving you are also receiving.

Going through all these stages takes time, and most of us enter marriage with some infantile love left in us. In fact, most of us never mature in every way. But some people are so seriously arrested in their emotional development that it would be nearly impossible for them to relate to others in an adult way.

With a little careful observation you should be able to identify whether your present relationship is at an infant, parent, buddy, adolescent, or mature stage. You can observe behavior and judge for yourself. But many young persons deliberately close their eyes to some of the danger signals. It is also exciting to be young and in love with love! They don't want any interruption to spoil the enchantment of the present experience. It is a little more difficult

to distinguish between the adolescent level of infatuation and the mature level of genuine love. The next section will help you understand those differences.

Love Versus Infatuation

A young person wrote Abigail Van Buren, the famous newspaper columnist, and asked how one knows when he is in love. Abby replied: "If you have to ask—you aren't." [4] The inadequacy of Abby's response surprises me, but many people, when asked how you know when you're in love say: "Oh, when it hits, you'll just know!" *No, you won't just know!* Infatuation is a strange mixture of sex and emotions. My dictionary defines the word as "completely carried away by unreasoning passion or attraction." It comes from a Latin word that means "silly or foolish." Differentiating between the emotions involved in love and infatuation is always complicated.

Love and infatuation do have one thing in common—strong feelings of affection for a member of the opposite sex, which complicates the matter of sorting out the differences because many of the symptoms overlap one another. The most passionate and blind infatuation may contain a portion of genuine love. And genuine love may include several symptoms found in infatuation. The differences between love and infatuation, then, are often found in *degree* rather than in definition. Therefore, one must examine all evidence with extreme caution.

Almost no studies have been conducted to determine the components, effects, or results of infatuation, although volumes have been devoted to love. This is unfortunate because infatuation causes no end of heartache for those caught in its trap of deception.

Love and infatuation share three similar symptoms: passion, nearness, and strange emotions. Passion may be present without genuine love. It is entirely possible to feel passionate or to have strong sexual feelings for a person you have not even met. Necking and petting increase the urgency of erotic feelings until sex may become a prominent part of your association together. But these feelings do not necessarily indicate genuine love. Sexual attraction can be as urgent in infatuation as it is in genuine love.

Likewise, the desire to be near one another constantly can be just as overwhelming in infatuation as in genuine love. You may wish to be together all the time, dreading the hour of parting. You may experience a feeling of emptiness after your friend has gone, but this does not necessarily mean that you have found real love. Longing for the other person may be just as strong in infatuation as in love.

Experiencing strange emotions when you think about the other person is not valid either. You may feel like walking on air when everything is going well with your love and downright ill when things go wrong. But this can happen just as frequently with real love as with infatuation, although funny feelings and strange emotions are probably more indicative of infatuation.

Greenhorn prospectors occasionally

mistook pyrite for gold. Fool's gold can be detected by popping it into a pan and putting it on a hot stove. It sends out a strong stench while it sizzles and smokes, but heat will not damage real gold. Unfortunately, you cannot put your love in a pan on a hot stove to see if it passes the test, but you can test your feelings by noticing the following clues. I have not listed them in order of importance, but you should consider each and every factor as objectively as you can.

Are You in Love or Star-struck?—Discerning the Difference

Love develops slowly; infatuation rapidly. Love *grows,* and growth requires time. Infatuation often hits suddenly. You cannot really know a person after only a few meetings. Many people wear masks and put on their best behavior at first. They try to be pleasant and agreeable at all times and keep such unpleasant traits as anger under control. For this reason it takes months and even years to know a person well. This is also why some people complain that they married a "stranger." Some people successfully hide their true personalities during courtship and reveal their true selves only after marriage.

Now you can understand why I cannot accept the "love-at-first-sight" theory. I can accept "like-at-first-sight" or even "like-very-much-at-first-sight," but "love," no. You may feel strongly attracted to a person you just met. You feel the chemistry working. You like what you see—body build, actions, and responses. You may like everything about the person. But there is still a great way to go before you can love that person.

Love ends slowly; infatuation ends rapidly. You cannot test this factor, of course, until the relationship ends. But in retrospect a person can ask two questions: How long did the romance last? And how long did it take to get over it?

Just as genuine love takes time to develop, so it also takes time for such feelings to vanish. It can happen in no other manner. If the two of you have grown together and shared many experiences together, you may not get over a breakup for a long period of time.

Infatuations end much the same way they begin—fast—with one exception. Infatuation will not end rapidly if you have become involved sexually. Sex complicates the emotional responses. A couple may stay together not because of the many interests shared but because of mutually satisfying sexual relations. Therefore, the length of time in recovering from a breakup does not indicate anything significant if the couple has had sex together. In such a relationship the lingering emotions need not imply that it was genuine love.

Love centers on one person only; infatuation may involve several persons. An infatuated person may be "in love" with two or more persons at the same time. These individuals may differ markedly in personality and temperament. For instance, a young woman may say she is in love with two fellows and find it impossible to choose between them. One is mature, stable, and responsible, whereas the other is an irresponsible, fun-loving spender. Most likely

"How do I love thee? Let me count the ways . . . ."

91

the girl really loves neither one. Chances are it is her adolescent responses that are drawing her to the fun-loving spender while her maturing emotions tell her that the qualities of the other fellow hold more importance. In her mind she combines the qualities of both and thinks she has fallen in love with both. Genuine love focuses on one person who embodies the qualities you have selected as essential. You no longer have to combine people to form an ideal.

Love motivates positive behavior; infatuation has a destructive effect. Love will have a constructive effect on your personality and bring out the very best in you. It will provide you with new energy, ambition, and interest in life. It promotes creativity and an interest in personal growth, improvement, and worthy causes. It engenders feelings of self-worth, trust, and security. Love will spur you on toward success. You will study harder, plan more effectively, and save more diligently. Life takes on additional purpose and meaning. You may daydream, but you stay within the bounds of reality by centering your thoughts on plans within reach. Your love will encourage you to function at your highest level. By contrast, infatuation has a destructive and disorganizing effect on the personality. You will find yourself less effective, less efficient, less able to reach your true potential. Family members or close friends may notice this effect immediately. They might say, "My, what's come over you? You won't go anywhere or do anything. What's the matter with you? Are you sick or something?" Then someone else will comment, "No, she's not sick. She's in love." But that observation misses the point. You are infatuated, not in love.

Infatuation thrives on unrealistic daydreams in which you imagine the two of you leading a beautiful, blissful life together in perfect agreement at all times. These daydreams cause you to forget the realities of life, school, work, study, responsibilities, and money.

If you are in love, you will naturally idealize about your love, but this will tend to grow out of an understanding and appreciation for the other person that you have checked out against real circumstances. If you are infatuated, you will idealize with complete disregard for reality.

Love recognizes the importance of compatability; infatuation disregards it. If you are in love, not only will the physical appearance and behavior of the other person attract you, but so also will his or her character, personality, emotions, ideas, and attitudes. You will be interested in the way he or she thinks and responds to situations. You will focus on the values you hold in common. How does the other person respond to personal success or failure? To the pitfalls and challenges of life? Is he or she kind, appreciative, and courteous? Do your attitudes on religion, school, family, sex, finances, and friends match? What interests do you share in common? Can you enjoy an evening with family or friends at home, or must you always go out somewhere? Are your backgrounds similar? The more you have in common in these areas, the better your chances for developing genuine love.

It may not sound very romantic or exciting, but a good marriage prospect might live next door to you. You grew up together, played together, went to the same school. Your family and social backgrounds are similar. Compatible personalities, along with common interests and values, go a long way toward developing a lasting love relationship.

Love recognizes faults; infatuation ignores them. Love will lead you to recognize the fine qualities in the other and help you build a relationship on those. But even though you recognize those good qualities and idealize about them to some degree, you do not see the person as faultless. You freely admit areas of his or her personality or character that fall short of perfection, but you see so much to respect and admire that you accept the person on the basis of the good qualities.

Infatuation, on the other hand, will keep you from seeing anything wrong with your friend. You idealize to such a degree that you will not admit that the other individual has any faults. You defend him or her against all critics. You admire one or two

qualities so much that you fool yourself into believing that these can outweigh all the faults or problems.

Love also recognizes all the good qualities, but it does not blind you to problem areas in the other person's personality. It will, however, enable you to love despite these faults.

Love survives separation; infatuation cannot. Love may even grow during a separation. Absence *does* make the heart grow fonder. If your love has been genuine, you will have been uniting your life more and more with your loved one. When he or she is separated from you, you will feel as though part of your own self is missing. Absence helps you recognize how much the relationship means to you.

Infatuation dies quickly once the other person fades from sight. Out of sight, out of mind holds because infatuation bases itself largely on physical attraction and one or two other qualities. Interest will die rather rapidly when the relationship is not sustained by contact. Infatuation cannot survive the test of time.

Love controls physical contact; infatuation exploits it. A couple in love tends to hold in check their expression of physical affection until relatively late in their relationship. Infatuation demands physical expression much earlier. Furthermore, physical contact makes up a smaller part of the total relationship for a couple in love, in contrast to an infatuated couple. The reason for this is that infatuation depends largely on physical attraction and the excitement felt when exploring the other person's physical equipment. The person experiencing this for the first time naturally concludes that this must be something very special because he has never before felt such a response.

Although genuine love includes physical attraction, it springs from many other factors as well. For the couple in love, physical contact usually has a deeper meaning than sheer pleasure. It expresses how they feel toward each other. Unfortunately, physical contact expressed in infatuation often becomes an end in itself. Pleasure dominates the experience.

Love is selfless; infatuation is selfish.

Being in love involves more than just the emotions. Genuine love gets off the feeling level and puts the principle of love to work in everyday life. This means that you will not only expect to be treated with love and consideration, but that you can also act with love and consideration *even when you don't feel like it.* Any of us can be loving when our needs are met and our partner behaves in a loving manner. But the test of love is whether you can be loving even when your partner has treated you unfairly, neglected your needs, or forgotten something you had asked him or her to do.

One of my favorite "Peanuts" cartoons shows Charlie Brown dressed in his pajamas and carrying a glass of water to Snoopy, who sprawls lazily on top of his dog house. The caption reads: "Love is getting someone a glass of water in the middle of the night." Charlie has the right idea here. It isn't easy to get up in the middle of the night and put someone else's needs before yours.

Infatuation is self-centered. You think more in terms of what the relationship can do for you than what you can do for the relationship or for the other person. You tend to feel great when your special friend accompanies you, because much of your feeling is related to the pride you feel when others realize that this person belongs to you.

Love brings the approval of family and friends; infatuation brings disapproval. When you truly love someone, your family and close friends will most likely approve of the relationship. They can see how well your personalities blend, the many interests you share, and how your relationship complements and motivates each other.

If your parents or friends do not approve—beware. If they feel convinced that you are about to make a big mistake, they may be right. They are extremely interested in your future welfare and don't want you to get hurt. Since they are not as emotionally involved in the situation as you, they may be able to see certain aspects you can't see. *Parental approval is a key clue.* Statistics show that those marriages which lack the blessing of parents have a high failure rate.[5]

When infatuation exists, your friends may not approve of your choice either. They may not come right out and say so, but you can often pick up cues that they wish you'd hurry and wake up to reality.

Strong evidence indicates that parents' and friends' approval indicates genuine love. Locke compared complaints registered by happily married persons with those of divorced persons. Divorced individuals were almost four times as likely to complain that they and their spouses had little in common with mutual friends. Locke also found that happily married couples were far less likely to have problems with each other's parents. If parents and friends object, take care. If they approve, take heart. The more they approve, and the more of them that approve, the better your chances for having found genuine love.

Love produces security; infatuation produces insecurity. If you are in love, you will tend to have a sense of security and trust after considering all the elements in your

relationship. An infatuated person, on the other hand, will probably struggle with feelings of insecurity and may attempt to control the loved one through jealousy. This does not mean that when you really love someone you will never feel jealous. It does mean that your feelings of jealousy will be less frequent and severe. Love trusts.

Some people feel flattered by their lover's signs of jealousy. They think it indicates true love and assume that the more jealous a lover is, the more they are loved. Jealousy, however, does not signify healthy emotions, but rather insecurity and a low self-image. Whatever the roots of jealousy, it will make you want to fence the other person in so you can keep him or her to yourself. In short, it makes you selfish and possessive.

Love recognizes realities; infatuation ignores them. Genuine love looks at problems squarely. It does not try to minimize their seriousness. Two high school students in love will strive to finish their education before they marry because they know their marriage will be stronger if they can build it on a solid educational foundation. They will not have to jump into a quick marriage for fear love will leave them.

Infatuation ignores the differences in social, racial, educational, or religious backgrounds. Sometimes infatuation grips a person who is already married or who finds himself or herself in a situation that precludes open dating. Infatuation argues that such things don't really matter. Surely if you love each other, things can be worked out.

A couple in love faces problems frankly and attempts to solve them. If certain problems seem to threaten their relationship, they discuss them openly and attempt to solve them intelligently. Under infatuation a couple will disregard or gloss over differences. A couple in love intelligently anticipates those problems most likely to occur.

Now that you have gotten a general picture of what kind of relationship you have, what should you do about it? The most important thing is to do nothing drastic—at least not right now. Even if you

"passed" with flying colors, hold back. Don't rush into any quickie commitments before you have applied the test of time. Remember, if you have found true love, it will still be there next week, the week after, and so on. You can avoid many heartaches by proceeding cautiously and slowly.

If your study has revealed that you are infatuated—or there's a good probability that you are—don't think that you must sever the relationship immediately, unless you've given the relationship a fair shake. Sometimes infatuation grows into real love, but if you move too fast in either direction you will never know for sure.

So relax and enjoy your relationship— even if it is only infatuation. *But recognize it for what it is,* and don't deceive yourself into thinking it is something it isn't. This may be one of several relationships you will have before making a final decision and settling down with a partner for life. What you can learn from your present involvement will prove valuable to you in future relationships.

CAUTION: Avoid any sexual encounters. It is normal and natural to have strong desires egging you on toward sexual intimacy. At times these urges may seem irresistible, but sex opens up a host of emotions and problems, which the next two chapters will discuss.

Have you analyzed your situation as carefully as you can but still can't decide whether or not you have found true love? Perhaps the more you try to figure it out, the more confused you get. If so, allow a little more time to pass. Time will give you experience. It will offer you more contact with your friend. It will provide more opportunities for you to find out what you need to know in order to make the final decision. After all is said and done, you have found genuine love when your mutual relationship fosters individual growth for both of you and increases the depth of your love for each other.

The Truth About "Falling in Love"

During a Compleat Marriage class, we asked people why they married. The

Looking Through the Keyhole at Love and Infatuation

INFATUATION . . .	LOVE . . .
1. is often based on nonsensical attributes, such as the way a person walks or laughs. Little things "send" you.	1. looks deeply into the compatibility of character traits, shared values, and common interests.
2. often depends largely on physical attraction—the chills, thrills, heartthrobs, and goose bumps felt when touching the other person.	2. considers other factors besides physical attraction. Physical attraction will make up a smaller portion of the total relationship.
3. often has a destructive and disorganizing effect on the personality, causing you to forget the realities of life.	3. brings out the best in you, promoting personal growth, self-respect, ambition, and improvement.
4. often ends rapidly—if you are not sexually involved. If sexually involved, this is not a valid sign.	4. takes time to develop and mature. Just as it takes time to grow, it also takes time for genuine love to end.
5. often keeps you idealizing the other person so that you are unwilling to admit any faults might exist.	5. recognizes fine qualities, but also recognizes qualities that are less than perfect.
6. often causes family and friends to disapprove of your choice.	6. brings approval of family and friends. They can see what your relationship does for both of you.
7. often dies quickly when the other person is gone.	7. can survive a separation.
8. often includes frequent quarrels, arguments, and misunderstandings as a consistent part of the relationship.	8. reduces tension as you work toward open discussion for solving problems without arguing.
9. is more interested in what you can get from the relationship.	9. is interested in sharing and giving to bring happiness and security to the other.

10. often includes frequent and severe feelings of jealousy.

10. promotes trust and security, which enables you to release the other person.

11. is generally used to describe past relationships.

11. usually describes present relationships.

12. often focuses on unsuitable persons.

12. is more often directed to suitable persons.

13. often includes frequent feelings of guilt, insecurity, and frustration.

13. is characterized by feelings of self-confidence, trust, and security.

14. is most frequent among young adolescents and immature persons.

14. grows over a period of time and comes with emotional and biological maturity.

15. can recur easily immediately after a previous love relationship has just ended.

15. will develop slowly following a previous love affair.

16. is often followed by boredom once sexual excitement dies off.

16. produces an ongoing sense of interest and joy when together.

17. requires that the couple must depend on external amusement in order to enjoy themselves.

17. sparks interest in each other and commonly shared activities.

18. changes your relationship very little even though you go together for a long time.

18. changes and grows deeper with ongoing association.

19. is often accompanied by shallow feelings and sensations that simply "send" you.

19. provides a climate of deepening feelings and growing intimacy as you share more of life with your lover.

20. often lasts only a short time.

20. tends to last for a long period of time.

21. often exploits the other person to your advantage.

21. protects, nurtures, and cares for the other person.

22. is always a poor basis for marriage.

22. is enough to build a marriage on—if all other factors are right.

majority of the couples answered, "Because we 'fell in love.' " They no doubt did. They married because they experienced a feeling that they interpreted as love. It is difficult, however, to state with any degree of accuracy precisely what love is. George Bernard Shaw said that love was the most misused and misunderstood word in our vocabulary. He may have been right. How would you define love? With which of the following definitions of love do you agree?

"When two people are under the influence of the most violent, most insane, most delusive, and most transient of passions, [and] they are required to swear that they will remain in that excited, abnormal, and exhausting condition continuously until death do them part."

"A state of perceptual anaesthesia."

"Love is a grave mental disease."

"Love is a fiend, a fire, a heaven, a hell,/Where pleasure, pain, and sad repentance dwell."

"Love is a feeling you feel when you feel you are going to get a feeling you never felt before."

"To love somebody is not just a strong feeling—it is a decision, it is a judgment, it is a promise."

"Love is an unconditional commitment to an imperfect person."

Furthermore, we use the term love in a great many different senses. We say, for example: "I love my parents"; "I love God"; "I love my dog"; "I love pizza." I assume that you do not have the same emotional response for your dog that you do for God. We talk about "falling in love," but the word *fall* has many meanings. We say: "Don't fall down"; a soldier "falls" in battle; the temperature "falls"; night "falls"; a nation may "fall"; a friend "falls" ill. What, then, does the expression *fall in love* really mean?

When we say that Sue and Tom have "fallen in love," we generally mean that an unexpected feeling has hit them, something over which they have no control. This, of course, relieves them from any responsibility connected with falling in love. But when a person "falls in love," the phrase should not imply that a couple has fallen down or fallen into a pit or a trap. A better meaning would be like that of "fall in line" or "fall heir to," a much less headlong process.

Another point. When we use the term, we usually mean that they have fallen in love only with their "hearts." But falling in love with the heart is only a portion of the love process. When you fall in love, you must fall in love with your heart *and* your head.

How much better it is to say that we "grow" into love. This is much nearer the truth, but it sounds so unromantic that we don't like to use the term. Although one may "fall" suddenly into a violent condition of infatuation, it takes time for love to develop. Love is complex. It does not strike suddenly or "fall" unexpectedly, as do stars. It comes only when two individuals have reoriented their lives, each with the other as a new focal point.

Perhaps you think of genuine love as a red-hot feeling that will burn steadily till the end of your lives together. But love neither stands still nor continues at the same level or intensity for a lifetime. We might compare the normal course of love to a wave, which rises and falls before it ultimately crashes on the beach. Most love begins strong. It may move to a quick conclusion or develop very slowly. The highest portion of the wave usually occurs at the beginning of "falling in love" or soon after.

If a couple who falls in love marry before they have ridden out the height of the wave, they may wake later to find themselves married to a totally unsuitable person. One disillusioned young bride described what happened.

Ku and I fell madly in love after we first met. We went together for about three months. We saw each other every spare moment and found it difficult to keep our hands off each other. We tried to hold our feelings in check because we didn't want to go too far.

Then we began to argue a lot and get on each other's nerves. We talked about it and decided that it was probably because of the sexual tension from our going so far but no farther. We decided

98

that if we would hurry up and get married, it would relieve the tension and we'd be much happier.

We were married right away, and for two months everything was near perfect. Now we have more quarrels than we ever had before. We found out the hard way that marriage is no solution to a dying affair.

In most marriages the love feelings tend to decrease very slowly after the first few years of mutual discovery have passed. Each new shared experience or understanding of one another naturally draws the couple together, so they ride the upward curve of the wave again, but such events and insights most likely will decrease in frequency as the years pass.

However, the longer one loves, the more difficult it is to stop loving. In the early days of dating, a minor crisis will often end the relationship before it barely has begun. If a young bride or groom were to discover that the other person had become unfaithful shortly after the wedding, it would likely end the marriage then and there. Yet my husband and I have worked with countless middle-aged mates who wait patiently for the unfaithful one to end the illicit affair and reestablish what they had going for them before it happened. The older couple has experienced a greater and deeper love that the younger couple has not yet discovered.

Although falling in love is an important element in the process of courtship, you must realize that falling in love is not enough. You need to check your love feelings against the realities of life.

A song says: "They tried to tell us we're too young, too young to really be in love . . ." I am not trying to tell you or any other young person that you are too young to be in love. (However, the younger you are, the more likely it is to be infatuation rather than love. But that's not the problem.) Anyone young or old can fall in love. The problem comes in trying to stay in love.

---

[1] Ray E. Short, *Sex, Love, or Infatuation: How Can I Really Know?* (Minneapolis: Augsburg Publishing House, 1978), p. 12.
[2] Portions of this test are taken from Dr. James Dobson's book *What Wives Wish Their Husband's Knew About Women* (Wheaton, IL: Tyndale House Publishers, 1975), p. 85.
[3] *Ibid.*, p. 21.
[4] The Fresno *Bee*, July 8, 1980.
[5] Short, *op. cit.*, p. 129.

Answers to the "What-Do-You-Know-About-Love Test from pages 85, 86.

All statements are false except numbers 10 and 19. If you scored 17 or higher, you have a pretty good understanding of genuine love. If you scored 15 to 17, you did well but could use a little help. If you scored 13 or below, you need definite help in understanding genuine love.

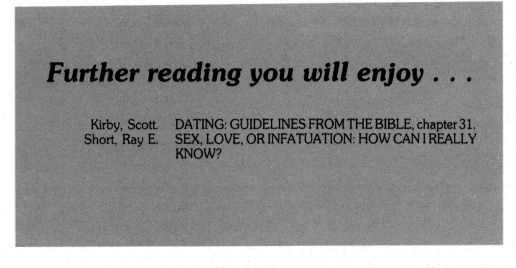

Further reading you will enjoy . . .

Kirby, Scott.   DATING: GUIDELINES FROM THE BIBLE, chapter 31.
Short, Ray E.   SEX, LOVE, OR INFATUATION: HOW CAN I REALLY KNOW?

Every young person,
whether male or female,
should have clearly defined standards
of sex conduct and then
stick by them.

Chapter at a Glance

I. **Petting Is the Most Popular Sport**

II. **Lines Guys Use**
   A. The "true love" approach
   B. The flattery approach
   C. The situational approach
   D. The big-shot approach
   E. The logical approach
   F. The abnormal approach
   G. The intellectual approach
   H. The threat approach
   I. The promises, promises approach

J. The guilt approach

III. **Why Gals Fall for These Lines**
   A. Carried away
   B. Inferiority complex
   C. Broken homes
   D. No father

IV. **Taming Petting**

V. **How Far Is Too Far?**
   A. Premarital sex
   B. Guilty conscience
   C. Undue sexual arousal
   D. Nudity
   E. Hurts relationship

Chapter 6

Touchy Situations

Statistics usually bore us, but you will probably find these figures on petting interesting. Next to dating, petting seems to be the most popular sport among young people. My research showed that 17 percent of the students surveyed had not engaged in petting and did not plan to; 27 percent had petted and never intended to do so again; approximately 43 percent had petted and intended to do it again; and 4 percent had no opportunity to pet. (Nine percent did not respond.)

When asked to indicate the most advanced level of physical affection they thought should occur during casual dating, 85 percent thought it should stop with holding hands and hugging and kissing. A scant 9 percent said it should end with light petting. And yet 17 percent of those who are presently having sex with each other report that they have only a "casual dating" relationship!

Fifty percent of those surveyed had had 1 to 2 petting partners; 28 percent had had 3 to 6. Most petting episodes took place in the car, although "at home" came in as a close second. Most students began petting at age 15 or 16. The greatest majority insisted that they petted in order to express love for their partners, closely followed by "we got carried away." Thirty percent felt petting had weakened their relationship, and an

---

VI. **Who Should Call a Halt and Why?**
   A. Shared responsibility
   B. The double standard
   C. Usually the female calls a halt

VII. **How to Put on the Brakes**
   A. Say No sincerely and politely
   B. Keep talking
   C. Avoid certain situations
   D. Plan dates
   E. Double date
   F. Reveal your values
   G. Keep an early curfew
   H. Plan after-date activities
   I. Use reason

   J. Dress modestly
   K. Set the limits
   L. Divert his attention
   M. Ask him to take you home
   N. Avoid dating "fast" guys
   O. Refrain from long Good nights

VIII. **Guidelines for Expressing Affection**
   A. The proper time and place
   B. The proper understanding
   C. The proper restraint

equal percentage thought it had strengthened their relationship. Sixty-six percent felt they were slightly, moderately, or very religious at the time of their most recent petting experience.

After these petting experiences, 31 percent felt positive about it and 29 percent felt negative. Those who had not participated in petting indicated overwhelmingly they had refrained because of personal values, not because of religious or family training. Less than 1 percent had discussed with their dating partner the possibility of limiting petting activities and decided to forego petting.

The respondents indicated they have engaged in petting even when they did not feel like it, for the following reasons (in descending order): "I didn't want to hurt the other's feelings"; "I felt pressured into it"; "I wanted to reassure the other person of love"; "I was afraid of losing the other person." Ninety-eight percent felt a girl did not need to pet on a date in order to be popular.

Forty-nine percent had engaged in petting to climax. The majority of young people considered "heavy petting" to mean petting to climax, and 10 percent considered it to be the same as sexual intercourse. Most of them did it for sheer sexual excitement and a lesser percentage to satisfy their partners. The survey showed that almost all who pet to climax in order to satisfy their partners are girls.

So much for the numbers! Now let's take a closer look at the practice of petting. Although the petting game is widespread, the rules vary tremendously. Young people tend to "wing it," making up their own rules as they go. Petting includes a wide range of body-exploring activities, and every group of young people seems to have its own definition of what constitutes light and heavy petting. I used the following definitions in my survey: "making out"—hugging and kissing without caressing or fondling of bodies; "light petting"—caressing each other's bodies outside of clothing; "heavy petting"—caressing each other's bodies underneath the clothing.

Whatever its definition, petting is an activity that says something important. Since most young people lack the ability to make flowery romantic speeches, they try to communicate what they feel through petting. They think that if they tried to put their feelings into words it would end up sounding corny and phony. They feel that their love is special, and they want to come across to their dating partner as sincere. They know that intercourse is the ultimate expression of love, and they aren't ready for that yet.

Petting goes a step beyond hugging and kissing but not as far as intercourse. When a couple engage in petting, they feel they are saying, "I love you and care about you. Someday our relationship may blossom into something more, but right now this is where things are."

But there's another factor. Although young people are reluctant to admit it, often they engage in petting because of the physical pleasure derived through sexual stimulation. They enjoy the pleasant sensations of the moment, and some get to the place where they look to such enjoyment as an end in itself. In these situations petting reflects self-love rather than love for the other. Under these circumstances petting violates the principles we expect to govern a relationship between a man and a woman. Particularly is this true during the casual dating stage, when the couple are not in love and have no plans to marry each other. Couples who engage in petting when they are not in love do so strictly for the fun of it. Yet sexual experimentation without love cheapens a relationship. To use another person to satisfy your own sexual desires of the moment is shoddy. The risks are high, and the rewards are low.

The game is risky because it caters to the temptation to take advantage of another person. People of all ages face the temptation to exploit others. But perhaps at no other time is a person more vulnerable to such exploitation than when involved in petting. The unloved feel loved, the ugly are made to feel beautiful, the lonely feel as though someone cares—all under the pretense of a love that may not even exist. A person's intense desire for someone else to care for him or her can easily translate the expression of lust into a message of caring, despite the falsity of motives.

The game is also risky because it leads many couples to intercourse. Such couples believe they can handle themselves and their emotions, so they begin petting and find it delightful. They also discover that in spite of all their good intentions, they have reached a point where they want to go on. They just can't stop.

Petting can also produce some permanent aftereffects in marriage. Psychologists and physicians have found that many of the women who cannot respond freely to sexual stimulation in marriage have the roots of their problems in early petting experiences. Some say that they got so used to responding to petting just so far and then stopping in order to keep from going all the way that later they still cannot go all the way.

And it has its price for the male too. Bad or early sex experiences can result in premature ejaculation, because he has gotten himself used to satisfying himself through quick sex. Trauma can also manifest itself in impotence, the inability to maintain an erection. Impotence is 90 percent a psychological reaction to a real or imaginary experience, and it can require extended periods of professional treatment.

Petting is not dirty. It will not give you a disease or make hair grow on your palms or curl your toes. Petting inside the bonds of marriage is a beautiful experience. It is the natural expression of love called foreplay, which leads to sexual intercourse. What, then, is the difference between petting and foreplay? Petting is the exploration of another's body by a couple who do not intend for intercourse to occur. And that's the trouble with petting. It doesn't stand alone. It is designed to move on to something else. By itself, outside of marriage, it is more frustrating than satisfying.

You should not view petting as an end in itself. It is a mistake to think of petting as only an adventure in the cool and calculated exploration of another person's body. Petting involves emotions and passions that all too quickly send inner controls into

oblivion. Petting is progressive. On your next date you will want to go a step farther in order to get the same thrills you enjoyed last time.

Petting might be likened to a bridge that spans the abyss between shunning all physical expressions of love on the one side and sexual intercourse on the other. Let's use this analogy, then. When petting, you could be one tenth or nine tenths of the way over the bridge. Persons who have never developed inner controls can find themselves across the bridge before they even realize it. Oh, it doesn't always happen all at once. It may take weeks or months, but those who begin a serious petting relationship will find out sooner or later how progressive it is.

Lines Guys Use

A professor who taught sex education classes at a large university asked his students to discuss the various approaches they had used to entice someone into petting or sexual encounters. At first these college-age young people laughed at the lines gradually exposed. Eventually, however, several of the guys complained that the discussion was ruining their sex lives! Follow-up reports confirmed there were no pregnancies during that session.

The role of lines in enticing young women into premature sexual activities is probably stronger than most people realize. Not only should a young lady know at what point to limit necking and petting, but she should also know how much stock to put in the man's persuasive words. Described briefly here are several of the more common approaches used by men.

The "True Love" Approach. One study revealed that the most prevalent line used is: "If you love me, you'll let me." Guys have used this one since the beginning of time. But if he does get what he wants, what proof will you have that he loves you when it is all over? More likely he used you to satisfy his own urgent needs. And furthermore, if he gets what he wants and doesn't leave you high and dry, you still won't have very much. Usually the guy who uses this line is a slow but steady operator who tends to hang in there till he gets what he wants. A good response to this line is "If you love me, you won't ask."

The Flattery Approach. "You have such a gorgeous body that I can hardly control myself!" Or "You're so beautiful!" or "You have such beautiful eyes!" Under questioning, the guys who use this line reveal they use it because they can think of little else to say. In other words, there is so little attraction between the two of you that he has to flatter you about your physical appearance in order to get what he wants. Of course, it reinforces what an attractive girl wants to hear, and even the most unattractive girl feels flattered. One study

106

showed that sexually aroused males rated women in pictures as much more attractive than did those males who were not sexually aroused when viewing the same pictures. The greater the sexual need, the better the female looks to a man!

The Situational Approach. "Everybody's doing it" is a line used by the situational-ethics crowd. These New Morality fellows try to imply that there is something the matter with a female who won't jump on the bandwagon, become mod, and live the way the rest of the world lives. They accuse her of possessing Victorian ideas. "Times have changed," they chant. "Live today and don't look back." They put such pressure on her that she begins to wonder whether she really might be missing something the rest of the crowd enjoys.

The Sympathy Approach. "Nobody but you understands me. Everybody is against me—my parents, the school, the law. All I need is you to help me, and everything will be OK." It doesn't take much of this approach to appeal to the mothering instincts of the average girl. You want to help this fellow who could amount to something if only he had an opportunity! You know his reputation isn't the best, but that could change if only others would give him a chance. Whatever the version, beware of this line. This guy has mastered the technique of playing on a woman's sympathies. Just as soon as you begin smothering him with sympathy he'll begin preparing you for the pushover!

The opposite version of the sympathy approach reads like this: "You poor little girl. Nobody has loved you as I do. You've had a rough deal so far. Your folks haven't been happy. But I'll show you real love, right now, in the back seat of this car . . ." Anytime sympathy is the primary motive, beware. This line poses a special danger for the young woman who comes from an unhappy home or who has never had a close relationship with her mother or father. This person is most vulnerable when she is feeling sorry for herself. You want a man to understand you, of course, but make sure he understands more about life than this.

The Big-Shot Approach. "Girls are standing in line for blocks to date me. You are a very lucky person, you know." He probably doesn't verbalize, but you get the idea through his words and actions. This guy is probably good-looking, tall, athletic, intelligent, personable, and popular with others. He has the ability to make you feel super special. You'll be especially vulnerable to this type if you are very young or inexperienced or if you have a good case of inferiority complex.

The Logical Approach. "I thought we were going to get married." "Who needs a slip of paper to legalize a love like ours?" "It's a good experience that will benefit our future together." This line comes on so gradually that it is often difficult to recognize. It occurs most often in long-term, steady relationships with a basically nice guy whom you "know" is right for you. A good response to this approach would be: "In case we ever changed our minds about each other, I wouldn't want you to feel obligated to me." Then be prepared for protests! The Sorenson report revealed that more than 33 percent of the sexually experienced girls believed when they first had sex that they would marry the fellow— but few of them did. However, only 7 percent of the sexually active fellows polled thought they would marry the young woman. One of two things was taking place—either she was fooling herself, or he wasn't telling the truth. Take your pick.

The Abnormal Approach. "What's the matter with you? Are you frigid or something?" "You don't want to be known as a cold cucumber, do you?" Every normal girl looks forward to a sexually complete relationship with her husband someday, but this guy plants seeds of doubt about her ability to function sexually. She wonders whether she might be undersexed or undesirable. WARNING: Fellows who use this approach generally believe that women are "things" to be "used" by males. Chances are that the "pro" with this line would and could make a gal frigid. (Remember, gals, that 99 percent of frigidity is located in the brain!)

The Intellectual Approach. Here the fellow promotes heavy "think" sessions regarding sex. He doesn't "do" anything at first—just gets you in the habit of verbalizing about sex. He's an excellent conversationalist who can wow you with phrases and ideas. His object is to lead you on in the natural sequence of events. Such discussions can be sexually enlightening and very stimulating. Some guys who use this approach are "innocents," and some are old smoothies. When things get too natural, better call a halt.

The Threat Approach. "If you don't, I'll date someone else." "If you aren't interested, I won't have any trouble finding someone who is." This fellow hopes to intimidate you by implying that unless you give in, you will have to sit at home alone for the rest of your life. He probably won't have any trouble finding a willing someone. But you know exactly what he wants from a relationship, and any girl will do. Tell this one that you'll pass his name around among your friends, then look for someone who will appreciate you and your standards.

The Promises, Promises Approach. "You won't get pregnant." "Even if you do, I'll take care of you." "We'll get married." Under the pressure of sexual tension, some guys will make promises that they could never keep. They may mean every word at the moment, but it would surprise you how quickly these fellows can forget all their promises once the desperately urgent sexual pressures have been relieved. Girls fall for promises because they desperately want to believe what the guy says. Girls, use a logical approach on him. Think it through. Is it possible you could get pregnant? Is he in a position to take care of you if you do? What does he mean by "take care of you"? Is he in a position to marry you?

The Guilt Approach. "I'm so tensed up I can't stand it! You've led me on. You can't stop now! I just gotta have it!" No, he doesn't "just gotta have it." If he doesn't get a sexual release right then, nothing bad will happen to him. He won't suddenly develop a hernia or suffer brain damage or have his growth stunted. The worst thing that might happen is that he might have to run around the block a time or two before he can go home, but that won't hurt him either.

There are many other "lines." The guys who use them run the gamut from those who know what they are doing to the totally inexperienced who stumble onto a young lady's weakness.

Now, I haven't intended to produce a negative image of males. They're really great—I'm married to one! Their tendencies are God-implanted, but these are powerful drives. The keen male sense is forever pursuing and trying to conquer. And the fact remains that it is the girl who gets hurt the worst—through pregnancy, yes, but also emotionally. Whereas the sexual encounter is a physical release for the male, it is a deeply emotional experience for the female. When sexually aroused, guys tend to say anything to get what they want. They will make verbal commitments, or promises, which they mean at the time, in order to obtain what they want. They do not consider this dishonest or lying when confronted later.

One fellow dated a girl for three years because he liked her breasts. Finally he broke up with her. Imagine! He hung on to the relationship for three years just so he could indulge himself in physical intimacies. Oh, what a man will do and say when his hormones get involved! Fellows, be honest with the girls you date.

Postscript: I do not wish to imply that young men have a monopoly on using "lines" or pressuring another for sex. During these times of sexual liberation, many young men report being pressured by their girlfriends for sexual activity. "Lines" can be a two-way street.

Why Gals Believe Them

From the time a girl shows an interest in boys, she begins to think about that special someone who will hold her tightly and profess the kind of love she has dreamed about. When this finally happens, she feels safe and protected and loved. The moment she has waited for has arrived. But hold it! At this point she has now become the most vulnerable. In order to keep her man, she may likely fall for almost anything.

Most young women innately understand

Don't Handle

1. Strongly agree
2. Mildly agree
3. Not sure
4. Mildly disagree
5. Strongly disagree

Read each of the following statements carefully. Respond to each statement according to the scale of 1 to 5 as shown at the left. Circle the appropriate number for each statement. Your responses should represent your personal opinion at the present time.

1 2 3 4 5   1. Petting has some of the same emotional effects on a couple as premarital sex.

1 2 3 4 5   2. Petting is progressive; each level of affection is enjoyable until the newness wears off.

1 2 3 4 5   3. It is up to the female to limit petting activities.

1 2 3 4 5   4. It is up to the male to limit petting activities.

1 2 3 4 5   5. Females usually engage in petting in order to feel loved.

1 2 3 4 5   6. Males usually engage in petting in order to get sex.

how to attract a fellow. They understand that their physical charms especially attract a man. And for the most part friends and society pressure them, push them, and chide them to get a boyfriend and get married. Every girl hopes she can entice a fellow far enough so that she can receive affection and have a dating relationship.

With this much established, let's take a look at some basic reasons why the feminine gender gives in to the approaches made by men.

We Got Carried Away. Pam, a truly fine gal, is going with Hal, a wholesome, well-liked guy. They believe that they have found genuine love. They are a first-rate couple and have held the line on physical intimacies. But one night they get carried away. Many girls get caught as Pam did. They need a little petting with their fellows in order to satisfy their need for emotional

intimacy and closeness. They have, of course, been taught that sex belongs in marriage, but if they can be swept off their emotional feet, seduced, or overwhelmed by the emotion of the moment, *when there was no planning in advance for the event,* it provides the excuse they need.

But getting carried away is no excuse at all. Each year more than one million U.S. teenage girls get pregnant, and three million people contract a sexually transmitted disease (two thirds of them persons under 24 years of age). Many of these girls got carried away, but no reason is big enough to wipe out the results that these girls suffered.

Inferiority Complex. Many studies indicate that inferiority complexes and sexual activity often go hand in hand. If a young woman feels terribly inadequate—that she isn't as attractive as other women, that she isn't accepted by others, that she isn't a part of the "in" crowd—she's on dangerous ground. In most cases she would give anything for attention, affection, and friendship. Madge had the reputation on campus for petting whenever she had the chance. One fellow described her as a "public neck." She longed to be popular, to matter to someone, but she had such a low opinion of herself, that she thought she had no other qualities to attract one. Unconsciously she said to herself: "If I can't interest a fellow any other way, at least I can use my body to attract one."

Those young people who have learned to appreciate in a healthy way their individual worth can more easily restrain their passions. The more a person accepts and respects himself or herself the less he or she needs to use sex as a means to affection. Feelings of self-worth allow a person to be patient and discriminating while progressing toward long-range goals.

Broken Homes. Girls with divorced or separated parents are three times as likely to be sexually permissive as young women from intact homes. These girls reflect the example and the teaching of their parents. One said: "At the time of my first encounter with sex, my parents were going into a hard time and almost divorced. This made me insecure and made me do anything to please my partner, because I wanted security, since there was none at the time in my home."

Girls reared in foster homes or by those other than their parents often show unrestrained sexual aggression. Strong consciences are developed under affectionate parents who consistently teach positive values and encourage restraint. Young people from happy homes are much less likely to be sexually permissive.

Girls Without a Father. Some girls overdo it—in the way they walk, the way they dress, the way they talk. Most likely such a person is starved for the male attention she never got at home. Her daddy was too busy, or maybe she never knew a real father because of divorce or desertion. So now she becomes a flirt. Studies of adolescent girls without fathers in the home have shown that teen girls behave differently around boys if they have not learned social skills from their fathers. In other words, girls learn to get along with boys by getting along with their fathers.

Girls whose parents had divorced were found to be a little too assertive in their interaction with boys. They were more seductive and sometimes promiscuous. The researchers concluded that this resulted from the tension these young ladies felt with the opposite sex. Tension produced action, so instead of relating easily and openly to boys, the girls responded more impulsively.

Certainly no one should blame a girl for such behavior when circumstances beyond her control have triggered it. But a young lady can learn where she is vulnerable and why she acts, talks, and behaves the way she does. FACT: Knowing yourself is more important than knowing more guys!

Guys and Petting—Taming the Beast in Him

Petting affects guys differently from the way it does gals. But since members of both sexes wear many masks, they often do not understand what the other is feeling.

Society rears boys to feel differently about themselves. We teach our boys to be strong, tough, forceful, aggressive, and capable of functioning in many manly ways. Being capable sexually is one of the most important tests of masculinity—especially during the teen years, when a fellow is trying to find himself. He needs to prove to himself and others that he can function like a man.

The male is stimulated sexually in ways that few females realize. He is more sex-driven than the female, and this holds true for him throughout life. Since God Himself implanted this desire for sexual pleasure, when a male acts in this manner he is responding in the way God planned. He is not being dirty or evil when he responds to sexual stimuli. He is being male, and that is good—to a point, at least!

Studies have consistently shown that males and females have little or no conception of the vast gulf between their own feelings and those of the opposite sex. Some men guilty of rape are caught because they return to the scene of their crime, assuming the woman enjoyed the experience and would like to repeat it. Peeping Toms are often caught because they make a noise to attract the woman's attention, thinking she will enjoy the attention!

I hope that the next two sections will help each sex recognize those forces which entice them and the opposite sex toward sexual behavior.

Males are more visually oriented than females. Most girls do not understand how their appearance affects fellows. Because women are not visually aroused merely by looking at the male body or the way he dresses, they have little realization of their effect on men. *Psychology Today*[1] reported the results of a study concerning clothes and adolescent behavior. It found that teenaged girls who wear skin-tight jeans and no bras think of themselves as being stylish. However, the young men read sexual come-ons into such dress. None of the teenagers said they felt that a guy's open shirt, tight pants, tight swim trunks, or jewelry indicated that he was on the prowl for sex. Both sexes agreed that a see-through blouse on a girl was probably a come-on, but the males tended to see other clothing as deliberately encouraging as well—a low-cut top, shorts, tight jeans, or no bra.

A young woman does not have to wear revealing clothing to play the teasing game. She can be totally clothed and still send out signals. In fact, some women could look sexy in a sack, and a loose woman looks loose regardless of what she wears. A fellow will read a lot into the movements of a girl's body. If she acts "come hither," she'll get that kind of treatment.

The choices a woman makes in regard to her clothing and behavior become signs for men to read. She is either saying: "I am a person of worth. I respect myself, and I expect others to respect me also. I have high ideals for myself and others," or "Hey, look at me! I'm available. I need attention! I'm ready and willing."

Since external stimuli easily arouse a male, sex lurks close to the surface of his thinking at all times. A billboard, a dirty joke, a suggestive picture, a movie, a television program, all help him along. Add music with suggestive lyrics and a girl, and you've got the whole plot.

For many males it innocently begins like this: He holds hands with her. She permits it, and they both enjoy it. In his mind he figures that if he can hold her hand, she will probably permit him to put his arm around her; and if he can get his arm around her, he knows he can kiss her. After he gets that far, he'll try French-kissing. If she allows that, he begins to dream about touching her breasts. If she allows her breasts to be touched, he will try to go further, until intercourse occurs.

After a few minutes of close body contact or prolonged kissing, the male will usually have an erection of the penis. This is not nasty or dirty. God designed the penis to become erect when mental or physical stimulus occurs. At this point the male is ready for sexual intercourse, although he does not *have* to engage in it. Nothing bad will happen to him if he doesn't, but he is ready nonetheless.

111

The erection occurred because he is thinking about sex. You see, it doesn't take long for a stimulus to propel him toward wanting to go further. Scripture, however, forbids intercourse outside of marriage and labels it either fornication or adultery. So unless he is married to her, the man is not at liberty to have sex with her if he has religious scruples.

If the couple have engaged in an extended period of petting, the man is very likely to experience an uncomfortable ache in his testes, or testicles, which hang inside the scrotum behind the penis. He may be hurting enough to use every means at his disposal to accomplish his purpose. Any words spoken at this time, any promises made, any vows taken, can be discounted. He is simply under too much pressure to think straight and will probably say anything to get what he wants.

This pressure buildup that he feels will not cause him any permanent damage or injure him in any way, despite his claims! He will not become sterile if he doesn't get the relief he wants, nor will he go bald, nor will his teeth fall out. The ache will usually pass in half an hour or so.

Males have a strong desire to prove their manhood. Most men feel the need to prove their masculinity. Many think the proof lies in having sexual relations and lots of them. These macho guys enjoy driving to the other side of town, where they are not known, and picking up a couple of girls. There is a lot of laughing, joking, and crude or suggestive talk about sex among such men. Their main objective is self-gratification. Their primary concern is to enhance their own immature and shaky egos. They show hardly any concern about what happens to the female involved or any consequences following their activity. Even the physical satisfaction is less important to this kind of person than the fact that they succeeded in exerting their masculine charm.

Peer pressure motivates many teenaged males. These fellows use sex as a means of improving their position with their crowd. Older males may exert pressure, and when others urge them on, such guys are afraid

not to take the dare. Often bets are wagered against a fellow's chances for dating, making out, or whatever with a gal. One of the strongest urges teenagers have is to conform to what the group is doing. So if all the others are engaging in sex—or they say they are—these fellows will want to do it too. This trait holds true for even the shyest guy in the group, the one of whom you would least suspect this to be true. After all, he feels the need to prove his masculinity more keenly than the others do.

Other men try to exploit women. Some devious males play at love as though it is a contest. They deliberately get girls into petting situations just to see how far they can go. One study investigated sexually experienced 20-year-old men. On the average, they had already enjoyed more than three partners each. Thirty-four percent had picked up women exclusively for sexual purposes or exploitative dates. They were using these women as a means to an end and reported having no feelings for the girls. Men who take advantage of the unwary always pose a challenge for any woman, however sophisticated.

Some young men use sex as a form of rebellion. Certain teenagers use sexual aggression as a means of rebelling against parents, teachers, church, or other symbols of authority. Most authority figures warn teenagers against premarital sex. Therefore, a fellow who resents authority and feels that those in power cannot force him to act against his own wishes may rebel just to show he is boss. Young people from overly strict homes frequently express their rebellion through sexual promiscuity.

Some need to show superiority. Some men may have a need to overpower females, particularly those females who may have given them vague feelings of inferiority. Boyd comes from a poor family, and all during his grade-school years his classmates ridiculed him. As a result, Boyd built up strong resentments and desired to prove himself better than his peers. In high school Boyd has worked hard to become a star football player. Now he can show the rich girls up. He begins dating them and always tries to go as far as he can sexually.

When he succeeds, Boyd feels that he is getting back at them for the embarrassment he felt in his younger days.

The adventure-loving male seeks thrills. The excitement of seeing if they can get away with it leads some men to sexual aggression. This "devil-may-care" attitude prompts them to drive fast, court danger, take risks with their lives—and win. Premarital sex offers several risks—detection, infection, and conception! To play the game and not get caught or hurt serves as a motivating force for some.

Gals and Petting—Taming the Tiger in Her

Fellows who do not really understand the female nature often assume that a woman is as eager to make out as they are. In actuality, females respond much more slowly. It isn't that a woman cannot respond; it is just that she takes longer.

Due to the erection of his penis, the male is much more aware of his sexual responses than the female is of hers. His responses are more localized than hers, but her responses are more complicated than his. He responds more to physical factors, whereas she responds to emotional ones. Men can have sexual relations with women they care little for, but females tend to want strong affection to precede sexual intimacy.

Petting for the female sets off a slow chain reaction of physical sensations. The first thing she might feel would be a general uneasiness, a restlessness, an excitement, and possibly a tightness in the throat. These feelings might be followed by a tingling in the spine or in other parts of the body or perhaps a choking sensation caused by the heart pumping faster and necessitating faster breathing. The woman may not recognize these sensations at first as a stirring up of sexual response. But it is important for her to realize that these first vague feelings of discomfort are the beginnings of physical desire.

So here we have a guy and a gal involved in petting. He's enjoying every minute of it and secretly hopes that maybe she'll get carried away and give him what he really wants. She probably isn't as aroused as he

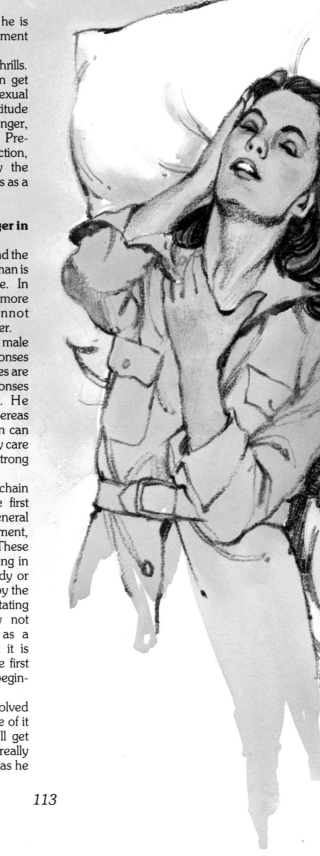

is. But that doesn't mean she isn't enjoying the episode. What she is enjoying, however, is not the physical thrills as much as the feeling of being "loved." Someone wants her, needs her, desires her, thinks she is attractive and sexy, and maybe even loves her.

Let's say that the gal suddenly decides that things have gone far enough, so she disengages herself. As she walks into the kitchen she feels little or nothing, because she was never that excited to begin with. But her boyfriend! He feels much different

She has left him feeling tense, uncomfortable, and somehow defeated. If he is a clever person—one who is determined to get his way sometime—he'll swallow his pride, repress his feelings, and vow to work on her another time when he can arouse her enough. Each encounter weakens the defense mechanisms.

Therefore a girl who allows prolonged kissing and caressing but who has no intention of following through is actually leading him on. But most women little understand what a man goes through when she permits intimacies that stop short of intercourse. One girl responded in the survey: "For me, the most of petting has been really boring. I rarely get stimulated. I usually just sit there waiting for it to end. I really wonder if the guy is getting anything out of it." You can rest assured that he didn't feel the same way; yet she was totally unaware of it!

I do not wish to leave the impression that a woman never enjoys petting episodes. The more experienced she becomes in petting, the better acquainted she will become with her body responses. She can begin to train and "will" her body to respond to sexual stimuli. Petting can be an extremely pleasurable and exciting adventure for the more experienced female, though not nearly as urgent as it is with the male.

Now let's consider some of the reasons why young ladies will engage in petting.

To get love. In the breast of every woman beats a consuming desire to be loved the way she has always dreamed of being loved. These dreams, which center on being cherished, protected, and cared for, begin in early adolescence and last till old age. This desire for love is the main goal of females and forms the core of their emotional security. Such a goal also puts her in competition with every other female for the attention of a male. This pressure is hard on a woman. It creates a state of mind that can quickly and easily believe a fellow when he says, "I love you." She believes it because she wants to believe it so badly.

Then when he goes on to argue that intercourse will make their love more secure, she finds his words persuasive because this is exactly what she wants to happen—not intercourse necessarily—but a love relationship. Therefore, women commonly color the facts to fool themselves into believing what they want to believe. Most males quickly learn this and use it to their advantage.

One other fact works against women and romance. Most single girls do not realize that the time when they feel the most romantic coincides with the time of the monthly cycle during which they are the most fertile. Just when intercourse appears most desirable, they have the least control and pregnancy is most likely to occur.

To gain popularity. Some young women think that being sexually cooperative will ensure popularity for them. Some of these girls are popular, you can be sure. But you should hear what the men say about them! Furthermore, their dates always end up doing the same thing in the same place. Hundreds of girls have complained as this one did: "When he wants to make out, he calls me; but when a nice event is scheduled, he takes somebody else."

To work out feelings of rebellion. Feelings of rebellion against parents or others can provide a springboard for sexual activity. The rebellious girl has something to prove to others. She has an ax to grind and lessons to teach adults. This young woman often has grown up under demanding or distrusting parents. She aches to get even with them for their lack of faith in her. Subconsciously she may even attempt to get pregnant—just to hurt them the way she feels they have hurt her. One girl wrote on the survey: "When I had sex the first time, it wasn't cuz I loved him. It was because I was bored and it was something new. Also I was feeling very radical and rebellious toward my parents and life in general, so nothing really mattered anyway."

To see how far they can go. Unscrupulous girls will lead men into situations just to see how far they can go. Such women do not and cannot really love the men they go out with. They are exploiting men for the sense of power they may gain over them. On a subconscious level they hate men, probably because their fathers neglected them during their childhood. This risky game experiences none of love's richness, no real satisfaction, no beauty, no permanence. Being seduced by such a woman is hardly a compliment, and a man who knows the difference between sex and love will hardly succumb.

CAUTION: A man can want sex without being in love, and his wanting sex affords no proof that he loves. He may interpret his strong sexual attraction as love and try to convince the woman that his love is the same as hers. She assumes that he would not ask unless he deeply loves her. She therefore gives in to his wishes, feeling they have sealed a compact through intercourse. But it only reinforces the observation that he gives love to get sex and she gives sex to get love.

When all is said and done, couples usually pet for *security—not love*. They feel they need to do it in order to tell the other person they love them, to have a basis for their relationship, or to hang on to someone. But unless a couple develop something besides physical intimacies, the relationship will crumble. Sex won't suffice when you have to live together daily. Sex cannot glue a marriage together. If you feel insecurities now and need to pet in order to build up your feelings of worth, then later you will have to find something else to help

you cope with your insecurities. Better to back off for a while from dating until you mature.

How Far Is Too Far?

Whenever I lecture about Touchy Situations, young people always ask the same questions: How far can I go? What's right and what's wrong? One 19-year-old said, "I have been going steady with a girl for nine months, and we both love each other. I would never touch her sex organs, but I rub her back and legs and we make out. I love God very much but don't know whether I have gone too far. Somehow I feel like I have disgraced my Lord. How far is too far?"

Young people want to know how far they can go and still stay within limits of propriety. Is it all right to kiss and hug? What about French kissing? Can I touch my girl as long as I stay above the waist? Can I go as far as the . . . or as far as the . . . How far can I go anyway?

God has not called upon me to set up a standard for couples to follow. But if I did produce such guidelines, an interesting phenomenon would occur as soon as most young couples got their hands on it. They would study it carefully to see where I drew the limits and immediately accelerate to that point, skipping all the preliminaries. That's human nature!

Tim Stafford talks about gray areas for which the Bible provides no clear-cut guidelines. He suggests that each individual must make independent decisions for himself. "Other than the warning against intercourse outside marriage, the Bible doesn't say much. There isn't a word about how far to go, or whether petting is right or wrong. That's not surprising. In Bible times, couples hardly saw each other before marriage. They certainly didn't get much opportunity to caress each other's bodies.

"Petting is defined many different ways. I'm talking about caressing breasts or genitals. Even within that definition there's much variety: a guy who touches his girlfriend's breasts through her clothes is in a different state from a couple lying together naked, doing everything but the act of

116

intercourse. But the Bible doesn't speak of any of this. Nor does it mention holding hands, kissing, hugging, French kissing, or caressing. All of this is a gray area. There are no specific Biblical guidelines for Christians.

"But people want guidelines. They want to know exactly how far they can go without sinning. I sympathize; I've felt the same way. But there isn't any answer. There really couldn't be; it's different with every relationship. Some relationships are casual; it's ridiculous to spend time making out. To do so would be simply to use each other.

"Also, people react differently to things. What's unbearably sexy to one person may be rather mild to another. And this is especially true between guys and girls. A girl may simply get a pleasant feeling from, say, a guy touching her breasts. But her partner may be going wild with desire.

"So I can't give any do's and don'ts. There is no magic line for how far you can go." [2]

Scripture does give us some guidelines, however, in governing relationships with the opposite sex. No, it doesn't say that hand-holding is OK, that kissing is OK, but that French kissing is wrong. But it does present some clear principles. On the basis of these standards you should be able to make some judgments concerning your own actions.

1. The Bible condemns sexual intercourse for unmarried people. In the New Testament the word *fornication* refers to sexual immorality in general (John 8:41; Acts 15:20-29; 21:25; Romans 1:29; 1 Corinthians 6:13, 18; 2 Corinthians 12:21; Ephesians 5:3). Two passages (Matthew 5:32; 19:9) use fornication as a synonym for adultery. In four passages both adultery and fornication are used together, indicating a definite distinction between the two words. (Matthew 15:19; Mark 7:21; 1 Corinthians 6:9; Galatians 5:19). Two references refer to voluntary sexual intercourse between unmarried people or between an unmarried person and a married person (1 Corinthians 7:2; 1 Thessalonians 4:3-5). In 1 Corinthians 5:1 Paul applies the word *fornication* to an incestuous relationship.

In the final analysis, then, 37 out of 39 Biblical passages exclude premarital sexual intercourse from God's plan for men and women. The two exceptions are where fornication is used as a synonym for adultery. God asks His children to confine sexual intercourse to marriage. Therefore, if any of your petting activities lead to sexual intercourse, you have gone too far.

2. If your conscience bothers you, you have gone too far. One teenager wrote: "I do regret some of the things I did, like petting. Although it was very light, I feel it was wrong—that I let my emotions take me away. Now I try not to get into a situation where it might happen, and I make it known to the guy that I am not that kind of girl and that some areas are off limits. If he doesn't like it, he can find someone else." This 18-year-old did not need anyone to spell out rules for her. She had settled on them herself when her conscience bothered her. One of the functions of the Holy Spirit is to convict us of sin through our consciences. If your conscience tells you that something you are doing is wrong, and you do it anyway, then it becomes a sin (see Romans 14:14, 23; 1 John 3:21).

Unfortunately we cannot always rely on the conscience to guide us. Such was the case with the young man who said: "I have had intercourse a couple of times and really am not ashamed of it. I think the Creator God gave us this beautiful ability to enjoy. Now, maybe I'm weird or something, but the way I figure it, what if I were to die tomorrow without experiencing this God-given ability? I have then missed life itself, for I'm not ashamed of it." Some people have abused their consciences for so long that they have become hardened. These persons need to go to God in repentance and ask Him for help in reestablishing standards in accordance with His will for their lives.

3. You have gone too far if you unduly arouse sexual desires. Once a guy and a gal pet to the point that either partner jeopardizes self-control, they have gone too far. The female may not always be aware in such cases of just how stimulated the male is. Almost all fellows have problems after

prolonged kissing, *whether she realizes it or not.* This point varies from person to person, of course. Normal interest and arousal is to be expected and should not be worried about unnecessarily. But if the tension becomes so strong that your passions begin to dictate your actions, then you are in trouble.

Josh McDowell refers to the Law of Diminishing Returns, which has to do with the progressiveness of physical contact. One kind of physical contact is enjoyable for a time, but then it gets boring. So you progress to the next level and stay there for a while till the newness wears off. Then you go a little farther, and so on. When each new thrill wears off, you have to go a little farther to get the same thrill. And before you know it you have gone too far.

Dating is a natural activity for young people today. It is also normal to have feelings for the person you are dating and to have inclinations to touch and to care for the person. And this is where the Law of Diminishing Returns comes into play. Thousands of people who thought they could stop petting anytime they wanted to have found out that they could not. Sexual stimulation constantly searches for deeper excitement.

4. You have gone too far when nudity is involved. The Old Testament on several occasions associates nakedness with illicit sexual conduct, and I would like to suggest that when an unmarried couple remove their clothing or caress under the clothing they have gone too far. Nearly half of the respondents in my survey indicated they had participated in petting to climax. Petting to climax (or mutual masturbation) involves manipulating the lover's genitals so as to attain climax without intercourse but protecting one's virginity. However, virginity is not just a technical term that applies to a membrane which has or has not been punctured. Virginity involves total chastity and purity. Petting to climax may or may not require total nudity, but the couple hold almost nothing back. The kind of intimacy required for mutual masturbation is the kind of intimacy that we should reserve for marriage. It is technically only a breath or

two away from intercourse, hence the term "technical virgin."

Petting to climax can provide a great deal of sexual gratification, but it has several hazards. One of the worst ones is that it may cause a complex. Humans have habitual ways of doing things. We get set in our ways. If an obsession or preoccupation sets in at this level, you might never be able to enjoy sex at its best. Why jeopardize tomorrow's sex for a few half-pleasures today?

And pregnancy *can* occur during mutual masturbation. It happens like this. The male sperm look much like small tadpoles. Their long tails allow them to swim when introduced to a moist medium. There are two-to-five-hundred million sperm in every male ejaculation. Since during heavy petting the female's genitals are likely to be moist, either the finger or genitals (in genital-to-genital petting) can transfer sperm to the area around the vagina. Thus it is possible for hundreds or thousands of live sperm to swim up the vagina, in through the cervix and uterus, and into the Fallopian tubes—even though there has been no penile insertion. Pregnancy by this method is infrequent, but it does happen.

In addition to mutual masturbation, a significant number of couples engage in oral sex—or kissing the genitals of a dating partner. During these petting episodes the mouth provides sexual pleasure by kissing, blowing on, or sucking the sexual organs. This activity may be continued to the point of orgasm. In my survey 28.6 percent reported having tried oral sex. The reasons reported for doing it were: "to satisfy my partner"; "for sexual excitement"; and "for experimentation." The long-term feelings of those who participated ranged from happy to mixed to guilty.

Kissing the genitals is a few degrees beyond mutual masturbation in the hierarchy of sexual experimentation. A person must overcome more inhibitions in order to expose himself or herself to such nudity and sexual openness. I neither condemn nor condone oral sex in marriage. But young people who engage in oral sex need to reckon with certain health factors. The

DEAR VAN PELTS:

I am 19 years old and single. When I was in high school all the girls I hung around with were always talking about how far they went with their boyfriends. At the time I had never gone "all the way" with a guy and I thought I was missing something. But I soon was to find out that I wasn't missing a thing.

I'd been dating one guy steadily for four months and we were doing some pretty heavy petting. But I would always find some excuse when it came to going "all the way." I was brought up in a very religious home and taught that sex was meant for married people only.

But then I thought, after all, my parents didn't realize how much things had changed. So when my boyfriend and I were out parking one night, I decided no matter what, I wasn't going to back out. I was going to go ahead and see what these other girls were talking about.

We had sex that night, and I still regret it to this day. I really thought I loved this guy, and we were thinking seriously about marriage. But after that I realized I didn't really love him as much as I thought. Soon we were bitter toward each other and constantly arguing about everything. Before long we broke off our relationship.

Since then I have dated several other guys, but it always seems like they are after one thing—you know what I mean. I would like to know how to respond to a suggestion for sexual contact.

DEAR 19 AND SINGLE:

We believe you could save yourself a lot of problems if you could learn some appropriate responses to head off trouble the minute it is suggested, especially if you have rehearsed in your mind the response beforehand. Here are some suggestions.

"I am really trying to be careful about physical commitments and I have a feeling you are that kind of person too. I'd like to ask you to help me keep that commitment."

"I don't think you can prove love by getting physical. I think love is helping another person grow to be the best kind of person he/she can be. I think we should do that for each other in a nonphysical way."

"I really like you and enjoy being with you, but I would really regret doing something that we might both be sorry for in the future."

Now create several of your own:

---

herpes simplex virus Type II causes genital *herpes.* The virus is passed from person to person through intercourse and oral-genital sex. Within a week following intimate sexual contact, fluid-filled blisters may develop in the area of the sex organs. The sores will heal on their own within two to four weeks, but the herpes virus remains in the nerve tissue, and the infected person will probably experience successive attacks of blisters and ulcers. Recent research indicates that genital herpes infection may make women more susceptible to cancer of the cervix, although the relationship has not yet been proved. Herpes differs from other forms of venereal disease in that at the time of writing *there is no cure for it.* If an expectant mother has an active infection of herpes simplex II in the vagina, her baby should be removed by Caesarean section; otherwise it may contract the disease during birth and perhaps die.

Such intimacies require a nakedness of the body and soul that should be saved for marriage only. The term "technical virgin" applies here also. Only a legalistic attitude would permit the idea that because you avoid penetration you also avoid fornication.

If you are involved in a relationship of mutual masturbation or oral sex, you should consider another factor: the more intense your relationship is with each other and the more its peculiar aspects fascinate you, the more likely you are to become psychologically stalled on the road to full sexual enjoyment in marriage.

5. You have gone too far if it hurts your relationship. One young lady wrote on her survey sheet: "It has been my opinion that if you do not pet, guys (at least ones worth worrying about) will respect you more and ask you out again. I had been going with a guy for about a year. Once when we were alone we engaged very briefly in light petting. We had never done so before. From then on things began to change between us. I firmly believe that we lost respect for each other, and this led to our breakup."

She made some good observations. Petting can hurt your relationship. How? Communication is one of the big problems in marriage today. Many couples have never developed the techniques necessary for getting and staying in touch with each other. Could it be that they never learned to communicate prior to marriage because they indulged so heavily in physical intimacies that the development of meaningful verbal communication was short-circuited?

When petting gets going, verbal communication shuts down. If a couple never really gets to know each other prior to marriage, after marriage they may find out that they never really had anything in common in the first place beyond sexual attraction. It is absolutely essential that a couple develop an intimate level of communication prior to beginning a sexual relationship lest sex become a substitute for verbal communication. After marriage sex is not enough, especially for the female.

I have never heard of a young person entering marriage with a guilt complex because he or she was a virgin. But many have requested counseling for the opposite reason. Sensitive and sensible young people distinguish between lighting the fires of sexual passion and a romantic embrace. If you can't, then you aren't mature enough to date.

Who Should Call a Halt and Why?

Over the years many researchers have asked young people who they think should draw the line when it comes to petting. The answers given reflect a gradual trend toward placing the responsibility on both. Fewer and fewer people now think that the woman must bear the full brunt of drawing the line. One study showed[3] that 83 percent of the men and 74 percent of the women said they felt it was the responsibility of both. Only 14 percent of the men and 26 percent of the women thought it chiefly the woman's responsibility. Apparently the men would, or do, accept more responsibility for limiting lovemaking than women give them credit for.

Petting behavior seems to be an area of dating in which communication breaks down, and it is not always clear even to the two involved which of them is taking the initiative and which is limiting. In one study of 3,100 students 14 percent of the men said they had drawn the line. However, only 4 percent of the women gave the men credit for having taken the responsibility!

Theoretically, the responsibility for calling a halt should be equally divided. However, for a couple who believe themselves to be seriously in love and who have unlimited opportunities to express affection, a natural and logical stopping place is difficult to find. Aroused sexual feelings respond reluctantly, if at all, to intelligence, reason, logic, ironclad decisions, previously determined guidelines, or anything else short of sexual release.

Usually, then, it is left to the female to call a halt. The male, being more aggressive, will usually proceed just about as far as she will allow. Society, parents, teachers, religious leaders, friends, relatives—all expect the female to say No when conditions require it. This double standard isn't fair, but it is a fact of life. And although the double standard isn't as strong today as it was a few years ago, it remains a factor that females must live with.

Frankly, as a female I am tired of the double standard. When our young men sow their wild oats, our system says, "Boys will be boys," but it brands young women who do likewise as "bad." This same system proposes equality in so many ways today that it has become nauseating; yet in one of the most basic and important aspects of our lives—our sexuality—the system remains silent. Then men who go through a great number of women and get a reputation for being fast will still insist on marrying a virgin. And where do they think they are going to find these virgins when they are so busy deflowering them?

We can erase the double standard in one of two ways: either both partners can willingly accept premarital sex in their partners, or both partners can demand virginity and purity prior to marriage. The latter choice has more advantages. In my estimation it is time for women to begin making some demands of their own. It is time for females to stop accepting soiled merchandise and insist upon purity and virginity in the men they choose to marry.

Culturally, as in other ways, the female has more to lose than the male when it comes to premarital sex, and others tend to blame her more than him if they learn of her behavior. There are two main reasons for this attitude, each with a long history.

1. Women can control their sexual impulses more easily than men. Fellows generally become sexually stimulated more

easily than do girls. He can become excited simply by watching a girl in a bikini or in a clinging dress with revealing lines. Add a few intense kisses and you have turned him on. A girl may consider all this next to meaningless and get no thrill at all. As his excitement mounts he feels less and less desire to stop. His natural urge is to proceed so that he can gain release from the mounting tension within him.

Because girls respond more slowly, it is left to them to apply the brakes. And, if she does not put on the brakes, often she is the one who bears the blame. Society rarely considers a fellow a poor prospect for marriage because he has made out with numerous girls. But few men want to marry women who have had as much sexual experience as they themselves have had.

2. The female runs the risk of pregnancy and suffers the greater social rejection when pregnancy results. More than one million unmarried teenagers become pregnant each year—most of whom thought they wouldn't get pregnant. But pregnancy is *always* possible—even when the couple take the best precautions. Forty percent of these teenagers marry the father of their child; 30 percent choose abortion; 10 percent miscarry; and the final 20 percent go ahead with the birth and either keep the child themselves or give it up for adoption.

Harry and I were teaching a Compleat Marriage Seminar in a northwestern city. In the home where we stayed lived a 16-year-old unwed girl in her eighth month of pregnancy. She lumbered out of the room after meeting us. The next day, after feeling more comfortable in our presence, she showed us a picture of her mom and dad. Her mom, a plump, happy woman, and her dad, a distinguished-looking minister, were more than 2,000 miles away, and she missed them.

"He wants to marry me," she confided, "but he's so stupid, I can't stand him. You know what? He can't even read simple words from the Bible like *redemption*. He stumbles all over such words. He's 19 and says he could support us, but I'll never marry him."

When asked what she planned to do with the baby, she replied, "I'm giving the baby up for adoption." She stopped, and then continued, "I'm taking correspondence now, and it's so boring." She found algebra particularly difficult. A tutor had come by occasionally to help her, but she still didn't understand it. And she missed her friends. "I don't have much fun. I can't go anyplace. Certainly no dates," she added with a bitter smile as she motioned to her body, large with child.

After our conversation, I reflected on how she was paying the ultimate price for engaging in premarital sex. The father of the child got off scot-free. No one exiled him 2,000 miles away from family and friends. He spent Christmas at home with his family. He didn't have to drop out of school and take one whole year by correspondence. He didn't have to stop dating for nine months. He didn't have to purchase a new wardrobe. Stretch marks won't scar his body, and he won't have to fight that extra padding of fat that many women find difficult to lose. He does not suffer the physical pain associated with birth or the emotional scars that remain when a young mother gives up her child to be raised by another mother.

Because it is a woman who gets pregnant, because it is a woman who carries the child in her body, because it is a woman who gives birth, it is she who has the most to lose and who takes the greatest risk in premarital sex. Therefore the final responsibility for calling a halt to petting rests with the women, in spite of the fact that ideally the couple should share the responsibility.

Putting on the brakes

Since society has laid the responsibility to hold the line on the female's shoulders, how do you do it? If a fellow's hands begin to roam, should you slap his hands, scratch his face, pull his hair, or laugh at him?

Since most men will go only as far as the female will allow him, he will begin by testing his ground. He starts off with hope in his heart until she calls his bluff. He will likely try to talk her into having sex, but he doesn't necessarily expect anything to happen. Furthermore it is not an insult to a fellow when a girl says No. When a young lady honestly and tactfully refuses, she does not really hurt or anger him. In fact, he may actually feel relieved if she refuses! Women underestimate their power to stop a man with a firm No. There are some gentle but

effective ways of doing this.

The most important point for a woman to understand in limiting petting activities is that she should say or do nothing that would damage the young man's ego, his feelings of self-worth, or his masculinity. Instead of discrediting his motives, assume that he really wants to show that he likes and cares for you. You might firmly take his hands and put them back in his lap as you continue talking. If possible (even though your heart is now in your throat) don't change the inflection of your voice or hint that anything unusual has happened.

Or you might say in a light-hearted, friendly manner, "Not so fast," or some other saucy remark that conveys the idea that you don't intend to proceed further at this point but clearly indicates that you place no judgment on his actions. The right kind of fellow will respect your wishes and appreciate your tact. He will understand that you can differentiate between his actions and him and that although you wish to discourage his actions, you do want to encourage your friendship.

Marianne wards off unwelcome behavior with a firm refusal to cooperate. Then she smiles and suggests an alternative activity: "Let's go get something to eat. I'm starved!" Or take a tip from Roberta. When her boyfriend begins to do something objectionable, she takes both his hands in both of hers, squeezes them affectionately while looking adoringly into his eyes, and says, "You're quite a guy!" This kind of gesture and remark lets him know that she won't permit him to go any further but that he is very special to her and that she likes him as a person.

Carla was snuggling close to her boyfriend in the car late one night. Both felt relaxed and happy—and very fond of each other. He began to kiss her, and she responded eagerly. Then something new came on the scene as his hands slipped under her blouse and his kiss took on an intensity that she had never known before. She struggled free of his embrace, shook her head, and with a nervous little laugh commented, "Wow, you're almost too much for me!" Learn to anticipate certain

"holds" and give the fellow a sense of being liked without anything too intense ever happening.

Other young women handle it other ways. One says that if a fellow tries it on her, she puts the key in the ignition and sweetly says, "Will you drive or shall I?" Another girl told me she begins to cry. Men get so frustrated over a woman's tears that in their frustration they forget about their own desires. Vivian takes a different turn. When a fellow's hands begin to wander, she firmly removes them and with mock surprise says, "What? This isn't Tuesday, is it?" This corny humor saves the situation. We are all very fragile during such moments. Only basic honesty, kindness, and a sense of humor can help us muddle through.

Two hundred college women listed fifteen techniques for controlling necking and petting on dates.

1. Be honest—say No sincerely and politely.
2. Keep talking. Maintain an interesting conversation.
3. Avoid situations that invite necking and petting.
4. Plan dates thoroughly.
5. Double date or date in groups.
6. Let the man know your attitudes from the start.
7. Abide by an early curfew.
8. Plan after-date activities.
9. Use reason; discuss your viewpoint.
10. Don't encourage necking or petting by your dress or actions.
11. Set a point beyond which you don't go.
12. Divert your date's attention.
13. Ask him to take you home.
14. Don't date fellows who seem overly interested in necking and petting.
15. Refrain from long "goodnights."

Having clearly thought out your own definite standards also helps. Christy and Gwen were classmates. Both were attractive, outgoing girls. Christy had definite and clear-cut standards—just so far and no farther. She entertained no ifs, ands, or buts about it. Gwen—well, she meant well, but she wasn't quite so sure. Christy's friends sometimes got annoyed with her and quit trying to coax her into doing what she didn't want to do. But Gwen always felt pressured and propositioned in ways that she found difficult and embarrassing. Christy got along happily and pleasantly with other young people because they accepted her standards. Gwen careered from one difficult predicament to another, partly because she had not really decided where she stood and what she wanted to do. The difference between the two girls was not one of standards only. Christy could be sure of her standards because she was sure of herself. Gwen's indecision about her own moral code reflected a basic indecision about herself.

Every young person, whether male or female, should have clearly defined standards of sex conduct and then stick by them.

Guidelines for Expressing Affection—What May Be "In" May Be "Out"

It is normal and natural that you and your dating partner should want to express affection for each other during the serious stages of dating. However, the way you express your affection during casual dating should differ from your expression in the more advanced stages of courtship. In earlier stages a couple *think* they love each other. In the latter stages genuine love is more certain, and the couple should be mature enough emotionally, socially, physically, and spiritually to shoulder the responsibilities of marriage. These are major and significant differences.

What demonstrations of affection are appropriate for each stage? A limited and controlled amount of affection is appropriate for young people in expressing love. And that's what this chapter is all about—helping young people decide what they want for each stage of their life. The guidelines fall into the following categories.

The Proper Time and Place. This does *not* include lovemaking in full (or partial) view of others on their way about the campus. Immature couples who engage in excessive public displays embarrass the institution, administration, faculty, and most of all the other students. Such behavior, whether it occurs on campus or in any other public place, is disrespectful, crude, vulgar, and cheap.

Genuine love is a private and personal experience. A portion of its beauty and innocence is lost when it has an audience. Such public love-making often degenerates into an attempt to use the other person for some purpose entirely unknown to true love—to boost one's ego in a showoff manner or to get even with someone else. Handholding, arms casually locked, a girl gently holding a young man's arm, and sitting closely together are usually proper, but even then young people will show discretion according to the time and place. You will want to use greater discretion when it comes to kissing and other physical intimacies in public.

Proper Understanding. Having a proper understanding means that a couple has come to terms with what they need to say to each other physically. They accept a kiss as an intimate expression of affection for one another but do not regard such behavior as an invitation to proceed to further levels of sexual exploitation. They understand that kissing arouses sexual desires and that two intelligent people who care for and respect each other will limit this expression of love.

Proper Restraint. This does not mean two hours of heavy petting while parked in a romantic spot! A couple who believe themselves to be in love should discuss their limitations and stay within those boundaries under all circumstances. (The next chapter will include more about this.)

It is in good taste, then, for a couple in the latter stages of courtship to practice limited forms of affection in private—and even more limited displays in public. It is unrealistic and perhaps even emotionally unhealthy to expect a mature couple to make their wedding kiss their first. Few extremes are good. But far better to err on the side of strictness here than permissiveness.

One needs to exercise respect and self-control for one's sweetheart during courtship. Where a couple do not practice such principles before marriage, any counselor can predict heartbreak ahead. Respect and self-control underlie the behavior of every couple with high ideals.

What you are will largely determine your ability to control your impulses to pet. When you begin the petting game, you encounter what you are at the core of your being. Long before you ever caress the erotic areas of another person's body, your total life experience has determined how far you will go. How do you feel about yourself? What takes first place in your life? Whom or what do you idolize? What do you expect from yourself in life? What are your values? What goals have you set for your life? In short, the sum total of your character begins to emerge now. You have started to write your life story.

If you commit your life to God, you can rest assured that He can and will help you control your sex life when you ask for His guidance. He will provide the strength to resist temptation and to keep sex under control. You do not have to battle your urges on your own. He will help you in this area of your life just as in all other areas.

A Teenager's Prayer

Walk with me, Christ!
I wonder—what was it like when You were young?
Was there an "in" crowd at Nazareth?
Were You on the fringe, just watching?

Did You walk alone through the springtime's glory?

Did You know the loneliness of being different?

Did You run down the hilly slopes filled with joy at just being alive?
Was the whole world brilliantly, beautifully waiting for You?

Did You know of the choices You had to make?

The world is waiting for me.
I'm on the brink of many choices and decisions;
Walk with me, Christ!

Life is fresh and tender and new—
I can feel the future approaching.

Lord, help me to keep the whiteness of my soul.
—Patricia Halbe

———

[1] Gail L. Zellman, Paula B. Johnson, Roseann Giarrusso, and Jacqueline D. Goodchilds, "Misreading the Signals." *Psychology Today,* October, 1980.
[2] Tim Stafford. *A Love Story* (Wheaton, Ill: Zondervan, 1977).
[3] Judson T. and Mary G Landis, *Building a Successful Marriage* (Englewood Cliffs, N.J.: Prentice-Hall, 1963).

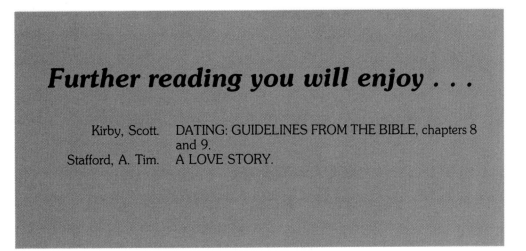

Further reading you will enjoy . . .

. . . By doing so, part of the mystery that surrounds the other person might also be lost and along with it something very precious to the couple should they eventually marry.

Chapter at a Glance

I. **Premarital Sex**
   A. A moral or psychological issue?
   B. Pious preaching won't work
   C. Premarital sex has good and bad
      aspects

II. **Advantages of Premarital Sex**
   A. Relationship to orgasm
   B. Sexual outlet
   C. Sexual experience
   D. Status
   E. Curb to homosexuality
   F. Fun

G. Learning situation
H. Emotional adjustment
I. Tests sexual compatibility

III. **Disadvantages of Premarital Sex**
   A. Can destroy relationships
   B. Can mask serious difficulties
   C. Can blur love with infatuation
   D. Can encourage poor sex habits
   E. Can produce guilt
   F. Destroys virginity
   G. Risks pregnancy
   H. Increases risk of cervical cancer
   I. Can spread sexually transmitted
      diseases

Chapter 7

Close Encounters of a Dangerous Kind

A recent television program on teenage sexuality reported that there is more sex, more pregnancies, more abortions, and fewer marriages today than ever before in history. More and more of today's young people question traditional morality. They judge premarital sex not in terms of whether it is right or wrong but whether it is a genuine expression of love that they should use in their relationship. This approach makes a psychological question out of what otherwise would be a moral one. No longer do young people ask, "Is it right or wrong?" but "Is it right for us in our relationship? Will it strengthen or weaken our relationship?"

Young people today, for the most part, remain unmoved by pious preaching. Honest answers based on proven facts, however, will impress contemporary young people. In the survey I conducted, one male said:

I believe that a very good topic on which to write would be the exact reasons why couples engage in sex before marriage. We can't solve the problem unless we know exactly the motives that are behind them. Maybe if all of the motives were brought to view, more people would realize the magnitude of social pressure and then decide for themselves.

If premarital sex has been proven helpful or harmful, young people want the evi-

---

J. Can predispose to divorce
K. Can increase likelihood of extra-marital sex
L. Can destroy reputation
M. Can destroy respect
N. Female response can be un-satisfying
O. Can result in male sexual dys-function
P. Destroys meaning of honey-moon
Q. Can be habit-forming
R. Can change attitudes
S. Erodes spirituality

T. Promiscuity only intensifies the problems

IV. **How to Keep From Going Too Far**

V. **How to Be Intimate Without Having Sex**

VI. **What About Living Together?**

VII. **What if You've Gone Too Far?**

VIII. **God's Plan for Sex**

dence. They want to know the reasons why.

The information presented in this chapter is straightforward, frank, and honest. Premarital sex has both good and bad aspects. You will need to examine the facts and see if the good outweighs the bad, or if the bad outweighs the good. In the long run you will make all the decisions anyway, so here I honestly try to present the facts. Some of the findings may surprise you.

The order in which I list these facts means little. Do not assume that just because one fact precedes another, it carries more weight. I have not ranked the facts in value from high to low. The facts presented may or may not stand alone. Read *all advantages* and *all the disadvantages* before you make a decision.

The Advantages of Premarital Sex— Yes, There Are Some!

Fact 1. The more premarital sexual experience women have prior to marriage, the more likely they are to experience a full orgasm during intercourse in the first year of marriage.[1] In the studies cited, this generalization held true both for those who had sexual relations with only their future spouse and also for those who had several partners. The fact is established: the more

complete the sexual activity before marriage for women, the greater the likelihood of achieving orgasm after marriage. But before you draw any conclusions, read on.

In spite of their ability to reach orgasm, far more of the wives in these studies had sex difficulties during the early days of marriage. Significant numbers reported long-term difficulties that began during the first two weeks of marriage. Others reported feeling like "sex servants." Perhaps a woman who fails to hold the line prior to marriage has little bargaining power in suppressing her husband's demands after marriage.

The American Institute of Family Relations questioned 2,000 women regarding their orgasmic response after marriage. Twenty-eight percent of the women who were virgins on their wedding day experienced orgasm compared with 39 percent of those with sexual experience prior to marriage. These differences disappeared quickly with experience during marriage. By the end of the first year the virgin wives equaled the nonvirgin wives in response.[2]

Fact 2. Premarital sex may satisfy a physiological need for a sexual outlet. A young man reaches his sexual peak between the ages of 19 and 29. During this time he experiences urgent sexual needs. We live in a very sex-conscious and sexually stimulating society. Sex outside marriage offers a convenient release for males. And although a young woman's needs are not as urgent as a man's, premarital sex can relieve her tension, as well as reassure her of love.

Fact 3. Premarital sex provides experience in sexual techniques. The old adage "Practice makes perfect" applies here in some cases. Repeating the experience may improve one's sexual ability.

Fact 4. Premarital sex may give a person status in some groups. Certain circles regard premarital sexual experience with awe and envy. The person may be regarded as having achieved manhood or womanhood. On the basis of this "accomplishment," the person might receive status and position that might otherwise be withheld.

Fact 5. Premarital sex experience might prevent the development of a homosexual relationship in a potential homosexual. A young person involved in a male-female relationship might not be as vulnerable to experimentation with a homosexual relationship should the opportunity present itself.

Fact 6. Premarital sex can be fun. Sex is one of the most pleasurable experiences given by God for men and women to enjoy. One of the purposes of sexual intercourse is that children may be born to the new union and become a delight to the parents. God could have accomplished this purpose by having a couple spit into a common receptacle. The female could then drink the contents and become pregnant. But His infinite mind conceived the idea of sex—the union between male and female that brings more physical pleasure than any other activity. Whether sex fulfills a desire to have children, satisfies the sex drive, reassures one another of love, or relaxes the nervous system, it all adds up to providing the most exciting physical experience known to humans. God created sex for our pleasure, and He wants us to delight in it. Sex is an enjoyable experience whether the couple engages in it prior to marriage or after.

Fact 7. Premarital sex provides the opportunity for a couple to learn about the response of the opposite sex. Males and females respond so very differently that it can take years for some husbands and wives to discover the individual tastes, preferences, and responses of their partner during the sex act. Premarital experimentation allows a couple to observe the reaction of the opposite sex. However, by so doing, part of the "mystery" that surrounds the other person might also be lost, and along with it something very precious to the couple should they eventually marry.

Fact 8. The younger a person is, the easier it is to make emotional and physical adjustments. All ages find certain adjustments difficult to make. But the older a person is, the more difficulty he or she has in making the emotional and physical adjustments necessary in the sexual relationship. Chances for successful adjustment are higher before a person gets too set in his or her ways. Consequently, early and frequent sex experience might help physical and emotional adjustment.

Fact 9. Premarital sex may test the capacities of two persons to adjust sexually should they marry. Before marriage, couples are anxious about their ability to function satisfactorily after marriage. However, human beings of almost any shape and size can mate successfully. The crucial factors in sexual compatibility are psychological and not anatomical or physiological. Naturally, a couple wants to know whether or not they are right for each another. But sexual compatibility cannot be measured by physique. When a male suggests testing the relationship by participating in sex, he assumes he has what it takes to make a good match but that the girl may not and could fail. But even if she did fail, his test would not prove that she lacked anything, since females do not respond as spontaneously to the sex act as do males.

In my opinion, these nine facts represent the sum total of advantages to premarital sex. Now read on.

A recent television program, One Day at a Time, depicted a situation in which the younger daughter was having a tête-á-tête with her mother about whether or not she should go all the way with her new flame. She asked her mother for reasons why she should not. Mother thought it over for a few minutes and with a shrug finally confessed that she couldn't think of any reasons against it. In the end the girl herself decided not to, but the idea that even a mother could not supply reasons against premarital sexual activity suggested to a million young persons that there is nothing wrong with premarital sex and even parents can't conjure up any good reasons against it.

I agree that young people must decide for themselves. But before you make that decision you should know the current information and facts so that you can decide intelligently.

During my teens, three basic reasons existed for not having sex before marriage: (1) pregnancy, (2) venereal disease, and (3) the Biblical condemnation. Of course, premarital sex does risk pregnancy and venereal disease, but the reasons for avoiding premarital sex go far beyond these considerations. With the help of a physician and a free clinic a couple can avoid having a baby. Antibiotics can cure most venereal diseases. But the timeless message of Scripture remains clear. The Bible clearly condemns sex prior to marriage. But Scripture also calls us to "reason together" (Isaiah 1:18).

I have tried to report the following facts as nonjudgmentally as possible.

The Disadvantages of Premarital Sex

Fact 1. Premarital sex tends to break up couples. Studies show that couples who engage in sex before marriage are more likely to break up than those who do not.[3]

Likewise, engaged couples who have intercourse are more likely to break their engagements. Why? One reason is that the male's need for marriage lessens when his sex needs are being satisfied outside marriage.

The first sex experiences together may be tremendous. However, since the biological force of sex attracted the partners to each another, once that force has been relieved, the power that drew the couple together wanes. Part of the sexual attraction between male and female is the desire to understand the mystery about the other person. Once the "ultimate" has been done, it leaves little curiosity to probe the mystery beyond. In time the relationship may tend to level off rather than deepen as the couple had imagined it would. Oh, the parties do not lose interest in sex. They continue to spend time engaging in it, but they sense that something is different. If a breakup occurs, it is far more painful than if they had never entered a sexual liaison.

Fact 2. Premarital sex can cover up serious difficulties. Couples who engage in intercourse tend to "neck their way" out of problems before marriage rather than talk them out or squarely face them. Premarital sex tends to mask areas of concern until after marriage.

Fact 3. Premarital sex makes it difficult to distinguish between real love and infatuation. Most young people find it difficult to distinguish between what feels good and genuine love. When there is no foundation for a relationship other than physical excitement, the ardor soon cools unless the couple stay together for sex. For instance, sometimes a girl will continue with a sexual relationship so she can keep him. Sometimes a guy will use a girl he barely likes just for the physical thrills. In most instances, the longer the courtship, the greater are a couple's chances of finding genuine love. But when a couple become sexually involved, they may stay together for the sex and not because they share common interests, goals, and values. Studies indicate that a sexual relationship may hold a couple together for three to five years, but no longer.[4]

Fact 4. Poor premarital sex habits often carry over into married sex. Premarital sex most often occurs under less-than-ideal conditions—the back seat of a car, under a blanket on the beach. Such poor conditions, plus the fear of discovery and the possibility of pregnancy, can start a chain reaction of poor habits and attitudes. In addition, the tension that often accompanies the need to perform or respond may reduce the level of pleasure. Occasionally it may produce anxiety to the point of partial or complete impotency (the inability to maintain erection) or anorgasmia (the inability to reach orgasm). Some studies[5] state that more than half of all American wives have such poor attitudes about sex that they cannot or will not enter the full enjoyment of sex with their husbands. Women, as well as men, tend to be hesitant and inhibited, and to harbor guilt and fears about past performances with previous partners. When this happens, the poor habits and attitudes adopted during their premarital experiences rob them of full sexual enjoyment.

Fact 5. Premarital sex may result in light-to-severe feelings of guilt. The Sorenson Report, the most complete sociological study of teenage sexuality to date, proved this point by asking girls to describe their reaction to their first sexual experience. The words *afraid, guilty, worried,* and *embarrassed* headed the list. Words like *happy, joyful,* and *satisfied* ranked much lower.

Women generally sense more guilt than do men when they break their moral codes. My survey included this statement: "Please take the remainder of the page to ask questions or relate stories pertaining to your experience with dating, petting, intercourse, and courtship." One 17-year-old female bitterly scribbled, "I don't want to remember. Use your imagination." *And the more devout the woman, the greater the likelihood she will experience regret and guilt following the incident.*[6]

When you indulge in premarital sex over and over again, the guilt, fear, and loss of self-respect are compounded. You feel

more and more remorse. It all catches up with you in time, and it is possible that you might forever associate these negative feelings with the sex act itself. Such feelings do not end once the marriage ceremony takes place, for most of us find it difficult to shake off previous attitudes. To the extent that you associated premarital sex with fear, guilt, and shame before marriage, to that same degree you will experience the same emotions after the wedding. Such attitudes may take months or even years of professional counseling to cure.

The disturbing factor about guilt is that you cannot predict in advance when it might hit. You may experience it immediately following the sexual encounter. Or later on regrets may gnaw at the conscience. Ernest Hemingway supposedly commented that "moral" means what you feel good after; "immoral" is what you feel bad after. Many young people continue with sexual relations because they don't feel guilty. But Hemingway's statement holds true only if you make that judgment once you can evaluate your total life. After only four months' experience it is pretty difficult for the average 18-year-old to decide what will make him or her happy at age 40 or on the judgment day. The conscience is not a totally reliable guide. It can be fooled.

One 19-year-old female said on the survey: "Guilt and fear are terrible, terrible things to live with. Thank God He forgives." Yes, God forgives, but humans have a hard time forgetting.

Fact 6. Premarital sex destroys virginity. Some people will overlook premarital sex experience, but a large portion of men still insist that their fiancées be virgins.

The May, 1979, *Medical Aspects of Human Sexuality* polled four hundred psychiatrists on the question of premarital sex and the teenager. One of the interesting concepts that the survey turned up was this:

"The majority of psychiatrists still believe, in keeping with the double standard of morality, that most boys still classify girls as 'good' or 'bad' depending on whether or not they are virginal." [7]

While some men seem bent on reducing the number of virgins in the population, they do not want to marry what they consider "soiled goods." They have a strange kind of logic that says, "*I* can have sex with the woman *you* want to marry, but *you* can't have sex with the woman *I* want to marry." Studies show that about half of all college-level males still expect to marry a

Oops!

1. Strongly agree
2. Mildly agree
3. Not sure
4. Mildly disagree
5. Strongly disagree

Read each of the following statements carefully. Respond to each statement according to the scale of 1 to 5 as shown at the left. Circle the appropriate number for each statement according to your present attitudes.

WHEN A GIRL BECOMES PREGNANT:

1 2 3 4 5   1. Abortion should be an option to consider.

1 2 3 4 5   2. The girl should be asked to withdraw from school.

1 2 3 4 5   3. The boy should be asked to withdraw from school.

1 2 3 4 5   4. The boy should marry the girl out of moral obligation to her and the baby.

1 2 3 4 5   5. Giving the child up for adoption is the best alternative.

1 2 3 4 5   6. Keeping the child and raising it alone should be the last alternative.

1 2 3 4 5   7. If I were a parent, I would accept the news about my son or daughter's premarital pregnancy warmly and offer both parents-to-be all the emotional and financial support they need.

virgin, or at least a woman who has limited her sexual activity to him.

A 19-year-old male in my survey told of his steady relationship with his girlfriend. It was his first experience of going steady, but she had had several other boyfriends and had indulged in sexual intercourse with the last one. He wrote: "At times I have a hard time relating to that fact. But so far I have survived mainly because she told me what happened and expressed regret."

Fact 7. Premarital sex risks pregnancy. Premarital sex *always* risks pregnancy regardless of the type of contraception used! About one third of all girls who engage in premarital sex end up pregnant,[8] and the number of illegitimate pregnancies continues to grow, especially among young teens. Between 1961 and 1974 the rate of unwed mothers between the ages of 14 and 17 increased 75 percent. One fifth of all births in the United States are to mothers still in their teens, and half of these mothers are under 18.[9] Furthermore, teenage pregnancies result in many complications for mother and child.[10] The surest way to avoid premarital pregnancy is total abstinence from sex.

Fact 8. Premarital sex increases the risk of cervical cancer among young women who engage in sex with multiple partners. About the time menstruation begins, the entire endocrine system is being stabilized and the finishing touches are being put upon the development of the uterus, Fallopian tubes, and ovaries. The cervix is extremely vulnerable during this time. If it is exposed to semen, whether from one or multiple partners, it can set the stage for carcinoma (cancer) of the cervix later on in life. Semen contains so-called "antigens" that sensitize the cervix and may cause abnormal development when a woman is exposed to it too early, too often, and by multiple sexual partners. Research shows that the younger a girl becomes sexually active and the more partners she has and the more frequent exposure during those years, the higher her chances are of contracting cervical cancer during ages 40 to 45.[11]

Fact 9. Premarital sex can result in sexually transmitted diseases. Every minute some teenager in the United States gets a sexually transmitted disease (also called venereal disease). These diseases spread from person to person almost exclusively through sexual intercourse, one infected person often spreading it to many others.

Syphilis kills four thousand people each year and cripples thousands of others. Although current medical skills could completely eradicate syphilis, more than two and a half million victims contract it each year.

About twenty-nine days after sexual contact, a cancerlike sore appears at the point of infection. This chancre (pronounced shanker) will disappear without treatment, but the disease remains. The second stage begins two to six months after the chancre appears. This stage can produce skin rashes over all or part of the body, baldness, sore throat, fever, and headaches.

An infected mother can transmit syphilis to her unborn child. The infectious agents pass from the mother's bloodstream into the bloodstream of the fetus. The child may be infected any time from three months to the time of delivery. If the mother's infection is not treated in the first three months, the probability of stillbirth quadruples. The possibility of infant death almost doubles, and up to 80 percent of the remaining children suffer from congenital syphilis, depending on the duration of the mother's infection.

The pain in 17-year-old Susan's abdomen became intolerable, and she could no longer attend school. She agreed to visit her doctor, who diagnosed her problem as gonorrhea, another sexually transmitted disease. Ordinarily, gonorrhea responds quickly and easily to penicillin and other antibiotics, but in Susan's case the virus lodged in her Fallopian tubes, forever denying her the privilege of having children under normal conditions. And no one was supposed to get hurt . . .

Males generally show the most symptoms with gonorrhea, but both males and females usually have a puslike discharge and feel a burning sensation during urination. The disease frequently causes sterility

since it infects the tubes that carry germ cells in both male and female. Women can contract gonorrhea and infect others yet never know they have it. When an infant passes through an infected birth canal during delivery, it can catch gonorrhea.

Now an outbreak of penicillin-resistant gonorrhea challenges public-health officials. The organism causing the disease produces a substance that breaks down penicillin. It could turn into a public-health disaster if this penicillin-resistant organism becomes the predominant strain. *The only sure way to avoid a sexually transmitted disease and its complications is complete abstinence till marriage.*

Any person who suspects that he or she might have a venereal disease should contact a physician or a public-health clinic immediately. The longer the victim waits, the worse a sexually transmitted disease gets. These diseases do not cure themselves, although the symptoms may disappear. The care that your local health department provides is absolutely free, and the records they keep are not made known to parents or to the public.

Fact 10. Those who have premarital sex are less happy in marriage and more prone to divorce. Chances for married happiness are greater when a couple waits to have sex until after marriage. Additionally, the more premarital sex a couple has, the less likely they will have a happy married life.[12] One reason for decreased marital happiness is that a couple's premarital sex experience often rises to haunt them. Also a person sometimes tends to compare the sexual performance of the spouse with that of previous partners. Naturally, if a couple is unhappy in marriage, they are more likely to seek divorce as an answer to their problems. Thus, the more premarital sex the couple engage in, the more likely they are to divorce.[13]

Fact 11. Premarital sex increases the likelihood of extramarital sex.

People who have had a variety of come-and-go lovers find it difficult to do an about-face at their wedding and commit themselves to a lifetime of fidelity within the sacred bonds of matrimony. Sexual appetites established before marriage affect us too strongly for that.

Studies relating premarital to extramarital coitus show that those who have had premarital experience are twice as likely to have extramarital affairs as those who are virgins at marriage. Furthermore, a greater proportion of those who have had extra-marital affairs think they will do so again.[14]

Fact 12. Premarital sex may hurt or destroy a reputation. When a young woman acquires a reputation for promiscuity, the fellows tend to think of her in this light rather than regard her as a total person. When a man acquires a reputation for promiscuity, he will have a difficult time convincing his prospective bride that he has honorable intentions and that he will maintain strict fidelity during the ensuing years of marriage. When it comes to reputation, however, a young woman probably has more to lose than a young man. Something in the male nature drives a man to brag about his conquests. The desire to impress friends motivates many fellows to have sex. Afterward, such a guy will tell his story with great glee—often naming names, dates, places, procedures, and embellishing the facts as he goes.

Fact 13. Premarital sex may cause one of the partners to lose respect for the other. Research clearly shows that the less serious the male is about the female, the more liberties he will try to take. If he respects the woman and values her friendship, he will generally exercise restraint. "After that, I lost all respect for her," guys commonly report after having had sex with a woman. Chances are, of course, that he never respected her to begin with. Other times disrespect follows a brag session with the guys. Even when a couple respect each other before the incident, it is highly unlikely that their friends will respect them. Friends often will view it as a lark and make lewd remarks. It will be difficult, if not impossible, for a guy to continue his respect for a girl when his friends speak of her with coarse and vulgar language.

Sometimes if a girl senses that a fellow's interest is dying and she might lose him, she may attempt to hold him by making

intercourse more available and by actually becoming sexually aggressive. If a woman lacks respect prior to marriage, how can a man be sure even after marriage that children born to their union are his? And how can she be sure he continues to remain faithful to her? Respect is a vital ingredient prior to and after marriage.

Fact 14. Sexual response for the female during premarital sex will likely be incomplete and unsatisfactory. Many women get *nothing* out of premarital intercourse. This may be due to her partner's ignorance regarding what preparation is necessary, or their haste, or difficulties arising from her reluctance. Girls engage in intercourse unwillingly much more frequently than do males.[15] Consequently, the woman's experience is frequently unsatisfactory. The sexual response system is much more complicated in the female than in the male, and it takes the average male time and patient understanding to learn how to arouse a female to her maximum level of responsiveness.

Furthermore, abundant evidence reveals that the average girl in her teens or early twenties has less capacity to respond sexually than she will have later in life. The odds are about one hundred to one that a girl will get little more out of the experience than being scared. It is highly unlikely that during a short period of sexual experimentation she will develop the capacity to have an orgasm. A woman is put together in such a way that her sexual needs are best met within the security of marriage and a trusting relationship with her husband. Her failure to respond may create anxiety about her sexual abilities, although there is no reason for such anxiety. And a woman who subconsciously worries about pregnancy (even when she and her partner use birth control measures) may hold back more than she should, which will inhibit her total enjoyment. Without abandonment and relaxation a woman's response mechanism will not reach its greatest capacity.

Fact 15. Premarital sex can result in sexual dysfunction for the male. One young man who experienced impotency (inability to maintain an erection) during the first year of marriage said, "My sex drive was greater while we were living together than it is now." Another young man admitted to his first bout with impotence after he and his girlfriend were "caught in the act" by her parents. A college student who began having intercourse with his fiancée just weeks before the wedding told his pastor, "I stay limp every time we go to bed, and my wife can't take it." The common denominator in each of these cases was premarital sex.

Premature ejaculation can also result from poor sex habits prior to marriage. A man suffering from this condition cannot withhold ejaculation long enough to bring a woman to climax at least fifty percent of the time. This problem plagues younger men more than older men and can often be traced to a history of heavy petting during the teen years, when he got used to ejaculating without vaginal penetration during a "quickie" rendezvous in a parked car where they feared interruption, or in a hurried pay-as-you-go establishment.

Retarded ejaculation, a less common malady, during which the male cannot proceed to ejaculation, also can be traced to promiscuity prior to marriage. Tim and Beverly LaHaye conducted a sex survey among 4,000 Christians and published the results in their best-selling book *The Act of Marriage*. The survey asked, "If you had your life to live over again, what one thing would you do differently?" The most popular answer was, "I would not have engaged in premarital sex." [16]

Fact 16. Premarital sex destroys the value and meaning of the honeymoon, one of the finest social developments of the twentieth century. The lingering memories of a happy and special honeymoon will bless a couple for many years. As married life progresses, a couple should be able to look back on the honeymoon as one of the choicest memories during their courtship and marriage. One study indicated that 87 percent of the couples who practiced self-control till marriage had a honeymoon, as compared with only 47 percent of couples who had been sexually intimate prior to marriage. [17] A 25-year-old married male stated on my

survey: "Premarital sex greatly took away my expectations of our honeymoon, and I was truly sorry that it had to be that way."

Fact 17. Premarital sex tends to be habit-forming. Ways of expressing affection learned in the past tend to become habitual. If your family greets loved ones warmly with hugs and kisses, you will continue this pattern all your life. Likewise a couple who hold hands as they walk down the street will tend to do so habitually. In much the same way, persons who have learned to pet to the point of intercourse find it extremely difficult to refrain during the rest of their courtship. They tend to expect and demand that level of expression to which they have become accustomed.

Fred and Nan had developed the habit of petting and could enjoy little else. All through the early part of the evening each was preoccupied with the thought of what would happen when they finally got off alone. Everything else faded out, and only petting seemed important. Finally their

relationship became so focused on petting that they decided to break up and not see each other as frequently. The first girls that Fred dated after he and Nan stopped going steady had quite a time with him, for he tried to fondle them in the same way he had Nan over the months. It wasn't that he cared especially for them, but rather that he had developed the petting habit to the place where any girl was a stimulus to the routine.

Fact 18. Premarital sex changes attitudes. It is impossible to predict prior to intercourse what your attitudes or the attitudes of your partner will be following the experience. However, you will not be the same persons afterward. Innumerable ramifications have occurred that you cannot alter. You may now look at yourself, your partner, and life through different eyes. For instance, as a result of intercourse a person may feel a strong attachment to the other party—an emotional bond that cannot be forgotten years later even though both individuals have married other persons. Or the female who submits reluctantly may begin to think of intimacy as a commercial enterprise in which sex is a masculine prerogative only. Some people feel used, dirty, and ashamed after premarital coitus. Others suffer from intense confusion and bewilderment. Still others feel that they have lost something that they can never reclaim.

Fact 19. Premarital sex erodes a relationship with God. It is difficult to listen to God's instructions about one area of your life and not listen to Him regarding another area. Studies show that premarital intercourse is less common among unmarried individuals with a strong religious upbringing. Premarital intercourse decreases as attendance at religious services rises. In a study at one university only 28 percent of the couples had participated in sex before marriage when both partners attended spiritual worship regularly.[18]

In my survey of 370 unmarried college students on conservative Christian campuses, 67 percent indicated that they had never had sexual intercourse. This may not sound like an astronomically high percentage for a Christian group, but many of these students stated that their sex experiences occurred prior to their conversion experience. Furthermore, many of the respondents were in their early twenties and several had already entered their thirties. The older the person, the greater the chances of having had premarital sex. In contrast, the national average for premarital sex among teenagers is purported to be around 50 percent. According to my calculations, 17 percent fewer students at a Christian college engage in premarital sex than do students on secular campuses, a fact that speaks well for religious educational institutions.

Maintaining a relationship with God may not rank high on your present list of priorities, but chances are that this factor will loom very large sometime in the near future—maybe after marriage as you gaze into the eyes of your firstborn child.

Fact 20. The greater the number of sexual encounters and partners, the greater the impact of all the disadvantages of premarital sex. It isn't just a matter of whether or not a young person engages in premarital sex, but how often and with how many partners it occurs. If a young person has sex with only one person before marriage, the disadvantages listed will apply, but the toll will not be as great as when there have been multiple partners.

I promised no preaching—only the facts. So I will merely ask: *Do you want to take these kinds of chances with your future?*

How to Keep From Going Too Far

If you want a healthy relationship with a member of the opposite sex, a relationship that does not commit you to a sexual involvement, how should you go about attaining it? Often couples rely on the fact that they are both deeply religious and therefore would never engage in such activities. This attitude has led to many unplanned pregnancies and premature marriages! The fact that you have high religious ideals does not inoculate you against sexual desire! Here are some concrete suggestions on how to avoid trouble in courtship.

Develop positive feelings of self-worth. Having positive feelings about yourself is the most important factor in avoiding premarital sex. If you live up to your own values, others will think highly of you, and inner conflicts will not tear you up inside. You will respond to others' opinions of you with personal integrity and self-confidence. Your appearance, abilities, or social acceptance will not unduly worry you, leaving you free to love, to work, and to play.

One self-respecting girl commented, "I have been choosing between varying courses of action since I was old enough to reason. My parents had confidence in me and my judgment from as early as I can remember. My friends and my church had the same high standards that my family held dear. There is no special virtue in my chastity. It is what I have chosen as the way I want for my life. I believe in fidelity—to my parents, to my sense of what is right, and to my future husband and our marriage. What others call 'fun' and 'messing around' I wouldn't find enjoyable, for I prefer keeping my life clean, open, and aboveboard."

Continue with an education after high school. Studies show that college-educated young people have a lower incidence of premarital sex than those who do not pursue higher education. The girl who visualizes herself as a teacher, a social worker, a lawyer, or nurse is not apt to rush off on paths that lead nowhere. The young man who lays plans to enter engineering, business, or computer processing has goals that cannot be easily disturbed. An unwanted pregnancy or forced marriage often does not mix with dreams of accomplishment.

Set up rules for conduct in advance. Think through your own standards, and develop criteria for your actions based on your personal values and the Word of God. This should be a standard you would be proud to discuss with your parents. Develop a specific plan to follow so that you can continue in a healthy, growing relationship with a member of the opposite sex without compromising yourself. After you have carefully thought out your standards, plan how you might maintain them. Think of the difference this could make in your relationship with your parents!

Talk it over with your dating partner. Open communication between dating partners regarding their sexual ideals and values is an excellent way of preventing arousing situations. This calls for planning and a determination to change the mood or behavior whenever either partner approaches dangerous ground. One engaged couple who on a few occasions had given in to their desire for sexual relations determined to call a halt to the practice until after marriage. Together they worked out a strategy of how to handle difficult situations in the future. They determined to curtail their time alone together so that they would have to limit their expressions of physical affection. They purposed to keep away from places where petting would be hard to resist. Instead they spent more time in activities that included things they could do together and with other couples. They took long drives, but avoided parking situations.

Choose your dates with care. Carefully select your dates from those persons who are similar to you in age, interests, and ideals. Avoid blind dates that someone you do not know or trust arranges. Blind dates arranged by a trusted friend might be acceptable.

Plan your dates carefully in advance. Dates should be creative and interesting. They should involve pleasant fellowship with others. Avoid dating situations in which you will have little or nothing to do. Before you go on a date know where you are going, who will be present, what activities are planned, and when you will return home.

Avoid situations designed to stimulate sexual pleasure. One young couple became converted and tried to stop what had become an intense physical relationship. In anguish the fellow sobbed, "We've tried to stop but we just can't!" He went on to say that he was living in a house trailer and almost every weekend his girlfriend came to see him so they could enjoy each other's company. They continued to sleep in the same bed, but she tried to sleep on her side and he on his and it just didn't work! They finally solved the problem when she began

To Get Down to the Nitty-Gritty

1. Definitely yes
2. Probably yes
3. Unsure
4. Probably not
5. Definitely not

Read each of the following statements carefully. Respond to each statement according to the scale of 1 to 5 as shown at the left. Circle the appropriate number for each statement according to your present attitudes.

1 2 3 4 5   1. After discussing the matter, my partner and I decided on a set limit of physical contact.

1 2 3 4 5   2. There is much conflict between my partner and me regarding how far we should go.

1 2 3 4 5   3. It is my parents who dictate to me how far I should go in a premarital relationship.

1 2 3 4 5   4. It is my own personal values that dictate how far I should go in premarital relationships.

1 2 3 4 5   5. I believe an open and honest discussion between my dating partner and I would help us determine how far we should go.

IF YOU ARE ALREADY SEXUALLY INVOLVED:

1 2 3 4 5   1. It has increased my love for my partner.

1 2 3 4 5   2. We are using contraception.

1 2 3 4 5   3. We sometimes turn to sex to patch up quarrels and misunderstandings.

1 2 3 4 5   4. I receive deep physical and emotional satisfaction from each sexual experience.

1 2 3 4 5   5. Should pregnancy occur I would be capable of accepting the emotional, social, spiritual, and financial responsibility for the child.

staying with a friend in town so they could avoid temptation.

You will not go to each other's home or apartment when no one else is there. This rule was firmly imbedded in my mind as a teenager, although I do not recall ever discussing it with my parents. On one occasion my boyfriend and I had arrived home before my parents, and I did not want to be alone with him in the house. So I did

having made any sexual advances. When asked why, he said, "I'd never try anything with her. She knows too much. Her dad is a doctor!"

Studies indicate that many young people who pride themselves on being up-to-date on sex information do not have reliable data on even the basic facts. What about you? Do you really know the score on sex? Have you taken a course in sex education recently? Have you read a good book on the physiology of reproduction? Do you know the correct names and functions of the reproductive organs? Do you know enough about anatomy and physiology to attain sexual harmony when you get married?

Your local library should have some authoritative books on the subject. Many high schools and colleges offer courses in marriage and family life. Some religious organizations sponsor discussion groups and seminars for their youth. Whatever avenue you choose, *get informed!*

Learn to control your sexual desires. You do not need to give in to your sexual urges just because you have them. The sex drive in both males and females can be denied expression for months, years, or even permanently with no adverse effects. Many men and women never marry or have intercourse, and they lead normal, happy, and productive lives.

I here refer to *sublimation.* Sublimation means that a person converts his or her drives and desires into acceptable outlets. It means that when you cannot or will not indulge your sexual urges, you will look for another form of expression. An unmarried woman can find an outlet for her sexual tension by becoming a schoolteacher and involving her life with her students—or she might take up writing, gardening, or tennis. A single man might pursue an occupation that will absorb his interests and much of his time. He can become involved in an active sport, community service, hobbies, service clubs, or religious work. To sublimate sexual energy means that you discover and develop interests and activities that give you enough personal satisfaction so that you can *redirect* your sexual energies. Thus you

some fast thinking and quickly suggested that we wash his car. We were merrily immersed in sudsy water and healthy conversation when my parents arrived.

Know the facts about sex. Some parents, educators, and church leaders believe that the best way to keep young people pure is to keep them ignorant. They pretend that sex doesn't exist in the hope that young people won't experiment. The truth of the matter is that sexual experimentation is highest among persons who have not had proper sexual instruction. Sexual curiosity can create problems.

Knowledge is your best safeguard. Many a fellow has said that the easiest score around is the girl who doesn't know what the score is. As one guy put it: "A girl who is really ignorant often lets a fellow go too far before she knows what's happening. Then she can't stop him." A sexually experienced man had dated a girl for some time without literally substitute other forms of expression for sexual urges.

Sublimation is more beneficial than repression. If you repress your sexual desires, you ignore them or pretend they are not there. Repression only delays the time when you must face the issue. In sublimation you recognize your drive and deal with it constructively. Sublimation of the sex drive does not mean that you reject sex, but rather that you accept it by taking charge of your sex urges.

It doesn't matter whether you are married or single. From time to time you will have to control your sexual desires. Even married people must do so. The physician may recommend that a pregnant woman avoid intercourse for several weeks prior to the birth of the baby, and for several weeks following delivery. A husband may take an extended business trip that separates him from his wife. Self-control must be exercised during such times.

Sex desires are very real, but they are more real when you sit around doing nothing. So take your mind off the subject and plunge into an absorbing activity. You will find it nearly impossible to concentrate on sex if you must practice for two hours a day in preparation for a swim meet, take an active role in church or synagogue leadership, or work on perfecting a part in an upcoming drama.

Ask God for guidance. Ask your heavenly Father to help you find His will for your life. If you and your date discuss and pray about your future together, it will produce a bond of conscience between you that can serve as a barrier against temptation. Discuss your relationship in terms of "we three—God, you, and I."

How to Be "Intimate" Without Having Sex!

"Have you heard about Ron and Susie?" whispered one pretty coed to another. "They've become intimate." If my guess is right, when you hear that a couple has become "intimate" you assume they have had sexual relations. But when you really become intimate with another person, it means more than just having sex with him

or her. In fact, it is possible to become intimate with a person of the opposite sex, the same sex, a roommate, a teacher, or any one of several persons and yet not be involved sexually.

How do you attain intimacy, then? Intimacy progresses through several stages. When you meet a person for the first time, you go from the stranger to the acquaintance stage. From these basic levels you may progress to friendship or even to a close friendship. At this point it is possible to move into intimacy. But we do not achieve intimacy overnight! It develops over a period of time as two people relate to each other in an atmosphere of caring and warmth. We can thus define an "intimate relationship" as one in which trust and honesty are evident in an atmosphere where both parties do not fear undue criticism of their thoughts, feelings, and worries.

Other expressions that might describe an intimate friendship include: caring, sharing, getting to know one another, physical attraction, giving of one's self, satisfying the other person's needs, satisfying your own needs, telling the other person things you've never told anyone else before, and openness. You can probably add to the list.

If you can achieve this kind of nonsexual intimacy with another person, you have reached the highest level of intimacy. Such a relationship springs from four factors.

1. Trust. Trust provides an atmosphere of freedom. Neither person experiences recrimination, criticism, or restraint. Each has complete confidence that he or she can bring to the surface all hidden thoughts and feelings with the assurance that the friend will accept them for what they are. Honesty and respect lay the foundations for trust.

2. Openness. Each person will feel that he or she can be himself or herself without pretending to be something else. Intimates share the unpleasant as well as pleasant aspects of their lives. Author John Powell describes openness when he writes:

If friendship and human love are to mature between any two persons, there must be absolute and honest mutual revelation; this kind of self-revelation can be achieved only through what we have called "gut level" communication. There is no other way, and all the reasons which we adduce to rationalize our cover-ups and dishonesty must be seen as delusions. It would be much better for me to tell you how I really feel about you than to enter into the stickiness and discomfort of a phoney relationship.

Dishonesty always has a way of coming back to haunt and trouble us. Even if I should have to tell you that I do not admire or love you emotionally, it would be much better than trying to deceive you and having to pay the ultimate price of all such deception, your greater hurt and mine. And you will have to tell me things, at times, that will be difficult for you to share. But, really, you have no choice, and if I want your friendship, I must be ready to accept you as you are. If either of us comes to the relationship without this determination of mutual honesty and openness, there can be no friendship, no growth; rather, there can be only a subject-object kind of thing that is typified by immature bickering, pouting, jealousy, anger, and accusation.[19]

Each person in an intimate relationship must feel that his or her feelings are important and that they are being given consideration. Out of such a relationship will grow respect for each other.

3. Freedom. Even in an intimate relationship you do not own each other. Each has the freedom to move in other directions with or without the other person. Independence is allowed for without accusations or mistrust. Since honesty, openness, and trust mark the relationship, there is no need to be suspicious or demanding. Each person has room to develop his or her own likes, dislikes, talents, and abilities without pressure from the other to conform to likes or beliefs.

4. Time. It takes time to develop an intimate relationship, and no one can rush it. Many couples achieve intimacy only after several years of marriage, and some never attain it.

It is possible and even desirable to achieve this kind of emotional intimacy without physical intimacy. Once a couple begins a sexual relationship, emotional intimacy tends to level off. If you need sex to express love, then you have formed a very superficial bond between you.

It is also possible to achieve physical intimacy without ever approaching emotional intimacy. Some of you have gone this route and know exactly what I mean. You move rapidly into a physically intimate stage too early, and you concluded that a passing infatuation was genuine love. Having a physically intimate relationship with someone does not provide an adequate basis for a "compleat" marriage. Any male and female can mate successfully provided they have the proper equipment and the opportunity for sex. But emotional intimacy requires more of a personal investment.

Society and the media have tried to

convey the idea that sex is the ultimate experience in life—that sex makes life worth living But sex has no corner on being the life experience, and certainly it cannot guarantee the caring and sharing relationship that we all desire. Developing a satisfying sexual relationship is an important part of marriage, but it is only one of a number of essential ingredients.

No one, of course, can achieve intimacy without personal cost. Sometimes cost must be measured in terms of hurt or pain should the friendship break up. But each relationship we develop with another person will provide such rewards as increased feelings of self-respect, knowledge of being loved and cared for, security, happiness, and the satisfaction of being trusted. The benefits should outweigh the pain.

Some people go through life without ever developing an intimate relationship with anyone. Oh, they want intimacy, but they refuse to give what is necessary to develop that kind of relationship. An intimate relationship can be destroyed also by peer or family pressure, needs or expectations not being met, the intrusion of another person, sex, changing values, differing beliefs, or by the feeling that you are being used.

Yes, you can develop intimacy without sex. At times you may find it difficult to refrain from sex when you are attracted emotionally and physically to a member of the opposite sex, but it is entirely possible and greatly advantageous to develop emotional intimacy first.

What About Living Together? What's Up About Bedding Down?

A few years ago I was invited to be the keynote speaker for a Human Sexuality Week at a large university. In addition to giving an evening presentation, I was also asked to present a workshop on marriage in the afternoon. At the close of the afternoon workshop I opened the floor for questions. Most of the questions came from a foursome seated at a table at the back of the room. One of the males in this group sneered as he asked, "Why bother to get married? What difference does that piece of paper make?"

As I grappled with this question, I had to decide whether or not to identify myself as a Christian who stands on Biblical and moral principles. I took a deep breath and replied, "I am a Christian and teach Biblical principles. The Bible advocates marriage between man and woman, and I can teach no other alternative. You have the right to choose the lifestyle you wish. I have chosen my lifestyle in accordance with what I feel is right. However, I respect your right to do as you wish. Your choice may differ from mine, but I stand on the Bible."

Once I took that position, the heckling stopped. During the evening lecture the foursome who had been sitting on the table manifested rapt attention. After the meeting one of the females from this group spoke to me earnestly. "I used to attend church as a child with my parents," she said, "and what you have said tonight rings true. I must rethink my values. Thank you for coming."

But aren't there any other reasons outside of Biblical ones for getting married? If two persons love each other, why can't they just live together without being bound by the Bible or guilt? Who needs a wedding anyway? What difference does a piece of paper make?

Yes, there are other reasons. First of all, a wedding means something to society, the state, and the church. It publicly declares that a new family has been established. Society and the community are interested in new families. Therefore a ceremony, court records, witnesses, the sanction of the church or state, and a minister or justice of the peace is required. Such formalities announce to the community that two persons have entered a new status.

Society also looks to the wedding as a safeguard for moral standards. Society attempts to protect property rights. According to the laws of the community, husband and wife have various rights to each other's property and to make joint purchases. The wedding also provides a legitimate name for children whom parents bring into the community.

Society also seeks to protect individuals

from abuse and exploitation. There are marriage laws that prevent bigamy, fraud, the use of force, as well as the marriage of children or of seriously incompetent persons. It preserves the kinship system that society holds dear. It guards the legality of the wedding agreement. Marriage has many built-in protections.

Perhaps you have considered living with someone without benefit of marriage. You may have toyed with the idea in order to avoid the tragedy of divorce. Before you decide, hear me out.

Living together enjoys a popularity today never heard of before. A study at Ohio State University found that between 1967 and 1973 the number of live-in couples increased by 267 percent![20] The latest census figures reveal that from 1971 to 1981 the number of unmarried couples living together jumped from 523,000 to 1,560,000—a 300 percent increase. Rarely have investigators discovered such a rapid change in any type of social behavior.

Research from a Boulder, Colorado study of unmarried couples who live together provides interesting information for anyone contemplating this alternative. In this study the most frequent reason given by women for living together was that they were looking forward to marriage. The males, however, verbalized their motives as "sexual convenience and pleasure." One male stated bluntly, "If you're living with a chick, it's a lot easier to get laid!" [21]

Another study revealed that the most common complaint of live-in women is: "I sometimes get the feeling I'm being used." It doesn't take some of these girls long to figure out just how, either! The male attitude is: "Why should I risk marriage when I can get everything I need without tying myself down to a lifelong commitment and responsibility?"

Journalist Sally Quinn wrote an article titled "Why Just Living Together Wasn't Enough for Sally Quinn." After living with Washington *Post* editor Ben Bradlee for five years, she changed her mind about getting married. On the occasion of their second wedding anniversary she reflected candidly and tenderly on why marriage became so

important and why many of her friends today are saying their vows too.

For years Ms. Quinn looked around at the examples of marriage she knew and didn't like what she saw—couples who stopped trying after a while, who took each other for granted, who didn't flirt or tease or do any of the fun things that people who lived together did. She liked what she saw in couples who lived together. There was life in those relationships, freedom. They stayed together because they wanted to. They had fun, excitement, romance, and adventure. They traveled, went out to dinner a lot, and took off on the spur of the moment if they felt like it.

What made her change her mind? Nothing major—just little things. She wanted to be not only loved but cherished. Then there were those little social problems that arose from time to time. What should she call Ben? Friend? Date? Escort? Certainly not husband. And how did they sleep when friends invited them to stay overnight? In separate bedrooms? In the same bed? Furthermore, they owned absolutely nothing together. So finally Sally Quinn told Ben she wanted to get married. He thought it over, and they got married a week later. Was she glad? Yes! She writes:

> Living together took up so much emotional energy. . . . Now I feel liberated to expend my emotional energy on other things, like loving completely, not holding back something in order to protect myself—just in case. It is so relaxing to be married." [22]

Marriage gives a couple the opportunity for happiness, though it does not provide them with the wherewithal to achieve it. There is no magic in the wedding itself to change persons or circumstances. There is no love potion that guarantees the couple will live together "happily ever after." No words spoken on the wedding day can teach the couple how to achieve lasting bliss. Whatever happiness they achieve will result from personal effort, knowledge, love, and commitment. The wedding makes few internal changes, but it does make dramatic changes in status, rights, and opportunities. Live-in lovers might find

"Wouldn't it have been nice if we'd been born before someone had invented sex?"

it possible to avoid divorce lawyers and alimony, but often there are no fewer tears, heartaches, or problems.

What to Do if You Have Already Gone Too Far

A young man set up an appointment with a school counselor. After being seated in the room, he could hardly speak because of his nerves. His throat was dry, and tears welled up in his eyes. Finally he began his story. "Three years ago I hired out to a family to do some repair work around their place for the summer. During the day while everyone else was away, the wife and mother of the family spent a good deal of time talking with me. She was very easy to talk with and very complimentary of my work. One day she suggested that we have intercourse. I felt so awful after the experience that I quit my job the next day and never went back to their home. That happened three years ago, but I still can't forget it. I want to find a nice girl and settle down to a happily married life, but I feel so unworthy. What can I do?"

147

What should you do if you have already gone too far? First of all, you do not need to feel unclean or subhuman. And you are not obligated to marry a person just because you have had intercourse together. Neither are you obligated to get married because pregnancy has resulted. For a couple to marry just to give a baby a name is one of the least valid reasons for marriage. A couple caught in this bind can find other options.

If you are already involved in a sexual relationship, the remedy will not be easy. But here are some suggestions:

Acknowledge your mistake. A girl came sobbing into her counselor's office with a story about how she and her boyfriend had "accidentally" gone "all the way." Let's look at her situation realistically. She should have said that she and her boyfriend had

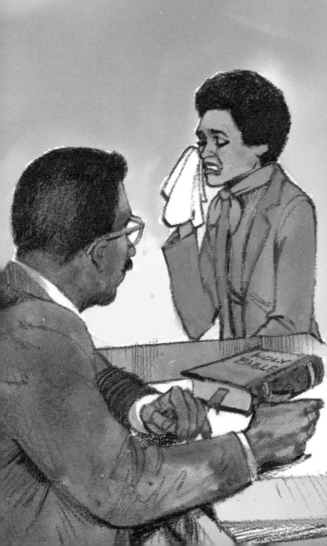

not *meant* to go all the way. Their emotions had gotten out of control and the inevitable happened. But this was no accident! Both parties freely and willfully made a series of decisions that permitted it to happen. They sought a place of privacy where they could spend time together alone. They also progressed from light petting activities to heavy petting. And they both agreed to sexual intercourse—she agreed when she permitted it.

To call this progression of activities an "accident" is a self-deceiving rationalization. The fact is that both partners refused to draw the line at several stopping points along the way. They threw moral and spiritual principles to the winds as a result of emotional and sexual arousal. This is not an accident but a *choice,* and the sooner a couple admits it the sooner they will be able to handle the problem and cope with the guilt connected with it.

Ask God for forgiveness. Once you can admit personal guilt, you can move to the second step and confess your wrong to your heavenly Father. How blessed religion is at this point! Confession is good for the soul, and we serve a God who will totally and completely forgive our sins when we truly repent. If we face up to our wrongs and are sincerely sorry, God has a wonderful way of using these experiences for our good. He can actually help us, through our mistakes, to become stronger, finer, and more complete persons. Your present attitudes toward the experience can help you grow to be a more loving, understanding, and sympathetic person when sin entraps and enslaves others.

So refuse to whip yourself endlessly with guilt. Forget the tears and sleepless nights. Stop punishing yourself. Stop cutting yourself off from spiritual activities because of your guilt feelings.

Stop seeing each other. If you are already involved in a sexual relationship and want to test whether it is genuine love or infatuation, there is only one way to find out. You must isolate the sexual factor. In any scientific experiment, the variable must be isolated. In this case the variable is sex. Studies indicate that a good sexual relationship can hold a couple together for some three to five years, but no longer if that is all they have going for them. For this reason alone, a couple should resist sexual relations early in a relationship. Sex deceives the emotions. A couple need to be very sure of other factors before clouding and complicating the picture with the powerful responses that surface when sex takes over. A couple who attempt to sidestep this act will only deceive themselves.

Refuse to see each other for a long period of time, preferably several months. You may write and phone each other, but you must avoid any opportunities to be alone together. Vowing to stay away from sex but continuing to see each other as before won't work. Once a couple has established a habit of having sex, it is next to impossible for them to be together without indulging in it. It's much like being addicted to a hard drug: During your serious moments you pledge that you will never again take the stuff, but when the craving hits, you can't control yourself.

You and your lover must initiate and carry out the decision not to see each other. It won't work if parents, a minister, or a friend tries to talk you into it. You would only rush back into each other's arms as soon as they turn their backs. Only you can make the decision to stay apart. This will be a difficult period, but it offers the only way for both of you to analyze the quality of your relationship.

Even though God may have forgiven your sins, you may still have to live with some of the consequences. If you lost your virginity so long ago you can't remember where or when, the fact remains that you are no longer a virgin. If you have had a venereal disease or became pregnant or caused someone to become pregnant or had an abortion or put a child up for adoption, the awful recollection of these things will recur from time to time. But God has an amazing way of healing such memories so they won't haunt you. When God says that He forgives your sins, He means that He not only forgives them but He *forgets* them, as well. He frees you to

begin again. Your slate is clean in His sight. It is as though it never happened.

Press forward in happiness, honesty, and earnestness. And on your wedding day as you approach the altar in your finest wedding attire, your face need not reveal any self-reproach about your past but only gratefulness to a heavenly Father who is big enough to forgive even sexual sins.

Double Protection

Let's assume that you have stayed with me so far. You've read everything I've written in this book, but you still wish to continue engaging in premarital sex. You plan to take advantage of the next situation that presents itself (and you know in your heart whether or not you will), or you plan to continue in the pattern you have already established for your life. The decision is up to you, of course, but I'm sorry that the defense of premarital chastity hasn't persuaded you.

But if you plan to proceed with premarital sex in spite of the evidence against it, will you at least proceed in the best way possible for both of you and for everyone else concerned? In other words, if you insist on indulging in sex before marriage, please use birth control measures!

And this means that *both of you should use something.* Unmarried sex calls for *double protection.* Male contraception should consist of condoms. Female contraception may include vaginal jellies or foams, or a physician might recommend an IUD, a diaphragm, or the Pill. (Do not try to obtain or use these last three items without medical supervision.) The Pill is the most effective method of birth control (outside of abstinence), but still one to five users in every thousand get pregnant. You could be one of those. So please avoid pregnancy at all costs. Double protect yourselves.

When you have to take the time for this double protection, you may find your desires cooling down and becoming easier to control. If you have to slow down and get ready for premarital sex, it gives you time to think. It isn't very romantic. It is more serious and businesslike than if you do not use any form of birth control, but, then, so is parenthood.

God's Plan for Sex

A prominent marriage counselor once said, "The only sound motive for a happy marriage is being overwhelmingly in love on a frankly sexual basis, centering about physical desire." Now, if he had stopped there, many of you could build a case for whatever you might want to condone. But he went on to add that, fundamental though sex is, "there is much more to a good marriage."

Sex by itself would be little more than animal appetite. Genuine love combines sexual desire with all the other components that build the highest kind of relationship between husband and wife. Love is friendship, tenderness, self-control, selflessness, kindness, and loyalty blended with sexual desire.

The sexual urge, separated from the other aspects of a relationship, selfishly desires to dominate, conquer, force, or surrender. By itself it is animal. Genuine love idealizes, controls, and conforms sexual desire to social living. Love is other-person-centered. Sex without love is self-centered, a craving for physical satisfaction, physical release. Love, on the other hand, craves an intimate sharing with another person.

Joe, a university honor student, was very popular with both sexes, having been voted most likely to succeed. In addition, he was voted best-dressed and best-looking! Joe really was intelligent, skilled, dependable, industrious, with a dynamite personality to boot. Single women found it difficult to think straight when they were around him, and it was common knowledge that married women had propositioned him. When Joe walked through an office, typewriters stopped clacking. When Joe walked into the cafeteria, the girls stopped eating. When Joe bounded onto the football field, not only the girls from his school cheered, but also the girls with the opposing team.

Furthermore, Joe loved God and possessed other rare and beautiful qualities that were a source of pride and joy to his family.

He listened to his father's advice, and because of his capabilities he became his father's favorite. Soon Joe's brothers began to hate him. Eventually they would not speak a kind word to him.

One night Joe had a rather unusual dream. He dreamed that he and his brothers were in a field binding sheaves. Suddenly his sheaf stood tall, and his brothers' sheaves bowed down to it. Then he had another dream in which the sun, moon, and eleven stars bowed to him. If his brothers hated him before, they now became more furious than ever. Their evil hearts carefully and deliberately plotted his murder.

You can find the rest of the story in Genesis 37 and on. It is a gripping and tragic story, the greatest rags-to-riches story ever told. Joseph's brothers sold him to a raucous bunch of merchants, who sold him again when they got to Egypt. Potiphar, chief of Pharaoh's Bureau of Investigation, bought him and placed him in charge of his entire household.

Before long, Potiphar's wife attempted to seduce Joseph. Even though she was married to a man with money and power, she was not blind to Joseph's masculine charms. For several weeks she plotted and planned. At all times dressing as attractively as possible, she made herself as available as she dared. One day she spent longer than usual fixing herself up. She applied her makeup just so, arranged her hair youthfully, bathed herself in perfume, slipped into her most revealing negligee, and invited Joseph to sleep with her.

Joseph, very much male, had 20/20 vision, and a good-looking woman had just offered herself to him. He had reached the age when a man's sexual desire runs at its peak.

Joseph did not have time to debate with himself about the proper course of action. He didn't play games, reasoning that Potiphar had given into his hand the entire house—and certainly Potiphar's wife was a part of his house. He didn't attempt to rationalize that the affair was of concern only to the two persons involved and that as long as no one else found out it wouldn't hurt anyone. He didn't argue with himself that she could get an abortion if worse came to worse.

He responded No! A thousand times *No!* But Joseph didn't make this decision when Potiphar's wife approached him. He had decided that long beforehand. He already knew what he would do. He did what he was used to doing.

In the face of temptation Joseph was able to look away. It wasn't because Potiphar's wife was unattractive that he fled, leaving his coat in her clutches. No, Joseph had learned to deny himself certain pleasures in order to attain his long-range goals. He knew the beauty of present sacrifice for future rewards.

Most of us seem to think that we can choose correctly at the very moment we must make the decision. But we don't really make the choice at that moment. Instead, we choose according to the way we have chosen a hundred times before. Our destiny is not that which we decide to do, but that which we have done. Our future actually lies behind us!

If you want to be a winner, as was Joseph, you, too, will have to give up some immediate pleasures for the sake of ultimate benefits. You will look away from wickedness rather than accept it as normal. Just as Joseph found and followed the law of chastity and purity, so you can find and live by a code of decency and morality in a world that places little or no value on these attributes.

---

[1] Paul H. Landis, *Making the Most of Marriage,* 3rd ed. (New York: Appleton-Century-Crofts, 1965), p. 394.

[2] *Ibid.*

[3] Richard F. Hettlinger, *Living With Sex: The Students' Dilemma* (Boston: Little, Brown and Co., 1972), chapter 10.

[4] Ray E. Short, *Sex, Love, or Infatuation: How Can I Really Know?* (Minneapolis: Augsburg Publishing House, 1978), p. 77.

[5] *Ibid.,* p. 93.

[6] Landis, *op. cit.,* p. 399.

[7] Alberta Mazat, *That Friday in Eden* (Mountain View, Calif.: Pacific Press, 1981), p. 104.

[8] Tim Stafford, *A Love Story* (Grand Rapids: Zondervan, 1977), p. 38.

[9] "The Shocking Statistics," *Woman's Day,* Oct. 11, 1979, p. 124.

[10] "Pregnant Teenagers: Do They Have Special Risks?" *Transition,* Nov. 1978, pp. 9-11.

[11] James A. Sebastian, Burton O. Leeb, and Richard See, "Cancer of the Cervix—A Sexually Transmitted Disease," *American Journal of Obstetrics and Gynecology,* July 15, 1978, pp. 620-623.

[12] Ernest Burgess and Paul Wallin, *Engagement and Marriage* (Philadelphia: J. B. Lippincott Co., 1953).

[13] *Ibid.*

[14] Landis, *op. cit.,* p. 397.

[15] Henry A. Bowman, *Marriage for Moderns,* 6th ed. (New York: McGraw-Hill, 1970), p. 132.

[16] Tim and Beverly LaHaye, *The Act of Marriage,* (Grand Rapids: Zondervan, 1976), p. 211.

[17] Eugene J. Kanin and David H. Howard, *American Sociological Review,* 23:5, 558.

[18] Robert O. Blood, *Marriage,* 2d ed. (New York: The Free Press, 1969), p. 134.

[19] John Powell, *Why Am I Afraid to Tell You Who I Am?* (Chicago: Argus Communications Co., 1969), pp. 62, 63.

[20] Short, *op. cit.,* p. 37.

[21] *Ibid.*

[22] Sally Quinn, "Why Just Living Together Wasn't Enough for Sally Quinn," Fresno *Bee,* Feb. 8, 1981.

Further reading you will enjoy . . .

McDowell, Josh, and Paul Lewis.   GIVERS, TAKERS, AND OTHER KINDS OF LOVERS.

Miles, Herbert J.   THE DATING GAME, chapter 8.

Wright, H. Norman.   DYNAMIC SEX.

The number of persons
that you could successfully mate with is great,
but this does not mean
that you could make a go of marriage
with just anyone.

Chapter at a Glance

Are You Fit to Be Tied?

The Scriptures read: "When I was a child, I used to speak as a child, think as a child, reason as a child; when I became a man, I did away with childish things" (1 Corinthians 13:11, N.A.S.B.).* Just as when you entered your teen years you put away certain toys that represented your childhood, so when you enter adulthood you will put away childish irresponsibility.

The process of growth from childhood into adulthood is often referred to as "maturing." It involves a series of steps that moves the individual from total dependence upon parents to the ability to be self-governing. You may find it difficult at times to see where you stand in this process,

because the child within you looks at himself from his own angle in the mirror! Only when you have grown sufficiently so that you can see yourself from a direct vantage point can you come face to face with your own behavior and thus view yourself as others see you.

If you are mature enough to marry, you will recognize marriage for what it is. You will realize that marriage is not an easy escape from reality or personal problems, but rather it may bring on new problems

---

* From the *New American Standard Bible,* © The Lockman Foundation, 1960, 1962, 1963, 1968, 1971, 1972, 1973, 1975. Used by permission.

and greater responsibilities. However, marriage also can bring great personal fulfillment and happiness. You will understand that marriage offers the most rewards when the relationship is a *mutual* meeting of personality needs. You will also realize that marriage is not just a private matter between two people, but rather it guarantees the stability of the community and protects the security of children born. If you are mature enough to marry, you will recognize these larger implications, as well as the meaning for your own personal life.

Maturity for marriage includes understanding the nature of love and how love develops slowly as you progress through adolescence and early adulthood. You will be able to recognize the various levels and types of love that you have experienced up to the present time. Each of your previous experiences with love should have taught you something valuable for the future. You probably realize by now that you have loved several persons with whom you could not live. You realize that love must be supported by common interests and goals, acceptance of each other, and mutual respect. You should be able to differentiate between romantic love (infatuation) as pictured in movies and fiction and the type of love that provides lasting happiness in marriage.

If mature, you will have developed a philosophy of life that will guide you through the future. You will have come to terms with your religious concepts, values, and goals, and you will live in accordance with what you believe to be right and good. You will have found your relationship with God to be workable, allowing you to cope with the problems in your life that will surface. Your exact course for the future may not be actually charted, but your direction will be set.

You will have accurately evaluated yourself and will be aware of your strengths and weaknesses. You will be working to improve weaknesses when possible. Weak areas that you cannot seem to change, you have learned to accept without excessive guilt or sorrow. You build on your strengths and make the most of what you have to work with. You recognize those areas where you have failed, but you have compensated by doing other things well. You can accept your limitations and appreciate your assets.

You will have taken a long hard look at your family background, the contribution it has made to making you what and who you are, and what it is from your background that you will bring to marriage. Research shows that the emotional climate of your parents' home greatly influences your chances for success in marriage. If unhappiness has marred your immediate past or if repeated marriage failures have dogged past generations, you will face this realistically and begin plotting constructive ways to overcome such obstacles to your future happiness. You do not blame your parents for their failures, and if you come from a happy family you will not take for granted that happiness is assured you. Instead, you will work hard at understanding the components of what makes for successful family living.

If you are mature, you will have learned to meet problems constructively. The frustrations of life will not throw you into fits of confusion, discouragement, or disorganization. You will learn from past experiences and use them as a means of growth to help you cope with emergencies and crises. Your ability to handle such situations will significantly affect your ability to build a successful marriage.

If you are mature, you will have learned about interpersonal relationships. You recognize that inner motivations prompt behavior in yourself and in others. You can see that aggressive and domineering behavior often covers up for insecurity and that heavy drinking, drug use, sex, and clinging dependence are usually methods of escape from problems in life. You recognize jealousy as an expression of insecurity or inadequacy. You know that criticism is an attempt to tear down others and build up self. An understanding of what influences behavior will help you in choosing a marriage partner and in all interpersonal relationships.

You will have achieved a degree of

independent thinking. You can think for yourself. You are past the immature stage of rebellion in which you threw overboard everything your parents had taught. You have formulated your own ideas based on your life experiences and attitudes so that you can make independent decisions.

You can accept responsibility for your own mistakes. You have outgrown blaming others for your weaknesses and refusing to recognize your own faults. When you make a mistake, you accept it and try to learn from the experience.

One 17-year-old put it this way: "I've tried to learn from my mistakes rather than trying to dodge what happens. Whenever I try to duck responsibility for what I've done by saying, 'Oh, well, it wasn't my fault anyway,' it seems the same thing happens again, only worse

Compatibility

How compatible are you with your future mate—REALLY? Do you have the same goals, interests, and values? Have you really thought about living with this person's character and personality traits for the rest of your life? Respond to the following statements and share your responses with one another.

1. The strong points I see in my partner are . . .

2. The reason I wish to marry is . . .

3. My partner and I have the following interests in common . . .

4. A good sense of humor in marriage is necessary because . . .

5. My partner's manners are . . .

6. My partner irritates me most when . . .

7. Our relationship has been the most successful in . . .

8. I am happiest in our relationship when . . .

9. I hurt the most when . . .

10. We differ about . . .

11. The goals toward which I think we should work in marriage are . . .

12. My friends think our relationship is . . .

13. My family thinks our relationship is . . .

14. In my free time the thing I like to do is . . .

15. On my days off I would expect to . . .

16. On a vacation I want most of all to . . .

the next time. It's easier to learn things the first time around rather than the hard way later on."

A young child wants what he wants when he wants it! But a mature person can want something and still make choices regarding it. He or she can look ahead and plan. She wants to get married now, but if they do he would have to give up his education. He wants a secure future, but is willing to take the time to train for that job. He has strong sexual desires for the girl he is dating, but he has chosen his values and puts his immediate desires aside for the good of their future. If you are mature, you won't deny all your desires and wants, but you are willing to wait and where necessary to make sacrifices today in order to achieve greater satisfaction later.

If you are mature, you can put the wants and needs of your partner before your own—at least part of the time. One Peanuts cartoon shows Charlie Brown talking with Lucy. Charlie says, "I'd like to be able to feel that I'm needed." Lucy says, "Don't forget, Charlie Brown, that people who are really needed are asked to do a lot of different things." He thinks it over and then quips, "I'd like to feel needed and yet not have to do anything." How often this kind of love and caring lures us! But it is totally unrealistic. The inability of partners to put themselves out for the other person, to think first of the needs of their partner, accounts for much marital agony.

You have also outgrown immature attitudes about sex. Some people think of sex as dirty or vulgar, secret, or sinful. If you are mature enough for marriage, you will have developed positive and wholesome attitudes about sex and will try to modify any attitudes that need changing. You may need counseling in order to accomplish this, or you might read good books on the subject, but you will take the necessary steps to correct your bad attitudes.

If you are mature, you will be able to assess your own level of maturity. If you are an immature person, you will be almost totally unaware of how much change or growth is necessary. The less mature you are, the more ready you will be to plunge

into marriage with little or no understanding of the responsibilities that accompany it. The mature person will not unduly fear the responsibility, but will face the facts and take steps to prepare for it.

How Can I Know if My Partner Is Ready for Marriage?

Naturally, the maturity that is expected of you is also expected of your partner. But since none of us ever reach the same level of maturity in the same area, this makes it difficult to judge whether someone else is mature. If only a genius would invent a device—a scale or indicator—upon which we could measure maturity and suitability! This genius would become a millionaire overnight and would save countless thousands from the untold heartache that selecting a mate by romance alone has caused.

Women seem to possess greater insight than men do when determining mate suitability. A study of marriage failures showed that 70 percent of the husbands whose marriages failed felt confident that their marriages would succeed. Only 48 percent of the wives felt this way. Even a girl's family and her best friends are better prophets than the boy's family and his friends.[1]

Marriage clinics can help young people make their final analysis. But most young people do not have access to such services, and the majority would not take advantage of them if they did. Most would rather trust romance along with the opinion of family and personal friends.

The fact that you are reading a book of this nature indicates that you want to avoid the mistakes and pitfalls others have fallen into. So for your benefit certain personality types[2] that should be avoided will be discussed here.

The Overly Possessive. A man will demonstrate jealous and/or demanding behavior in an attempt to reinforce his own shaky self-image. He will try to dominate the female so he can build his sense of security. In marriage he will allow his wife little opportunity to exercise a will of her

own. The overly possessive woman may play the role of the "clinging vine" or the "mother-knows-best" little dictator. She will be jealous of every aspect of her husband's life—his job, his male friends, his parents and family, and above all else, his female acquaintances. She will attempt to keep him tied to her apron strings and yet tell the world that it is what he wants and it is for their best good.

The Continually Dissatisfied. The male will likely be overly ambitious and work toward goals he cannot define. He moves from one job, school, and community to another in an attempt to find the solution. He refuses to work diligently toward a chosen goal. The continually dissatisfied female may hold marital and social expectations that only a bionic man could satisfy. Movies, television programs, and fictitious love stories have fed her unrealistic expec-

tations, and no one could possibly measure up.

The Temperamental. The temperamental man is self-centered and moody. He thinks himself superior to others and imposes on everyone. In marriage he will do all the taking and will allow his wife to be nurse, mother, and constant admirer, although he gives nothing in return. The temperamental woman is dramatic and unconventional. She needs an audience in order to function and finds the routine of homemaking and parenthood a bore.

The Superior. The superior male knows something about everything and dominates every conversation, as long as it remains on a superficial level. He has a sharp wit that he might even turn on his friends. His aggressive behavior usually covers up a very shaky, frightened self underneath. If anyone called his bluff, he might end up a broken person, and his wife would end up pampering and humoring a bitter and frustrated man.

The superior female succeeds in everything she tackles—career, homemaking, and mothering. She works hard at being a success to overcompensate for the many inadequacies she feels keenly about. She is likely to be highly competitive even in marriage with her husband. She sees her husband, friends, and even her children as threats to her own status. If she does not reach her goals, she will blame her marriage, her husband, and her children.

The Overly Meticulous. The overly meticulous dresses faultlessly and has fastidious personal habits. Frequently he has been a bachelor for a number of years or one whose mother was "perfect" at everything. He cannot tolerate anything less than perfect in a mate, so very few people appeal to him. Whenever a personal problem confronts him, his frustration level increases along with his demands.

The Flirt. The "ladies man" enjoys charming the female gender and avoids his own sex. He wows the gals, and they usually consider him quite a "catch." His flirtatious ways are frequently an attempt to reassure himself of his masculinity and emotional maturity, for he usually harbors grave doubts about his maleness. Since most of his charm is put-on, he usually is a real failure in the emotional and sexual intimacy of marriage.

The female flirt never tires of playing the "come hither" game. She is overly clothes-conscious and fails to handle the routine of daily life well after marriage. Her continuous flirtations constantly embarrass her husband. As she begins to lose her youth and beauty, she is a likely candidate for an affair, in which she attempts to prove that she is still attractive, sought after, and desirable.

The danger signals connected with these personality types do not always show up early in a relationship. Therefore, I always recommend long periods of courtship prior to engagement. The people who rush toward marriage without recognizing danger signals often are the least prepared for it.

In fact, some people marry quickly to avoid facing the danger signals. A compulsive mechanism inside them drives them to the altar regardless of all obstacles. Others marry with the hope that matrimony will provide a way out of difficult situations. Such persons ignore doubtful elements in a relationship. Factors motivating individuals toward such a decision might include the

"We could elope . . . and live under the Big Top."

divorce of parents, a death in the family, a difficult step-parent situation, and uncertainty about educational or future goals. These persons do not want to evaluate their chances for success in marriage and reject any idea that might frustrate their plans to race into marriage.

Other people are just plain reckless. They make hasty decisions in all areas of life without weighing the consequences. They throw caution to the wind and act without thinking. Such persons tend to have a history of failures in life, and only when it is too late can they see that they overlooked important considerations before making their choice.

Still others ignore all warning signals in a relationship because of their romantic ideas about love. They blindly blunder on, holding on to their fairy-tale ideas and refusing any evidence that their marriage might not be wise.

The following list of mild social characteristics that betray an immature individual may help save you from a disastrous marriage.

Mild Social Characteristics[3]

1. Shows fear and anxiety when faced with a new or unusual social situation that holds no real threat; expresses an unprovoked sense of guilt that seems to have no reason at all for asserting itself.

2. Experiences frequent instances of emotion and excitement that are more intense than the situation calls for or that are not appropriate to the situation; is given to frequent hysterical laughter or tears or general excitement.

3. Has phobias; shows fear or unwarranted disgust toward certain objects, situations, or ideas to which people do not ordinarily so react.

4. Is ritual-ridden; daily life is unnaturally patterned around the exacting performance of specific tasks in a specific way.

5. Has uncontrollable impulses—suddenly-felt desires to do particular things regardless of consequences.

6. Has an obsession with state of health—a hypochondriacal concern about

his own health, frequently accompanied by a limitless number of complaints with the area of pain shifting frequently.

7. Has deep moods of depression, often accompanied by unwarranted feelings of guilt.

The persons showing the above characteristics are marginal in their marriageability quotient. In addition, you should entirely avoid marrying some personality types. It is always risky to classify personality types because of the difficulty in sizing people up and putting them into slots. However, an understanding of how maladjusted persons act and the extremes that characterize their behavior will indicate that any person who approaches these extremes will make a difficult, if not impossible, mate.

Serious Social Characteristics of a Maladjusted Person[4]

1. Shows extreme shyness, submissiveness, and inability to relax in the presence of others.

2. Shows hostility and antagonism toward others, society, government, authority, and the world in general.

3. Expresses suspicion and extreme skepticism concerning new people, ideas, and values.

4. Makes a conspicuous display in clothing, possessions, and finances in order to impress others—even strangers.

5. Shows arrogance and an attitude of condescension around even long-time acquaintances.

6. Is given to boisterous behavior regardless of the mood or purpose of the group in which he finds himself.

7. Is preoccupied with sex or sex-linked subjects or shows a strong aversion to sex.

8. Has an insatiable yearning for excitement and adventure and cannot enjoy quiet times or more subtle forms of pleasure.

9. Makes tactless and embarrassing public displays of affection for friends of either sex.

10. Is given to lying or distorting facts in order to put himself and his accomplishments in a more favorable light.

11. Shows an overeagerness to please everyone, even strangers, by doing their

bidding, agreeing with their opinions, et cetera.

12. Shows extreme dependence, and desires to have everything settled and unchanging.

These symptoms should never be ignored in mate selection, especially if they tend to be extreme.

Personality testing, which can help you understand yourself and your partner, along with a counselor's advice, will generally prove helpful. But there is still no substitute for a long period of steady dating, followed by an engagement period of at least six months to test the compatability of personality types. Only after a long acquaintance will put-ons slip and the real self emerge.

If you are in a serious dating relationship and your partner exhibits any one of the factors mentioned, you should investigate what makes him or her act this way.

The Most Important Factor When Choosing a Mate

If you are a normal young person, you are looking for the "ideal mate." You want to find that special person created just for you—in other words, "made in heaven." However, the theory that somewhere on earth is your "one and only" rests on very shaky evidence.

A well-adjusted person can marry any one of several persons and be happy. Probably an immature person could never be happily married to anyone. Marriage does not make an immature person mature, but happy and mature people do make successful marriages.

Although the number of persons that you could successfully mate with is great, this does not mean that you could make a go of marriage with just anyone. You must still choose wisely. What, then, should you look for in an ideal mate? Ten special factors can tell you more about a person's marriage-ability than anything else.[5] Here they are.

1. Superior happiness of parents.
2. Childhood happiness.
3. Lack of conflict with mother.
4. Home discipline that was firm but not harsh.

5. Strong attachment to mother.
6. Strong attachment to father.
7. Lack of conflict with father.
8. Parental frankness about matters of sex.
9. Infrequency and mildness of childhood punishment.
10. Premarital attitude toward sex that is free from disgust or aversion.

Interpersonal relationships during the early years, the example parents have provided, and the attitudes and training they have passed along to their children are the most important issues in preparation for marriage. Many different studies have pointed out the importance of these factors, and you should not overlook them when you select a mate.

Happiness runs in families—and so does divorce and unhappiness. The early years of life at home with your parents can predispose you toward a successful marriage. You have learned from your parents how to settle problems when they arise, how to communicate, how to maintain a proper role relationship between husband and wife, how to relate to children, how to handle finances, and how to handle all other issues of life.

Most likely the pattern you have already learned, you will carry into your own marriage. If you were raised in a family of constant bickering between parents, brothers, and sisters, you will probably carry the same behavior over into your own relationship. If your parents showed their superior happiness through loving words, kind deeds, and deep affection, you will likely experience the same bliss.

But suppose you didn't have a happy home. What then? If you are willing to study and prepare yourself for marriage, you can overcome any handicaps in your background. Studies show that when a person deliberately prepares for marriage through classes, reading, and personality testing, the cycle of marriage failure can be broken. When couples deliberately prepared for marriage in order to break the cycle of unhappiness in their backgrounds, 90 percent rated their marriages as happy or very happy. Even if, with the passing years, the

10 percent who rated their marriages as only average or unhappy should divorce (and this is very unlikely), the divorce rate would still be only half as high as that of their parents.

You are not absolutely bound by your background. You are no more guaranteed a happy marriage if your parents were very happy than you are guaranteed a poor marriage if your parents were very unhappy. What is necessary, though, is that regardless of your background you approach marriage intelligently and work together toward building a happy and successful relationship.

The Best Age to Marry

How old should a person be before he or she gets married? To a large degree the laws of the land settle this question. The legal age ranges from 14 to 18 for young men and 12 to 18 for young women with written permission from their parents. Only when they reach 18 (21 in Puerto Rico) are they allowed to decide for themselves. But are the laws of the land an adequate guide for a successful marriage?

Pity Mary Lou, who "fell in love" at 15, married at 16, and by 18 described herself as "an old married lady before my time." She said, "Here I am with two babies, a tired husband, and nothing to live for but more work than I can manage. I've been nowhere, seen nothing, and am nothing but a drudge. Other girls my age have dates and good times, get to graduate from high school, go on to college, and make something of themselves. But not me. I had to marry the first man who came along—even before I knew what I was doing or even who I was."

Many teenagers never actually *choose* marriage—they are forced or drift into it. "Everyone sort of expected us to marry," confessed Tim, a 19-year-old who had gone steady with Carla since he was 15. "I was tired of her even before I married her, but I had gone so far that I felt I couldn't back out of it."

All studies to date conclude that early marriages are not as stable as those of more mature persons. Estimates indicate that more than 30,000 12-to-15-year-olds marry each year. Teenagers who marry are more than twice as likely to get divorced as the rest of the population. More than half of all marriages are between teenagers. The bride is pregnant in an estimated 50 percent of all teenage marriages, and those teen brides who are not pregnant at the time of their wedding usually become pregnant soon after. Teen husbands find it difficult to support a family because of their limited earning power as a result of a lack of experience and education. Teenagers who drop out of school to marry rarely go back. Put all this together and you find that almost 60 percent of all teenage marriages end in divorce.

What is the ideal age for marrying, then? Age 22 for women and 24 for men seems to ensure the best success. Grooms under 24 are usually unstable, and the percentage of unsuccessful marriages when the groom is 19 or younger is very high. Marriages between couples 18 to 23 years of age still have a very high divorce rate. Couples who are 25 years of age or older have better than a 70 percent chance of success. And, according to psychologist Joyce Brothers, the happiest couples marry after age 28.

In early marriage it is common for one of the partners to lose interest in the other. The person you are in love with at 18 may not be the person you are in love with at age 21. Changing personalities and values also complicate matters. A couple of years during the critical maturing process can drastically change one's thinking and attitudes toward life. Lack of an adequate income also causes major problems.

It is best if both of you are about the same age or if the male is two or three years older. If the woman is slightly older, there will be

no special problem unless one or the other is especially sensitive about it.

As people grow older, age differences become less important. But if at the time of marriage one of you is as much as eight to ten years older than the other, you should take a careful look at the problems that might arise. For instance, physical activities may vary; interests may differ since the younger person may wish to go out more; and attitudes toward life may be different, because a young person usually thinks of life as being much more simple than it actually is.

A girl may actually marry an older man to obtain a substitute parent or because she may think it is her only chance to marry. The relationship can then take on the character of a father-daughter role (or a mother-son role when the wife is older).

One young bride who had married a much older man returned from her honeymoon visibly upset. She went straight to her pastor and reported that she hadn't yet recovered from the first night, when her husband removed his false teeth and put them in a glass on the motel dresser. He requested soft lighting during their love-making, but those infernal choppers leering at her from the dresser cut her response to nil. She knew he had false teeth, but she had never inquired what he did with them at night!

Campus Nuptials

Many couples now in college are trying to decide whether to marry immediately or to postpone marriage until they complete their education. Let's look at the facts regarding student marriages.

Certain studies[6] have revealed that married students make better grades than single students do! Several factors can explain this. A married woman who continues her college education while taking up home-making duties must know her goals and have a strong desire to achieve them. Therefore she might excel over the single girl who doesn't know why she is in college or what she plans to do with her future. Married men, too, seem to have more clearly defined educational goals. Since

they have less time for outside social activities that require time and energy, they devote more time to their studies than they did when they were single.

All right, married students achieve more, but are they happier? It is difficult to get accurate information on this question, since couples must rate themselves and since they have not been married very long. But all studies point to the fact that about three quarters of the couples who respond to "Knowing what you know now, would you marry before finishing college if you were unmarried?" said that they would do it all over again.

The remaining quarter said they had encountered too many hassles earning a living, finding housing, and doing satisfactory college work. These were the reasons they listed, but the real reasons may lie hidden. Many of the couples who doubted the wisdom of their college marriage felt dissatisfied with their marriage for other reasons. The truth of the matter is that if they had waited until after college to marry, they probably would not have married at all.

Marriage while in college has some advantages, one of the biggest being the emotional security that marriage provides. Married college men feel that being married gave their lives stability, more purpose, and made it easier for them to settle down to work. Almost all husbands surveyed felt that their wives helped rather than hindered them. Only a few complained of their wives having too much company, interrupting their study, or wanting to go out evenings.

College marriages, however, have some disadvantages that are not necessarily present in other marriages. While dating during college years, young people may find someone they want to marry and yet not be ready to settle down to one partner even if they are in love. Single girls on campus often complain that married men "don't act like they are married." These men were not ready to give up their single ways for marriage. They probably got swept along into marriage after a short engagement, without realizing what it would mean to be a married student.

Facing Problems

Let's pretend during the following exercise that you are married and the following circumstances come into your life. Write down how you think you would respond to the following problems if they came into your life. Discuss your responses with your partner.

1. major trouble with in-laws

2. birth of a handicapped child

3. husband's loss of job

4. personal injury or major illness

5. an unexpected and unwelcome pregnancy

6. unreconciled sexual difficulties

Most couples who marry during college years postpone having children until after graduation. They dismiss the thought of any unplanned pregnancy interrupting their well-laid plans. But for reasons that are not completely clear, and in spite of the Pill, about one third of all pregnancies among college students are unplanned. Whether these student couples have inadequate knowledge or are careless is beside the point. Students who marry must consider the possibility of parenthood despite the best contraception available.

The success of a college marriage depends to a great degree on how the couple organize their time and divide their responsibilities. If both partners are in school and have children, they may need to be Superman and Wonder Woman in order to keep up with it all. To study, to participate in some social activities, to maintain a home even if there is plenty of money and no babies, requires unselfish cooperation and the sacrifice of personal preferences.

Money matters cause another concern. Some parents continue to support their married children in college. But problems may arise from this generous act. Few parents can look upon their children as married adults as long as they are contributing to their support! And the in-laws who do not contribute to the support may often complicate the situation. Young people may accept parental support, but they are not often willing to accept any interference

that may come with it. Many misunderstandings arise from this arrangement and contribute to disappointment for the parents and unhappiness for the children.

Young people will continue to marry while in college. Nevertheless, those who are considering such a marriage need to take a long, hard look at the facts. Yes, they can make it if they choose not to wait until they have completed their education, but they will have to work harder at succeeding than other couples do. This often sounds easier before marriage than it does after marriage.

Religion and Mate Choice

Most couples are married by a minister, priest, or rabbi rather than by a justice of the peace. Why? Is religion an important factor in marriage? In what ways do the religious beliefs of a couple affect their lives after marriage? What consequences follow? What are the chances for a happy marriage when one marries out of his or her professed faith? What significance do religion and spiritual values have on a couple, their marriage, and the children born to them?

Years of research have indicated that those who belong to no religious group have a greater marriage risk than those who do. In marriages where one person is religious and the other not, the divorce and juvenile delinquency rates are generally twice as high as in marriages where both partners share the same faith.[7]

Even during the engagement period, a couple's involvement in spiritual activities can contribute to a successful relationship. When the girl attends the church or the synagogue more frequently than the fellow, more than half of the engagements are broken. This also holds true of engagements in which neither party attends religious services. Fewer broken engagements occur among couples who worship together once a month or more.

The same factors that make for a successful engagement also influence marital happiness. Couples who attend their church or synagogue regularly after marriage report a higher degree of marital satisfaction. Without a doubt, religion makes a significant contribution to the success of marriage.

Commonly during the dating period a couple can get so completely wrapped up in each other and so emotionally satisfied with their mutual love that they overlook the place of religion in their lives. It all begins with a dating relationship that was never meant to become serious in the first place! After the honeymoon, however, the couple often wish to develop a social life similar to that which they enjoyed prior to marriage. It is natural at this time for each partner to turn to the church or synagogue in order to satisfy a need to share activities with those of like faith. If the couple agree in this area of their life, there is little problem. If they come from different religious backgrounds, the odds are against them.

All research shows that mixed-faith marriages experience trouble sooner than do other marriages. Such couples also seek separations sooner after the wedding than do same-faith couples. Why is the divorce rate higher in mixed-faith marriages? One reason is that during courtship a couple finds it difficult to think realistically about marriage. It is easy to minimize the difficulties likely to be encountered. When a couple have not dealt with realities, large conflicts can develop after the honeymoon glow has died down.

The four most common causes of conflict in mixed-faith marriages, in order of their frequency, are:

Conflict Over What Religion the Children Will Follow. The religious training of children causes the most trouble. If a couple already disagree over religious matters, all is compounded when children enter the family. Now the question of whether or not they will provide religious training for their children comes up. And if so, which religion?

Young unmarried couples find it difficult to project themselves into the future and predict how they will handle the children when they arrive, but after the birth of a child many people find that things begin to matter to them that didn't before.

Even a person who seemingly has lost interest in religion prior to or during the early years of marriage may find it difficult to remain entirely indifferent about the training of his or her own children. He or she may never find the time to train the children in his or her own faith, but may deeply resent their being schooled in a different faith.

Paul Landis explored who took the responsibility for religious training in homes of mixed-faith couples. In more than a third of the cases, the mother took all the responsibility. In most of the other cases, the child was exposed to both faiths, sometimes by one parent, sometimes by both. In a few cases, the child was actually taken to both religious services in turn. A group of students who reflected on the mixed-faith marriages of their parents were inclined to feel that, in general, *it had been a serious handicap in their home lives.* Another study showed that six out of ten children from mixed-faith homes ended up rejecting all religion.[8]

Some religions differ vastly from others. For instance, many faiths say "grace" before meals. In others, family devotions take top priority. Personal Bible study and prayer are a must for others. Still other religions provide their own parochial school system, and the question arises whether the children will be sent to public or church school. To a parent of a differing faith or with little interest in spiritual matters, such matters may seem unnecessary and the effort may not seem worthwhile. Insistence on any spiritual item can compound an already touchy problem.

Conflict Over Church Attendance. Many times it is only *after marriage* that a couple realize how deeply imbedded the standards and values of their faith are in their lives. A person whose life has centered around religion may find his faith more firmly grounded than he had realized. He may have been quite casual about religious matters prior to marriage, but when his goals come into direct conflict with the person he loves, he is more aware of his values than ever before.

If a couple share the same religious ideals, church or synagogue fellowship and activities will form an important aspect of their social life. If a couple come from different religious backgrounds, they will tend to compete with each other for loyalty to his or her religious affiliation. Each one begins to invent excuses for not participating in the spiritual activities of the other. Soon the more liberal of the two begins to feel little tolerance for what he considers the narrow-minded views of his spouse's religion. It is equally difficult for the one raised in a strict religious environment to liberalize his views. The stage is now set for major conflicts regarding attendance at places of amusement that the more strict of the two considers questionable or outright sinful.

There is always the chance that a person whose life has been built around religious values but who has slipped away from them during adolescence and the young adult years will come to realize after marriage that the partner with whom he has chosen to live does not share the goals and values he cherishes. This awakening comes as a shock to many young couples once the glamour of the wedding and newness of each other wear off.

According to studies of couples who do not share the same religious background, their interest in religion usually decreases after marriage. Many times this is the only known way to keep peace. Even though it brings little satisfaction, it at least reduces the tension.

Couples whose marriages begin to fail attend worship services less frequently than those with happy marriages despite the fact that religious organizations are supposed to help people in trouble. Most individuals feel ashamed to face a seemingly judgmental congregation. Yet church or synagogue attendance does foster marital stability. The unhappiest married couples have no religion at all. Close behind are mixed-faith marriages in which one partner fails to share the other's religious interests. This leads to one important conclusion: Religion contributes to marital stability and success when it is shared by husband and wife.

Conflict Over Interference by In-laws in Religious Matters. The attitudes of both sets of in-laws also come into play and contribute to marital conflict. Both sets of grandparents will be watching and waiting to see if their grandchild is brought up in the "right" church. They may also feel compelled to apply pressure on the parents to see that they comply.

It is possible that each set of grandparents might begin to give the children religious gifts in order to indoctrinate the child—books, figurines, wall hangings, et cetera. Pressure in opposition to what the parent is teaching leads to confusion and disillusionment. Children may conclude that religion isn't worth the conflict and wash their hands of any religion.

Conflict Over Size of Family and/or Spacing of Children. Although this issue causes the least amount of conflict, it can produce significant problems. Some deeply spiritual individuals feel that the world is approaching the end of time. Thus they question the advisability of bringing children into the world during the "last days." Other religious groups discourage contraception. Statistics indicate that couples of mixed-faith marriages have fewer children, presumably because of the many problems encountered while raising them.

If you are, or have been, a loyal member of any religious group, you should think twice before marrying someone outside your faith or someone who has no interest in religious matters. Remember, your spiritual loyalties and attitudes have been built into you during your early childhood days. These particular values run too deep to be ignored or easily discarded.

Despite all the difficulties cited, many persons willingly face the risks of a no-faith or mixed-faith marriage. If you are seriously considering such a union, you owe it to your future to weigh the issues *before* you marry. Here are some specific questions that you should ask: Is one of you willing to adapt to the other's religion? If not, will you each attend religious meetings separately or take turns going to the other's place of worship? Will one of you break with your religion

Spiritual Roots

Respond separately to the following statements on spiritual compatibility and then compare your responses with your partner's.

1. My spiritual inclinations are . . .
   a. very strong
   b. moderately strong
   c. slightly strong
   d. not strong

2. My dating partner and I attend church together . . .
   a. regularly
   b. occasionally
   c. rarely
   d. on religious holidays
   e. never

3. Establishing a strong Christian marriage is _____ important to me.
   a. very
   b. moderately
   c. slightly
   d. not

4. It will be _____ important for me and my future family to attend church together.
   a. very
   b. moderately
   c. slightly
   d. not

5. The spiritual growth of the children should be the responsibility of . . .
   a. he
   b. she
   c. alternate
   d. both
   e. no one

altogether? If you do this, how will you feel about it? How might you feel about it a few years from now? If each of you agrees to maintain your present religious affiliation, what will you do about social activities? In which religion will the children be raised? Will they attend one place of worship, both places, or no place? When they are old enough to attend school, will they attend a parochial school? If so, which one?

What will you do about tithes and offerings? How will your decisions affect your parents and friends? Will you be able to withstand the pressures of devout parents and grandparents who will urge you to rear your children in their particular faith? If you have decided that religion will not be a part of your married life, what will you do when a crisis overtakes you—the death of a parent, child, or other loved one? Might you revert to the faith of your childhood then?

In addition to examining your own attitudes, look carefully at the religious values of your sweetheart. Does he/she attend religious services only to please parents or only to see friends? Does your sweetheart ridicule or respect and uphold religious ideals? Do you pray together? Will you ever have the joy of thanking God for His blessings and seeking His help during difficult times? Tim LaHaye reports that there is only one divorce in 1,026 marriages when the husband and wife pray together regularly.

Can you picture yourselves together in the evening having family devotions with the children? Or would you end up arguing over whose beliefs are right or wrong? Will you attend religious services together? Or will your spouse begin to make excuses and sleep in, until pretty soon you will know the pattern well? Think of attending worship services alone for a year, five years, a lifetime.

My parents did not hold the same religious values. Because my father tended to give my mother control of our religious training, my sister and I were raised in my mother's faith and continue in it yet. My parents' home was relatively happy; yet I shall never forget when, after my father's death, my mother confided: "In spite of the many years your father and I spent together and the joys that we shared, if I had it to do all over again, I would never have married him, because of the religion factor alone." Their difference in perspective caused countless problems that I was aware of and many more that I had no knowledge of.

Religion is an asset to marriage. The committed religious person has a greater chance for marital happiness when married to an individual of like interests. The virtues extolled in the Bible—meekness, kindness, consideration for others, helpfulness, selflessness—help make a well-adjusted personality. Those who have captured such values and have learned how to apply them in real-life situations will make good prospects for marriage. This does not imply that a nonreligious person cannot possess such characteristics. It means only there is greater likelihood of a person's having them if he or she belongs to a group that teaches and practices such values.

Marrying a Divorced Person

A young woman visited her minister for what she considered routine premarital counseling. She chatted happily about her wedding plans and asked for any advice he might give her. She also requested that he not reveal her plans to her mother, whom she had not told of the engagement because she didn't know how to break the news that her fiancé had only recently been divorced. A divorce had never marred her family, and she felt her mother might be prejudiced concerning her desire to marry a divorced person. The young woman said, "His past has no bearing on our future together. That is over and done with. It was not his fault. Divorce is so common now, and it would be silly to reject him just because he had been married before!"

It is easy for a person who has never been married to take this view; nevertheless, marriage to a divorced person is not the same as when both partners are marrying for the first time. Let's take a look at some of the differences.

1. Society looks at second marriages differently from the way it does first marriages. Society and traditional religious

groups smile with approval on first marriages. The marriage is actively supported and celebrated with an enthusiasm that is somewhat lacking when a second marriage is involved. The difference may be slight, but it is there. Even if the disapproval does not appear obvious, many friends and relatives assume an attitude of "Let's wait and see what happens here." They don't manifest the optimistic acceptance that usually accompanies first marriages. Take, for example, the shower given by friends. If neither the bride nor the groom has been married before, friends almost always give a shower. If both have been married before, only about one third receive showers. Family, friends, and society come to the aid of first marriages more often than they do second marriages.

2. Family opposition. There is a strong likelihood of family opposition when one partner has been divorced. The family of the previously unmarried person often tends to view the marriage with mingled hope and fear for the future, whether or not the fears are justified. The family of the divorced person cannot help but make comparisons between the new choice and the former mate. Is the present choice better than the former one? The first marriage and divorce are facts of life that will enter all relationships with family and former friends, even though the couple feel that "all that is in the past."

3. Children. If the previous marriage has produced children, additional factors must be considered. If the divorced person has visitation rights one day per week, the new spouse must adjust for the days when the children will visit. The divorced person will have to contact the former partner to arrange these visits. The divorced person may have a financial responsibility for the children, and these financial pressures may be severe. Few men earn enough money to support two families adequately. The new wife may have to help her husband meet his financial obligations to a first family. We know a couple both of whom have married before and brought children to the present marriage. One of the partners said to me, "When children are involved, divorce is never over."

4. The person may be less tolerant of difficulties the second time around. The very fact that a person has gone through a divorce makes the individual more susceptible to divorce again. A pattern has now been established for life. The barriers against divorce have been broken down. There is also the possibility that the divorced person is a relatively unmarriageable type or a difficult marriage type. Perhaps the divorced person runs from problems instead of facing them squarely and attempting a solution. Should serious problems arise, this type of person will likely seek divorce again.

If you are considering marrying a divorced person, you need to be particularly alert in evaluating his or her personality and adjustability. Statistically speaking, you must realize that the divorced person poses a greater marriage risk than one who has not been married, and the divorced woman is an even greater risk than the divorced man.

Divorced people have a higher rate of marriage failure because (1) they tend to marry divorced persons; (2) they have less hesitation to divorce a second time, since they have broken down the barriers against it; (3) they may habitually try to escape from problem situations rather than work through them; (4) they may hurt so badly from the trauma of divorce that they compensate by rebounding rapidly into a new love experience. This last point may be the most important factor. Studies show that divorced people tend to remarry after shorter acquaintance and with shorter engagements (or more often with no engagement period at all) than with first marriages.

When considering marriage to a divorced person, one should contemplate how much the divorced individual has learned from his or her marriage failure. Does the person feel totally blameless, that it was all the mate's fault? If so, it is doubtful that such an individual is a good prospect for marriage. Those who have failed once should learn from experience and pinpoint areas that demand improvement. It *is* possible to learn through bitter experiences how to make a better choice the second time around and work more effectively at building a successful relationship. Ask yourself: "What has this person learned that might have helped the first marriage succeed and that will make our marriage better?"

Interracial Marriages

Whether or not a person should marry someone of another nationality or race greatly interests young people. Colleges and universities nowadays have students from many ethnic and racial backgrounds, providing the opportunity for a high degree of social contact among groups of different races. As a result, interracial marriages in America have become more frequent in recent years. The most controversial of all marital unions, and the ones with the strongest social stigma in our society, have been those between blacks and whites.

Interracial marriages raise several important issues. They often mean breaking with one's own family and social patterns. Why has this person chosen an individual of a different race and cultural background from his own? Why has he or she chosen to risk the criticism of family and friends by marrying outside his or her own racial group? The question of motivation is crucial.

A simple answer might be that love knows no barriers, does not recognize color or creed. But other factors must certainly influence the final decision also. Is one or both partners highly idealistic and willing to risk personal discomfort or ostracism in order to demonstrate the freedom and individuality in which they sincerely believe? Or could they be rebelling against parents, friends, church, or social control? Could the motivating factor be a step up in social status?

The reaction of family and friends to a mixed racial marriage is one of the most crucial issues. In black-white marriages the family of the black spouse seem to respond more positively to the marriage than do the family members of the white spouse. Black-white couples usually find it easier to live in a black neighborhood, and in most cases this leads to closer contacts with parents of the black spouse. Indeed, all social contacts tend to run in the same direction—the couple forms more black friends than white. Unfortunately, the interracial couple cannot always enjoy the best of both cultures with equal ease.

Another monster also rears its ugly head. Most likely a couple from two different social, cultural, and educational backgrounds will also have wide variances in values. The things important to one partner may not seem important to the other. Any couple, but especially an interracial couple, should carefully and thoughtfully discuss values prior to marriage.

How stable are interracial marriages? Is the rate of divorce higher when partners of two different races marry? Research on this point is sketchy and not too helpful. Furthermore, most interracial marriages involving blacks usually include divorced persons, and divorced persons distort the statistics. Taking this factor into consideration, it still seems safe to conclude that interracial marriages have a higher-than-average failure rate.[9]

Finally, we must consider the children. Can a child born to racially different persons have an opportunity for a normal and emotionally healthy childhood? Will there be adequate occasions for friendship and interaction with other children in both cultures? When the child has reached dating age, will he or she be able to have a normal dating relationship with one or the other race? Will the child have adequate educational opportunities?

There are no simple answers to these questions. The national trend is toward greater acceptance of people from different races. But even then progress is slow. Prejudice does not die overnight.

The couple considering an interracial marriage should think over all these conditions very carefully. Prejudice may not often rear its ugly head on college campuses in or near large cities. Thus in such communities interracial couples may feel less tension. But in most parts of the country the majority of those whom interracial couples meet will not approve of such marriages. They will have to earn any recognition or acceptance the hard way.

Don't Jump the Gun

Josh McDowell, national chairman of Campus Crusade for Christ, relates an experience from his seminary days, when he was dating Paula, a "fantastic girl"—one with everything a guy could desire (and he did mean *everything*). Paula even had neat parents, and that meant a lot to Josh because of the way he had been brought up. They dated for two and a half years and had a beautiful time together. Their likes and dislikes matched. They got along well. Everyone kept telling them how right they were for each other. Even the seminary professors got their word in: "Josh, you better marry Paula. She'd make a tremendous Christian worker's wife." They really put him under pressure.

Paula and Josh began to talk of marriage just before he left for Canada to direct a crusade there. Paula was in her junior year at a State college in southern California. But in various ways God began to indicate that Paula was not the one for Josh, that He would take Paula out of Josh's life.

Josh found this very hard to accept. Paula was everything he ever desired in a woman. He began to think he'd done something wrong and that this was God's way of punishing him. So he began to look for ways of trying to please God and appease His disfavor. Josh offered to attend church more often, read the Bible more, or share his faith with six more souls.

Since he and Paula had a very "open" relationship with each other, Josh arranged a speaking itinerary that took him to southern California. On his last evening in California he took Paula to a Mexican restaurant for dinner so they could talk. Josh hesitated to bare his soul, though, because he did not want to hurt her, and, also, he did not want to hurt himself. When he began to share with Paula what he felt God had shown him, an amazing thing happened. God had revealed to Paula the same thing! She had felt reluctant to share this with Josh because she didn't want to hurt him or herself! They sat there and bawled like babies while deciding to call it quits. Everyone in the restaurant stared at them as they tried to eat their tear-soaked enchiladas.

After supper they strolled through Balboa Park and reminisced about the wonderful times they'd shared together. They laughed and had a marvelous time. Josh put on such a good front that Paula didn't even think the breakup bothered him.

The next morning Paula and her parents picked Josh up at his motel and drove him to the airport so he could fly back to Canada. Everything seemed normal while he rode in the car. Even at the airport while he waited for the plane he acted casual. But when he kissed Paula goodbye, he swore to God that he would never go through a similar experience again as long as he lived. And as he turned to leave, his legs felt like crooked noodles. His stomach turned so queasy he thought he would vomit on the runway. More than anything else he wanted to run back to her and say, "Paula, let's get married," and he knew she would have said, "Yes." They'd forget the ministry, forget school. They could make it. They'd buy a functional house, have some functional kids, get a functional dog, and just *function*.

He felt so upset when he got to the plane that he had to pull himself up the steps of the plane with both hands. The plane was full, and he felt foolish crying like a baby as he stumbled toward the back of the plane and the only available seat. The flight attendant trailed behind him holding his briefcase—like a mother carrying her child's lunch bucket!

Once Josh settled into his seat he began to doubt God and to curse Him. Where was God's love now? Where was His plan for Josh's life? "If you love me so much, why are you taking away someone who means so much to me, God?" He almost turned his back on God. He considered chucking Christianity, the ministry, everything. For three-and-a-half hours he struggled.

Then the Holy Spirit began to help him recall scriptures he'd hidden in his mind: "For God so loved . . . [Josh] that he gave . . ."; "No good thing will he withhold from them that walk uprightly"; "All things work together for good to them that love God." He began to ponder that last text—"All things work together for good . . ." It didn't say, "All things are good . . . ," only that "all things work together for good." "No good thing will he withhold from them that walk uprightly."

Josh reviewed his life. "I've loved you, God. By the power of the Holy Spirit I've tried to walk uprightly. And You say You will withhold no good thing. But Paula looks like a pretty good thing to me. You've been faithful before, Lord. Then that must mean that the one You want me to marry must be better than Paula! Wow!"

Gradually Josh became convinced that God loved him and that He was taking Paula out of his life because He had someone else for him. Not someone better than Paula, but someone better for him than Paula. And suddenly he could hardly wait for God to reveal His plan to him.

After Paula and Josh broke off their relationship, Bob, one of Josh's friends, began dating Paula. He told Paula that he had been in love with her for more than a year. But he had so trusted God with his life that he never revealed his feelings to Josh or Paula until after the breakup. He trusted God that far! He asked Paula to pray about their relationship and future together. He knew that if it was God's will that they share their lives, God would give her love for him.

Paula didn't know what to make of the whole situation, because she was still hurting from the breakup with Josh. But she did pray about it, and they got married several months later. They continue to enjoy a beautiful relationship together.

Later Josh and Paula discussed the events that followed their breakup. They could have married and would have had, in their own words, "a fantastic relationship." But they never could have had what Paula and Bob have now.

Of course, eventually Josh met the girl of his dreams, the person he felt that God had in mind for him.

Many people can't wait, and so they get married on the basis of the same type of love that Josh and Paula had for each other. But they fail to develop a better and higher kind of love. Be patient. If anything can withstand testing, love can. Allow God to work in your behalf. Remember, God always bestows the best on those who leave the choice to Him. Don't jump the gun!

――――――
[1] Paul H. Landis, *Making the Most of Marriage* (New York: Appleton-Century-Crofts, 1965), p. 260.
[2] *Ibid.*, p. 268.
[3] *Ibid.*, p. 272.
[4] *Ibid.*, pp. 272, 273.
[5] *Ibid.*, p. 263.
[6] *Ibid.*, p. 141.
[7] *Ibid.*, p. 283.
[8] *Ibid.*, p. 291.
[9] Robert K. Kelley, *Courtship, Marriage, and the Family*, 2d ed. (New York: Harcourt Brace Jovanovich, Inc., 1974), p. 283.

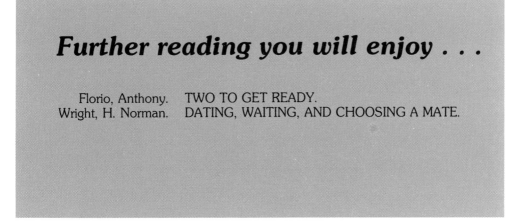

Further reading you will enjoy . . .

Florio, Anthony.   TWO TO GET READY.
Wright, H. Norman.   DATING, WAITING, AND CHOOSING A MATE.

No matter how long
a couple have gone together,
engagement introduces
a new twist.

Chapter at a Glance

I. **The Purpose of Engagement**
   A. Public notice
   B. Wedding plans
   C. Future plans
   D. Tests loyalty

II. **Length of Engagement**
   A. Long engagements
   B. Short engagements

III. **How Intimate Should Engagement Be?**
   A. Does the ceremony make any difference?
   B. How a Christian marriage is formed
      1. Mutual love
      2. Mutual freedom
      3. Approval of society
      4. Conformity to Bible standards
      5. Sexual intercourse
   C. Dealing with growing sexual tension

IV. **See Your Doctor**

V. **Premarital Guidance**
   A. Benefits all couples

Chapter 9

Two to Get Ready

A fellow and a girl met, began dating, and fell in love. They had a healthy relationship. Her parents lived at the beach year-round, so many of their activities revolved around boating, waterskiing, marshmallow roasts, and walks on the beach. A few weeks after they met, he popped the question, and she accepted.

But since he was in the military service and she was entering a two-year nursing program, they faced a long engagement. Their parents told them that a two-year engagement would be difficult, but the young couple knew their own minds.

She went off to study nursing some 1,200 miles away. He served his country. They wrote each other almost every day. He romanced her with flowers every month and phoned often. Even then they found the separation was difficult. When she returned home for Christmas vacation, they decided (with the aid of some pressure from relatives) to get married on New Year's Day. The ten remaining days were spent working out the details for their whirlwind wedding. They enjoyed a lovely wedding in the home of the bride, overlooking the bay.

This couple made several grave errors. First, she became engaged "on the rebound"—trying to fall in love after a traumatic broken relationship with someone else. They did not know each other

---

B. When to begin
C. Topics to cover
D. Advantages
  1. Clarifies marriage relationship
  2. Smooths adjustment
  3. Increases chances of happiness
  4. Increases chances of success
  5. More inclined to seek needed help

VI. **The Past—What to Tell**
  A. Why tell?

B. How much to tell?

VII. **Quarreling**
  A. Strain prior to the wedding
  B. Disagreements over
    1. Manners
    2. Values
    3. Family

VIII. **Broken Engagements**
  A. Why they are broken
  B. How to break an engagement
  C. What to expect after breaking up

IX. **Your Parents' View of Courtship**

Hollins, Liddle

Bass Scholes

long enough prior to becoming serious, and they became engaged with no wedding in sight—just "some day" a couple of years down the road. They were separated during their entire engagement period, planned a quicky wedding, had no time for premarital counseling, and couldn't afford a honeymoon.

I know this couple. The "she" is me, and the "he" is Harry. We've made it. But . . . if we had it to do all over again, we would want to do it right.

The Purpose of Engagement

When you become engaged, it will be one of the happiest days of your life. The congratulations and good wishes from your friends will sound like music to your ears. You will feel that you have finally arrived and that overnight you have attained a new status.

This special relationship to the one you love will bring you peculiar satisfactions. A deep sense of commitment and belonging that going steady or having an "understanding" doesn't have goes with becoming engaged. In addition, family and friends now openly accept the fact that the two of you belong together.

Becoming engaged is so satisfying and thrilling in itself that some young people fail to pay enough attention to what it really stands for in relationship to their future lives. Engagement is a serious step. You plan to link your entire future with another person in marriage, which can never really be undone. Even divorce cannot undo the decision you have made.

Many couples think that the only purpose of the engagement period is to have time to plan the wedding. Wedding plans are important, but they constitute only a small portion of what should take place during the period of engagement. First of all, engagement serves as public notice to family and friends that a couple intend to marry. Often the local newspaper prints engagement news. A formal announcement in such a manner notifies everyone that other eligibles have dropped out of the picture and the future now belongs to the two of you.

The public announcement also solemnizes the engagement. It gives family and friends the opportunity to adjust to the fact that a new family will soon form. Walter Trobisch writes that in some African tribes the entire village dances along with the groom when he leaves his village to go to another for his bride. African tribes demand no legal documents (nor were there any in Old Testament times), but the entire tribe recognizes the new status of the couple and stands behind their marriage. The society reinforces the responsibility of the couple to each other, to any children born to their union, and to the community. Making a promise public tends to strengthen the intentions of keeping it. The more people who know about what you promise to do, the more likely you will follow through. Thus, a secret engagement is no engagement at all. When you keep an engagement secret *for any reason*, somebody is fooling somebody.

Another purpose for a period of engagement is to plan the wedding. After a couple announce their engagement, they can begin planning in earnest for the wedding. Since the wedding itself requires many decisions, wise couples start their planning a number of months in advance. Organizing and administering a wedding is hectic enough without trying to make last-minute decisions. A church wedding usually requires at least six months of planning.

Setting the date for the wedding means balancing numerous factors. The date should allow ample preparation time. It takes into account the bride's menstrual cycle to prevent interference with sexual relations during the honeymoon. (It is possible now to use medication to postpone menstruation if desired.) It takes into account the many relatives and friends who will attend. It must also take into consideration the minister and the facilities for the wedding and reception.

An afternoon wedding is preferable to an evening wedding. The couple need ample time after the reception to get away to the honeymoon spot, (or wherever they will spend their wedding night), unpack, freshen up, and have dinner together before retiring. Most couples leave the reception in a total state of exhaustion owing to the frenzy of the wedding preparations, the ceremony itself, and then the reception. They need some time to calm their nerves and to restore their blood sugar levels to normal by eating a good meal. The night before the wedding avoid all parties that might run till the wee hours of the morning.

The engagement period also provides the opportunity for a couple to discuss the future and lay plans for the first year of marriage. Many things you may have discussed before, but now you will talk more intimately and specifically than previously. Some of the questions that you will discuss include: Do you plan to have children? If so, when and how many? Will the wife work outside the home? If so, will she continue to work after the children arrive? What methods of birth control will be used? How will the two of you support yourselves? Where will you live after the wedding, and how will you furnish the place? What type of wedding will you have? When will it take place and where? Who will perform the ceremony? Whom and how many will you invite? Will you have a honeymoon? If so, where will you go? How long will it last, and how much should you spend? What are your attitudes toward the sexual side of marriage? Should you seek premarital counseling from a minister? What plans for money and material things best suit your temperaments and circumstances?

Finally, the engagement period provides a time frame in which to test sincerity. In an age where morals and values have slipped, where relationships are more casual and temporary, someone with ulterior motives could utilize an engagement for personal gratification. A man might use it to persuade a woman to enter a sexual relationship with him. A woman might use the engagement period to further her status among her friends although she has no serious intention of marrying the man.

Consequently the engagement period offers time for critical and final investigation. This is your last chance to check out your loved one. You have already made certain investigations or you would never have reached the engagement stage, but now you check and recheck your reactions to each other. Now is the time to bring out any unresolved differences and conflicts that may have plagued your relationship. It is also time to reveal any hidden secrets that should be brought out before marriage. (How and what to tell will be discussed later.) It also allows time for each of you to get acquainted with the other person's family.

However, the engagement period must not last indefinitely. A couple should not become engaged until they know at least what month the wedding will take place. To become engaged with no end in sight destroys the transitional meaning of the custom. Engagement is not an end in itself but a commitment to get married. Its meaning becomes distorted when there is no goal in sight.

Why not elope? One good reason is that those who elope do not have the sort of marriage that produces statistical evidence for endurance. A study of 730 couples who ran off for a surprise wedding indicates they did not fare as well as a like number of pairs who got married in traditional ceremonies. The trouble with elopements, the researchers say, is that they involve a high proportion of people who just want to escape from something.

Length of Engagement

"Me, I don't believe in long engagements," Susan snapped emphatically. "I say once you've decided to make the plunge, then go ahead and get it over with!'' Susan wants to rush into marriage the same way she rushes to a sale on clothes, and inevitably, she ends up with a multitude of misfits in her wardrobe. Hasty marriages after short engagements have a poor success rate.

Many studies through the years have tried to determine the correlation between the length of engagement and happiness in marriage. The majority of studies show that an engagement of two or more years has the highest rate of success, whereas engagements of six months or less have the highest number of failures. Whether these findings are still valid today is open to question.

Many of the issues that used to be discussed only after a couple was formally engaged are now settled during the ''engaged-to-be-engaged'' stage. Many couples discuss intimacies that once were talked about only after engagement. Even if this is true, one thing remains certain: a fairly long engagement might cure many fly-by-night romances that should never result in marriage.

If a couple has known each other for a long period of time and have gone together for a couple of years, a long engagement is not as important as if they had a short courtship prior to engagement. The real question is not How long should the engagement be? but How long have you gone together and how well do you know each other? Getting to know the other person is the most valuable portion of any relationship, and you simply cannot hurry the process.

It takes time for two people to understand the attitudes and viewpoints of the other. Take the matter of having children. A couple engaged only a short period of time may repeat clichés such as ''When we have children, we will . . .'' ''Our children will . . .''—all in a romantic, idealized way without ever touching on basic issues. The couple may have drastic differences of opinion about *what* is to happen ''when we have children.'' A lack of time does not allow discussion on this vital topic to take place.

Each may assume that the other holds the same values regarding family life with children, when in reality those values may differ widely. A longer engagement provides the opportunity for misconstrued ideas on this and other subjects to surface. The couple can then talk honestly about their feelings. They may end up compromising so they can marry with an understanding on the issue even though they do not feel the same way about the matter. Or with time they may realize that their ideas are too divergent. In either case, a short engagement would push them into a commitment before they have time to think objectively about the matter.

On the other hand, a couple could be engaged for two or more years and still not be prepared for marriage. One young wife went for counseling after only six months of marriage. She had been engaged for more than two years and sobbed bitterly because she thought such a long engagement would guarantee happiness. The counselor learned that although the couple had been engaged for a long period of time, their actual time together amounted only to about 30 days! Furthermore, most of their dates had been formal occasions when each was dressed in his or her best. They had found little time to get to see each another as they really were in real-life situations. This couple proceeded through a relatively long engagement without coming out of their artificial world long enough to build a sound relationship.

Most engagements last less than a year, the average running between 6 and 10 months, allowing ample time to accomplish everything that needs to be done. Please note: *Such a length of time is ideal, provided the couple have known each other at least two years prior to engagement.* At least six months is needed to complete all the functions of engagement and to get ready for marriage. Engagements of more than a year tend to lose their momentum. A couple can retain a sense of anticipation through one cycle of seasons, but hardly more than that.

The crucial factor in marital success is not how long you have been engaged but the total length of time the two of you have known each other and explored personalities, values, and backgrounds. A courtship of around three years might ensure the best success.

It follows, then, that it is better to have the engagement relatively brief rather than to have the period of acquaintance brief and the engagement long. However, it is preferable to have a long engagement than a premature marriage.

How long is too long for an engagement? The answer involves many variables. Much depends upon personalities, the reason for the delay in wedding plans, how often the couple see each other. However, an engagement is too long if it generates an excessive amount of nervous tension; if the couple experience excessive frustration; if they grow irritable; if they are getting to the point where they cannot keep petting within the limits they originally set; if they become indifferent to each other; or if they become tempted to plunge into marrige impulsively while disregarding the serious consideration that originally led them to postpone their wedding.

How Intimate Should Engagement Be?

Let's say that you've held to your guidelines so far, but now you're engaged. You find it more and more difficult to keep from going all the way. Your expressions of physical affection step up as the wedding approaches. You work on plans for the wedding, honeymoon, and married living,

and as you share in anticipation more and more aspects of life the temptation to "jump the gun" mounts.

Have you ever wondered what difference it makes whether a couple has intercourse three months, three weeks, or three days before the wedding, or waits until after the ceremony? Such a question implies that there is no difference between a couple who has intercourse before marriage and a couple who waits until after marriage. Let's take a look at several significant factors.

1. Before marriage a couple remain dependent on separate economic systems. Generally their parents continue to provide food, clothing, shelter, and protection. Marriage, however, forms a new economic unit separate from dependence on others.

2. Before marriage each is more or less emotionally dependent on parents and/or others. After marriage that dependence is transferred to another.

3. Before marriage each is legally identified with his or her own family. They are separate individuals legally free to act according to the laws of the land. After marriage they are legally responsible and bound to each other.

4. Before marriage society has not accepted them as a family unit. Others still see them as members of their respective families. After their marriage society considers them a family.

5. Should pregnancy occur before marriage, the couple faces a mountain of legal, personal, emotional, social, and spiritual problems. Marriage provides the atmosphere for even an unplanned baby to be cared for, loved, accepted, and nurtured.

Dr. Derrick Baily in *The Mystery of Love and Marriage,* states that a Christian marriage is formed when (a) a couple truly love each other; (b) each acts freely, deliberately, rationally, and responsibly; (c) each acts with the knowledge and approval of society; (d) each acts in conformity with Biblical standards; and (e) sexual intercourse unites their lives.

According to this definition of a Christian marriage, an engaged couple would violate the definition on three counts if they had

Who Does What?

1. Strongly agree
2. Mildly agree
3. Not sure
4. Mildly disagree
5. Strongly disagree

After marriage you will be involved in an endless number of activities and responsibilities that will require task assignments. It is imperative that you deliberately and mutually develop guidelines for determining roles and responsibilities in the husband-wife relationship. Read each of the following statements carefully. Respond to the statements according to the scale of 1 to 5 as shown at the left. Circle the appropriate number for each statement. Share your responses with your partner.

1 2 3 4 5   1. The husband should help regularly with the dishes.

1 2 3 4 5   2. It is all right for the wife to initiate lovemaking with her husband.

1 2 3 4 5   3. The husband and wife should plan the budget and manage money matters together.

1 2 3 4 5   4. A wife who has special talent should have a career.

1 2 3 4 5   5. The husband should take his wife out twice a month.

1 2 3 4 5   6. Money that the wife earns is her money.

premarital sex: (1) they acted without the knowledge or approval of society—no license, public announcement, or marriage ceremony; (2) they desecrated Biblical sexual standards; and (3) their decision was not rational or responsible when they risked the possibility of a child born out of wedlock. More likely they decided under the heat of aroused passions.

Claiming the rights and privileges of marriage prior to the ceremony might be likened to an Inauguration ceremony. Can you imagine the confusion and hubbub resulting from a President-elect's attempting to move into the White House and assume the Presidential role before it was legal?

Furthermore, as many as two thirds of all engagements are broken. Some persons become engaged five or six times before they actually marry. If they have sexual relations with each of these partners just because engagement has taken place, the risks and difficulties are greatly increased. Broken engagements are always traumatic, but when sex has become part of the relationship, a breakup is even more difficult.

One of the greatest dangers of sex during engagement is that a couple totally unsuited for each other may find themselves held together because of sex. John and Lois announced their engagement and entered into a sexual relationship immediately. In time, John sensed Lois was not right for him. But having a strong sense of honor, he went through with the wedding anyway. Later John suffered a complete breakdown as he faced divorce. Had he not felt bound by a sexual relationship, he would have felt freer to stop the wedding and thus have prevented a tragedy.

Sexual intimacy also prevents a couple from grappling realistically with problems and issues that they should discuss and settle prior to marriage. When quarrels do occur, they are covered up with intimacies. Sex becomes a way of avoiding important issues.

Another reason for waiting is that intercourse before marriage—even when a couple are engaged—often occurs under rather unfavorable conditions. Stolen moments in the back seat of a car, in the bedroom of parents' homes, in a motel room, on a blanket in the woods, leave something to be desired. The risk of detection runs high in their minds. And when a couple has crossed the boundaries that they said they would not cross, guilt feelings and resentment can follow. Fear of pregnancy can also take away much of the satisfaction.

Let's assume you have decided that sex must wait for you and your loved one until after marriage, but how far should you go in other physical intimacies? Even normal expressions of kissing and embracing can be highly stimulating. As a result, one or both of you may be stimulated beyond the point where you feel comfortable. This is how many couples get swept into intercourse.

Engaged couples need to know that their desire for intimacy is expected to increase during the period of engagement. Freer expression of affection between engaged partners is normal because you are now in a transition period between courtship and marriage. Provided your engagement does not drag out for too long, this increased intimacy is acceptable because it leads toward free and unrestricted expressions in marriage.

Furthermore, an engaged couple should expect sexual tension to increase. It is this tension that spurs the desire for marriage. However, if the tension increases to the point where it affects a couple's emotional equilibrium and causes them to allow physical appeal to dominate their thinking and behavior, they are increasing their problems rather than allowing the natural transition to proceed.

The solution to the problem is not easy and is highly individualized. Each couple must discover experiences that allow them to express their affection for each other, that allow them to get to know each other better, and that will help them with their marriage preparation. And they should avoid that which confuses them, disturbs them, and sidetracks or disorganizes the final stages of their preparation. Whatever leads them to a happier, less strained and less fearful relationship they should continue. Whatever increases tension, worry, or guilt they should stop.

Physical intimacies may become almost an obsession with some engaged couples. They may think of it too much, anticipate it, plan for it, daydream about it. No matter how intimate their contact may be and no matter how far they go to find satisfaction, they still seem frustrated. Thus the tension they are trying to relieve makes them irritable. The problem is very real but thinking about it too much may defeat their purpose. Instead of improving the situation, they drift into an endless spiral and become confused.

Either together or with a counselor a couple caught in such a bind should attempt to reach a reasonable plan. Analyzing and controlling the initial steps that lead to increased intimacy and frustration may help. Participating in new and fascinating activities, classes, hobbies, or interests may also disperse some of the accumulating nervous energy. Then, without continually questioning the pros and cons of their relationship, they should tenaciously adhere to the solution they agreed upon.

RULE OF THUMB: Think through your limits, discuss them with your sweetheart, and follow through with a change of activity. The problems caused by this buildup of sexual tension is one of the main reasons I recommend *long courtships* and *short engagements*. Self-control is possible and necessary.

It's Time to See the Doctor

Both the prospective bride and the groom should have a thorough physical examination. At the time of this writing, 37 States require a physical exam for both men and women and 45 States require blood tests for venereal disease. But in too many cases the physician gives only the Wasserman test for syphilis and a very superficial physical examination. In a majority of cases the exam does not even include a pelvic examination of the bride to determine whether she would have problems in bearing children.

If the physican conducts an examination, it is usually just prior to the wedding. A much better practice is to make this appointment at least *three months* before the wedding date. Each partner may wish to see his or her family physician, but ultimately both should see one physician together. This gives the doctor an opportunity to discover any conspicuous physical or psychological factors that might need correction prior to the wedding. It also gives the couple time to correct problems or to receive counsel. In cases where special treatment becomes necessary, it can be completed prior to marriage.

The examination should consist of an initial interview together. The doctor should take the premarital history separately. The menstrual history of the prospective bride is extremely important. Following the exam the physician should allow time for any questions to be discussed separately and for

a final consultation together.

He should provide an opportunity to ask questions about sex in marriage. The physician may or may not be trained in giving such help. He often has information regarding the functions of sex, but sex is also psychological. Many physicians are not in a position to give advice on this important aspect. But a couple should not hesitate to ask about any matter that they do not clearly understand. This will, of course, be gone over in great detail during a premarital counseling session with their pastor.

The couple should also discuss with the physician his recommendation for the type of contraception they should use. If the woman will use contraceptive pills, she should begin taking them approximately one month before the wedding date. Some physicians advise beginning two to three months prior to the wedding, thus allowing time to get past any disturbing symptoms that might occur with the first use of the Pill.

Young women sometimes worry about menstruating during their honeymoon. A doctor can administer hormones to the bride a month before the wedding date in order to postpone menstruation for a short time. This is not absolutely necessary, but you may want to discuss it with your physican.

At any rate, family planning is a fundamental question at any premarital consultation. The couple must decide upon the means of contraception, whether they will share the responsibility, or whether, for the time being, it will be borne by one person only. The doctor's advice on the type of contraceptive to use will probably follow the physical examinations. He will likely do a sperm count on the male and test for cervical cancer in the female.

A premarital examination may cost you quite a bit, but it is an obligation that a couple owe to themselves, and to the children that will be born to their union in the years to come.

Premarital Guidance

Young people often get pushed into an engagement when they don't actually intend for it to happen. This may result from

the pressure of family or friends. Perhaps they have gone together for so long that everyone just expects it to happen. Or maybe everyone else in their crowd was planning for marriage, and they got caught up in the plans of others. A young woman is particularly prone to be influenced by the wedding plans of her friends—by attending showers, discussing bridesmaid's dresses, and being involved in the general planning of weddings. This surrounds her with an aura of excitement and romanticism that she finds difficult to resist. However, getting married takes the kind of maturity that means using your head as well as your heart.

Premarital guidance would benefit all couples. Many couples think of counseling as remedial. They avoid it because they don't think anything in their relationship needs fixing. When carried out properly, premarital guidance encourages a couple to carefully observe themselves, each other, and their relationship. Many couples think that premarital guidance will consist of little more than dry presentations of boring facts, which in most cases predict doom for their plans. Any guidance that includes little more than the "facts-of-marriage" would be superficial. It would not allow a couple the opportunity to explore their relationship as they should.

Couples should consider starting their guidance at the time they announce their engagement. It is best to conduct the counseling no later than four to six months before the wedding. This allows time for the couple to think through, discuss, and correct any potential problems. It gives opportunity to uncover any negative personality traits and hidden deficiencies.

Premarital guidance should consist of a series of interviews, discussions, and consultations between the couple and an experienced professional, who in most cases will be the minister who marries them. The session should include discussion of assigned outside reading, written homework and workbook activities, and selected cassette tapes. Ideally the guidance will extend over six sessions and cover the following topics: (1) the purpose of engage-ment, status of the present relationship, previous marital history (if any), temperament testing; (2) scoring and discussion of temperament testing, family backgrounds, religion; (3) discussion of individual needs in marriage as found in love, acceptance, appreciation, and communication; (4) discussion of individual needs in marriage as found in understanding the opposite sex, roles, and finances; (5) discussion of sexual adjustment, contraception, children; and (6) discussion of leisure time, housing, employment, health, and education. Plans regarding the wedding itself may be discussed as they come up or as the wedding draws closer.

Such an approach to marriage may sound clinical, hard-nosed, and even unromantic, but pastors report that where such a program of intense premarital guidance has been initiated, the divorce rate for such couples falls to 3 or 5 percent. Compare this with the national average of 50 percent!

Complete and thorough premarital guidance has several advantages:

1. You will have a clear understanding of what is involved in the marriage relationship and how to maintain it. The two of you, as a prepared couple, will have a great advantage over the unprepared couple. You will understand what marriage involves and the adjustments that you must make. Perhaps most important, you will take a good look at yourselves and at each other as persons, fully understanding what resources you have to work with. You will understand the roles each of you must assume.

2. You will be able to adjust to marriage more smoothly and quickly. The first few weeks of married life are critical. You will find help in deciding many important issues, such as: who will lead, how arguments are settled, how household duties are divided, how money is managed, how sexual needs are met, how leisure time is spent, and much more. The way these patterns develop will greatly influence your future happiness. Bad habits are not easy to change later. It is much easier to establish good habits and be off to a promising beginning than try to undo poor habits later on, after the motivation for change has

declined.

3. Your chances for a happy marriage will be greater. Premarital guidance is one of the best ways of ensuring that your marriage will work. There are enough mediocre marriages in existence today, the kind where the couple share the same roof but few intimacies. They communicate, but only about routine matters. They never really get to know each other. You can ensure this will not happen to you if you take the time prior to marriage to develop the full potential for your relationship. A compleat marriage is seldom attained by chance.

4. You will increase your chances of being successful parents. Many couples fail to recognize the critical connection between marriage and parenthood. These two phases of life are intimately bound together. As a child grows up, he needs more than two parents—he needs two parents who love each other. The greatest gift parents can give their child is that of a happy marriage.

5. You will be more inclined to seek marriage counseling should you ever need it in years to come. The average couple grapples with a problem for seven years before they seek professional counseling. The longer the delay in seeking professional advice, the less that can be done to help. Attitudes of hostility and resentment may have already destroyed or poisoned the love relationship. It is difficult, if not impossible, to help such people. The couple who seek premarital counseling show a much deeper commitment to marriage than couples who do not, and they are less apt to get into trouble. But if they do, they are more likely to seek help before the destructive process begins.

No matter how long a couple have gone together, engagement introduces a new twist. They have seen a great deal of each other and yet may not really know each other. The responsibilities of making a home and having children may not even have entered their heads. Engagement, with the impending nearness of marriage, brings some sobering realizations.

Many couples wish to skip premarital preparation. After all, who can be more sure of love and happiness than they! Parents and others who urge them to get such help are prophets of doom, not personally involved, don't really know what they know about each other, et cetera. They are so sure about each other! But so were the nearly 1.2 million couples who were divorced in 1980.

If a couple will not spend time nurturing their relationship prior to marriage, they will not spend time following marriage to nurture the relationship. Some professionals have gone as far as to suggest that a couple who refuse to invest the time and energy in premarital preparation should not be allowed to solemnize their vows in the church or synagogue. You see, these religious institutions exist not just to conduct weddings but to foster growth and development prior to and during marriage.

Outside your commitment to God, your marriage is more valuable than careers, education, money, social involvements, or friends. Your marriage is one of life's three greatest decisions. Make sure you avail yourself of premarital guidance.

The Past—How Much Should I Tell?

During the engagement period, or even before, a young couple usually feel a strong urge to confess their past to each other. Although both usually have a need to do so, male and female do it for different reasons—she to test his love and he to relieve guilt feelings.

This desire to reveal the past is a normal phase in the development of love, particularly for the male. It can actually be an asset not only for him but for the couple's future together. It indicates that they have achieved a level of intimacy in which they can now share carefully guarded secrets with each other. It indicates a strong sense of mutual need and trust.

But how much should one reveal to one's sweetheart? There is no pat answer to this question, for it depends on a number of varying factors. But before you tell all, consider the following questions: Why do I feel I need to tell so much? What has caused the question to be raised? How long ago did the incident occur? What is the possibility of discovery if I don't tell? What is the possibility of my repeating this kind of behavior? What is my attitude toward the incident? What has taken place since the incident?

If the only purpose of confessing is to dump a load of guilt or to relive with pleasure past experiences, it might be better to search for a counselor and spare your loved one. Confessions made for no better reasons than these could cause unhappiness for the other and could even raise doubts about the wisdom of the marriage. Sometimes even insignificant past events can be magnified in the mind of the other and begin to haunt and plague the mind with thoughts and misgivings.

No one is under obligation to bring all the skeletons out of the closet just because an engagement has taken place. Certain things, however, should be confessed if they would affect the couple's future relationship, or, if found out later, would make for trouble in marriage. For instance, if either has had a venereal disease, given birth or fathered a child out of wedlock, been previously married, served time in prison, suffered a nervous breakdown, or suspects hereditary defects, such things should be known prior to marriage. Anything that might be readily learned from a third party should also be told.

Whatever is revealed should be told *before* the wedding. When things are revealed after the wedding, the other person may feel trapped. Relate the confession as information that will further the adjustment and future happiness of both of you. Take into consideration the effect it will have on the other person, as well as on yourself.

Findings indicate that almost all engaged persons confess serious problems in their background. And it seems that when one breaks down and confesses things about the past, it very often prompts the other to tell things also. Only a minute portion of couples studied regret having told about the past.

If you have serious doubts about confessing something, you should consult with a counselor or clergyman first. It is often useful to get the advice of a third party before taking the risk of revealing something that has little or no significance on the relationship and which might even create barriers.

If you suspect your fiancé(e) of some past indiscretions, it is better to allow it to be told voluntarily. Don't try to pry it out through curious questions. Such prying implies a lack of trust. Once your sweetheart has volunteered the information, accept what

Can This Engagement Be Saved?

Tom & Pat went to high school together. They dated seriously during their senior year, and when Tom received a scholarship to study in England, he asked Pat to marry him after he graduated from college. Pat's parents are really in favor of the marriage. Tom and Pat have seen each other only during summer vacations since Tom has been in England. Tom is now a senior and will be returning to the States. Wedding plans are in progress. Pat appears to be excited and has helped her mother with the plans. Tom has not really said much of anything, even in his letters, except that he is planning to go through with the wedding. Tom and Pat are your best friends. What advice would you like to share with them?

you have heard as the truth and drop the subject.

Quarreling and the Engaged Couple

Susan ran to her dormitory room in tears. "Dick and I just had a terrible argument over something," she sobbed to her roommate. "He wouldn't give an inch, and we had a terrible fight. I can't believe this has happened to us, of all people!"

Engagements seldom run smoothly and afford the perfect bliss you might expect. And the reason is simple. As your relationship grows more intimate and you spend more and more time together, all formality falls aside, and disagreements, quarrels, and even fights may begin. About two thirds of all engaged couples report at least some strain prior to the wedding.

The most frequent disagreements seem to center on (1) manners and conventionality, (2) values and philosophy of life, and (3) methods of dealing with each other's families. The latter problem indicates that many in-law problems begin long before the wedding.

A couple can handle such problems in a variety of ways. If they deal with a problem squarely and resolve it constructively, then they know that they can deal with issues after marriage and find a workable solution. Problems handled in such a manner will strengthen their relationship. In cases where arguments and conflicts increase in number and intensity, a couple should take a second look at the advisability of marriage.

About 50 percent of all engaged couples report some doubt in their minds about whether they are making the right choice. About half of those wish they had never become engaged and at one time or another seriously consider breaking the engagement. One fourth to one third of all engaged couples break off at least temporarily.

If this period of hesitation ever strikes you, seek out a person in whom you have confidence and discuss the advisability of continuing with your plans for marriage. Parents, relatives, friends, doctors, and ministers are concerned persons to whom you may turn.

Broken Engagements

The wedding will begin within minutes. The flower-filled sanctuary holds a capacity crowd of smiling guests. The organ swells and then diminishes as the clergyman, groom, and groomsmen enter from a side door. A moment of hushed silence hangs over the congregation before the organ thunders with the opening strains of the wedding march. The guests turn to watch the bridesmaids proceed down the aisle and take their places at the front. Anticipation builds as everyone tries to be first to catch a glimpse of the radiant bride as she enters on the arm of her father. Here she comes, down the aisle. She gives her hand to the man who is about to become her husband . . . and both of them know they are making a terrible mistake.

They've known each other for years. After several months of steady dating they entered a year's engagement. They came from similar backgrounds. They had attended the same small-town church during their teen years, but they hadn't begun dating until they went away to a large college. They were not prepared for life on an impersonal campus. It was different from the friendly country atmosphere they were used to. So they gravitated to each other in an effort to belong to someone or something. What began as a casual friendship mushroomed into an overwhelming infatuation. They announced their engagement during Christmas vacation and laid plans to get married the following summer. By spring their relationship included frequent sexual relations.

When the school year ended and they both returned home, their romance began to cool even though wedding preparations proceeded. He could not bring himself to call off the wedding because he felt responsible for drawing her into a sexual relationship. She felt guilty because she had violated her personal code of ethics and felt she was already committed to him because of sexual involvement. Each was a very private person who kept his thoughts to himself, so they went through with the wedding, but it brought them years of untold heartache.

Could such a thing happen in your life? Never! you say. But the couple in the story didn't think so either, at least not until the time they reached college.

Not only is it unwise to go through with a marriage after you have discovered that you do not want to share the rest of your life with that individual, but it is also an act of gross irresponsibility. No self-sacrificing attitude will suffice. To link yourself with someone you don't love is a cruel act. And to bring children into such an atmosphere is almost criminal. If at any time during the engagement period you have serious questions about the advisability of your upcoming marriage, then don't go through with it!

Engagement is not a sealed contract that links a couple's destiny forever. It is entirely possible that as a couple come to know each other better during engagement, they may find they are not as well-suited as they had imagined and may decide to break their promise to marry. In this way engagement differs from yesteryear when a promise to marry was considered a legal contract that must culminate in marriage. Today society considers it a time of intimate acquaintance during which a couple evaluate the desirability of marriage. If either person at any time has serious questions, it is far better to break an engagement than to proceed into a marriage that might end in divorce.

It is difficult, however, to break an engagement once family, friends, the church, and the community know about it. Engagement is an emotional involvement that is hard to sever. Sometimes couples feel trapped by family, friends, possessions that are now involved, sexual involvement, or pregnancy.

Research indicates that men more often feel trapped by an engagement than do women, particularly where sexual experience has entered the picture. And if the affair has been of long duration, he may feel it unfair to drop her after having kept her off the marriage market so long.

Why Engagements Are Broken

The most frequent reason given for broken engagements is loss of interest. Young people of courtship age change and mature so rapidly that the couple who become engaged during the high school years but who do not plan to marry until after graduation from college often find that the other person fails to measure up later on. The expectations for the ideal mate at 22 usually bear little resemblance to the person dated at 18. The younger the couple at the time of engagement, the more likely they are to change their attitudes toward each other and the greater the probability that the engagement will not last.

Another common reason given by young people is that one or both are not yet ready for marriage. Studies show that most of these love relationships began before the couple were 18 years old. As the couple grow older they realize they have become serious before they were ready for marriage. When young people begin college, they not only mature, but their interests and values change also.

Incompatability is yet another reason. An engaged couple spend more time together than they did when they were dating. Now they can see each other in more varied and real-life situations. During the stage of dating it is easy to be on good behavior, but during the more intimate contact of engagement each has the opportunity to become familiar with everyday behavior. He may observe her laziness and selfishness in her

own home and come to realize that these personality traits are a part of her. She may come to see that although he has always treated her with extreme courtesy and thoughtfulness, he shows little consideration for his mother.

Habits and behavioral tendencies have a way of revealing themselves *if given enough time.* The couple who spend enough time together will be able to determine the attitudes of the loved one about goals, likes and dislikes concerning people and activities, as well as values, character, and interests. The longer the period of engagement, the greater the opportunity to be realistic about compatability.

Many "mixed" engagements do not survive the contrast in backgrounds. When a couple of different races or religion date, they frequently think the differences between them matter little. But as they approach the reality of marriage, each may come to the realization that it may be more difficult than they thought to push aside their differences. The reaction of family and friends to such an engagement can also be a contributing factor.

A FINAL NOTE: *Beware of a person with a history of broken engagements.* This may be evidence of recklessness or immaturity, impulsiveness or using others for exploitive purposes without serious intentions of marriage.

How to Break an Engagement

A broken engagement is distressing, but not as painful as a broken marriage. It is better that a couple learn before their wedding that they cannot live together than to blindly forge ahead with plans and discover this later. The purpose of engagement is to enable a couple to make the final adjustments in their relationship before the wedding. It is only natural that some of these attempts will fail.

There are a few ways to lessen the pain of engagement, and the emotional reaction that follows a broken engagement will depend somewhat on the way the break is made. There are cruel ways to break up just as there are cruel ways to carry out all other social relationships.

If you are involved in breaking an engagement, reread the section titled "Breaking Up Is Hard to Do," as well as the following section, which will help you minimize a difficult situation.

The time to break an engagement is as soon as either party wishes to break it. This does not mean that a couple should break up every time they have a quarrel and then patch up their differences and announce that their engagement is on again. This would make a farce of what the word *engagement* stands for. But when either one has carefully decided that he or she cannot go on with the wedding plans, the other should be notified immediately. The news will be unpleasant for both parties and will be extremely galling to the unsuspecting person. But the longer the break is postponed, the greater the hurt is likely to be. Furthermore, the longer the delay, the greater the front the breaker must put up.

Talk it over calmly. As soon as you realize that a breakup is inevitable, try to discuss the situation reasonably with your fiancé(e). Continuing with someone after this point is cruel. Let your fiancé(e) know how you feel. Discuss the matter as openly as you can. By all means do everything you can to help the other person save face. If either of you feels you are being jilted for someone else, your pride will hurt all the more. It is unkind to leave the other person with the feeling that there is something seriously wrong with his or her personality. Whatever you say or do, allow the other to feel that he or she is an attractive person even though the relationship didn't work.

The situation is greatly complicated when one still cares deeply for the other and does not wish to break the engagement or if one breaks off without discussing the matter with the other. However, even when deeply hurt feelings are involved, restrain yourself from saying things about the other person that you might later regret. Don't deliberately rub salt in the other person's emotional wounds.

Inform family and friends. You must tell of the change of plans as soon as possible, particularly if wedding plans are in progress.

The news can leak out more gradually to friends. If relatives or friends try to get you to patch things up again, you may want to see a counselor or talk the situation over with your pastor. Such a decision would clarify your own thinking and satisfy most friends or relatives who felt the break was hasty or ill-advised.

Return all gifts. Any wedding gifts that you have already received should be returned with a simple note stating that plans have changed and that you are returning the gift with many thanks for the giver's thoughtfulness. Even when gifts have been personalized, such as monogrammed linens or other articles, you need do nothing more than return the gifts and inform the giver that there has been a change in plans.

If your ex-fiancé(e) should threaten to tell things that might damage your reputation or do something violent, try to look at such threats as objectively as you can. Usually there is little chance that the person will carry out such threats. When a child doesn't get his way, he threatens to run away from home. However, he seldom gets more than a few blocks away. It is likely to be the same story here. Furthermore, a person who makes such threats gives strong evidence of immaturity and instability. This is proof positive that the engagement should be broken. Marriage will not cure such an immature person.

191

or both parties. In fact, the breakup of love affairs is one of the most severe emotional crises facing young people today. Ailing love affairs were one of the most serious problems I had to deal with during my stint as a girl's dean at a boarding school.

For some people there is almost a feeling of relief when the engagement finally ends. In many cases the breakup takes place during the "understanding" period prior to official engagement, when both are not as deeply involved as in the formal engagement stage. However, if there has been a formal engagement and both are totally committed to the planned marriage, the results will be more serious.

When involved in the emotional turmoil that results after a broken engagement, the experience will appear totally unique. Some will feel that no other human being has ever experienced quite so much pain or such an ordeal. Although it is little consolation at the time, others have gone through a similar experience and survived.

The trauma following a breakup seems to follow a rather specific pattern. More than half of one group surveyed said they felt "indifferent" toward the former loved one and no serious trauma remained. About 15 percent indicated they felt a temporary flare-up of love that soon faded into indifference. Another 15 percent vacillated between hurt and love before tapering off into indifference. Eleven percent said their love actually turned into dislike. Ninety percent of the group ultimately achieved indifference (a normal state of adjustment) after breaking up.

One does not reach this desired state of indifference overnight, however. Some people have recovered in a week. Others said it took two years or longer. The most reliable research indicates that the average young person will get over the emotional effects of a breakup in less than six months.

Afterward most young people tend to remember the relationship as a pleasant one, and most begin dating someone else as an aftereffect. Some continue to dream about their lost love. Young ladies treasure keepsakes from the relationship, but few fellows do. Some say they try to avoid

A Note to the Brokenhearted

Much has been written about the brokenhearted. Both story and song often bemoan the loss of a loved one and how there will never be another to replace such a love. Such ideas come from the myth that for every person there is a "one-and-only," but this simply isn't true. Within a given range of compatibility and background factors, any number of persons can fall in love, marry, and find happiness.

Nevertheless, when an emotional commitment has been made, whether there had been a formal or an informal engagement, a parting of the ways involves trauma for one seeing the other person again, while others admit going out of their way to meet the other.

A young person who has dated widely before becoming engaged can probably face the future easier. Those with little or no previous dating experience are the ones most likely to suffer serious hurt. The latter person has the least confidence in his or her ability to attract another love.

Even if you manage to get over a broken engagement with a minimum of pain, there are still some questions to answer. "What will I do now?" comes first. Getting back into circulation takes time and effort. And you must decide whether you will date immediately or rest up for a while.

At any cost, avoid marriage on the rebound. These marriages have little chance of succeeding because they usually aren't based on long acquaintance and matched backgrounds, values, and maturity. The person who chooses this way out usually does so out of hurt and loneliness. It is a way to prove to one's self and others that somebody cares and wants him or her. Naturally, one's pride and self-confidence will hit rock bottom after a breakup, but marrying someone on the rebound will only intensify an already confused situation.

The best course to follow then is to S-L-O-W D-O-W-N! Feel free to rejoin your old crowd or to apply yourself to a few new and absorbing tasks. Reject the idea of throwing yourself into a mad frenzy of dates and parties or of getting even with your former love. Give yourself time to think things over, heal, and get the other person out of your mind. Put reminders of the past away. When you do begin dating again, date several persons rather than just one. This protects you from a steady relationship before you have had a chance to recover. (You don't want to have a relapse!)

Love has some brutal aspects to it. Breaking off is heartbreaking. In our romance-minded culture many love affairs do come to an untimely and unexpected end. If you are the victim and are hurting right now, you may have a hard time believing that within a short period of time you will recover and give dating another try,

but it will happen. Just give it a few weeks—or months.

Courtship From Your Parents' Point of View

No one cares more about your final choice of a marital partner than do your parents. In fact, whether you realize it or not, your parents have been going along with you on all your dates. Not literally, but figuratively. Your dating days take your parents back a few years to the days when they courted each other. They relive, if only for a few minutes, memories from their youth, and they feel young once again.

When you and your sweetheart dash off together, your parents' hearts and prayers follow you. Even though they lead busy lives, always at the back of their minds is you—your happiness, your safety, and your future. Even if your parents have gone to bed before you return at night, they sleep lightly. They rest peacefully only when they know you have returned safely.

Why do your parents act this way? Because they love you and care for you more than anyone else on earth. It was they who gave you life. You are their own flesh and blood—a part of them. They raised you from infancy, loved you, held you, cuddled you. They soothed your hurts and kissed your tears. You belong to them by virtue of a blood relationship that can never be broken. Long after you have married and are gone from home, there will still be bonds of love that tie you to your parents in innumerable ways.

Your parents also have a tremendous investment of time and money in you. By the time you graduate from high school, they will have devoted eighteen years of their lives to your upbringing. They have given some of the best years of their lives to caring for your needs. In addition to time, they have given unselfishly of their money to provide you with food, clothing, shelter, and many of the pleasures of life.

Your parents have been responsible for you a long time. Ever since you were born they have protected you from getting hurt. They look to your future in the same way. They don't want to see you get hurt in your choice of a life mate.

Your parents can also see things about your future that you can't see. They have faced some of the same problems you are facing now. They can also, because of their experience, foresee certain problems you might encounter in the future. Because of their special love and concern for you, they will probably point out certain pitfalls they want you to beware of.

Because your parents are not directly involved in your situation, they can be more realistic than you. They can get a broad overview of the total picture. To you, your future marriage may be mostly a matter of being in love. But your parents know that marriage must combine love *and* action. They may detect underlying attitudes that would keep you from having a happy marriage. They may try to get you to slow down and think things through calmly and rationally. You may wish to forge ahead, feeling that you know your own mind—you *know* you can make a go of it.

Your parents really do not wish to restrict your happiness, but they want to help you achieve lasting happiness. They sometimes hope to pass on to you insights and lessons they may have learned—the hard way. They hope to spare you future complications that they know will surely follow if you make the wrong choices now. It is only natural for your parents to want to derive pleasure from your marriage. They look forward to the possibility of grandchildren.

They also hope and dream that your conduct and your choices will be a credit to your family. What does this mean? Your parents hope that you have instilled enough values and standards so that as you set up a home of your own you will be a credit to them, the community, the church, and society. They hope you will choose a mate who will fit into the family, someone they can be proud of.

I can hear some of your arguments already: "I don't respect my parents. They have made a mess out of their lives, so why should they try to tell me what to do?" "Why should I listen to my parents? They tell me what not to do and turn around and do it themselves." "My parents don't even try to understand me. So why should I listen to them?"

Even under such conditions what would happen if you tried to listen to your parents? The Scriptures are very clear on this point. "'Honor [revere and respect as God's appointed representatives over you] your father and mother . . ., that it may be well with you and that you may live long on the earth" Ephesians 6:2, 3, R.S.V.).* In addition to the Bible's promise of a long and happy life, you would also probably witness tears of pure joy and pride on your parents' faces on your wedding day. They will whisper through their hugs and tears, "This is the happiest day of our lives. We couldn't be happier with the choice you have made. You have our richest blessings."

Contrast this picture with the sorrowful scenes you will likely encounter if you marry without your parents' approval. Think of the pain as you are torn in different directions by loyalty to your parents and love for your sweetheart.

The same holds true even if you have gone through a rebellious phase in which you have been reacting negatively to your parents' wishes. This will greatly affect your courtship and your marriage. The same forces that caused you to react negatively to your parents will cause you to treat your future in-laws in much the same manner. You may become involved in trying to enlist your fiancé(e) in the battle against your own parents, thus driving a wedge between them. If you have any unsolved conflicts at home now, do all within your power to solve them before you marry. Your parents and your future in-laws will play a bigger role in your married life than you can imagine now.

Your impending wedding marks a turning point in the lives of your parents, as well as in your own. If you are the first child in your family to marry, your parents are entering the launching phase of the family cycle. In a sense your approaching marriage is a bereavement to them. They are happy, of course, with your newfound joy. But they also realize you will soon leave home forever, and this knowledge leaves an empty void.

If you have been away to college, the way has been paved for your final departure. Nevertheless, until now the family ties have remained unbroken. Home has always been the place where you could come for vacations or when you were in need or in trouble. Now that you are about to get married, your parents realize that you will transfer your loyalty and dependence to another home. This is as it should be, but as a result life will never look the same again to your parents.

Their reaction to the impact of the wedding will depend somewhat on their personalities. If your mother has devoted the better part of a quarter of a century to you and you alone, the effect can be drastic, as her tears bear witness. Dads, too, feel deeply involved with a child they've nourished, enjoyed, and worried about for twenty years or more.

Your wedding will likely be the major social event in your parents' lives to date. See to it that they have some say, and take their wishes into consideration. The wedding may be yours, but they are your parents and care more about your future than anyone else on earth. If there is a conflict of opinion on how big the wedding should be, where it should be, who should be invited, et cetera, bend a little. Your parents have been looking forward to your wedding day longer than you have.

They may want to do certain things in a certain way in order to impress others. This may seem selfish and irrelevent to you. But if it means a great deal to your parents, try to meet them at least halfway in granting their wishes. Your parents want your wedding to be the most memorable occasion of your life, but they also want it to be attractive and memorable to others. Don't disregard their wishes and feelings. Hard feelings that begin here may never be completely overcome.

A friend of mine is a florist by trade. Can you imagine the plans and dreams she had for her own daughter's wedding as she carefully planned for the weddings of others? Can you also imagine her disappointment when her only daughter opted for a midnight elopement? Her only daughter . . . all those plans and dreams . . . a bitter disappointment.

Your parents care about you, your fiancé(e), and your wedding. Avoid doing anything at this point that would cause a rift between you. They want you to be happy, well-liked, successful. Your parents are well aware, through experience, that your choice of a life mate will play the primary role in your future happiness. Take time to look at the total picture from *their* point of view.

---

* From the Revised Standard Version of the Bible, copyrighted 1946, 1952 © 1971, 1973.

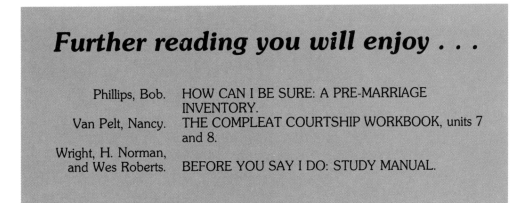

Further reading you will enjoy . . .

Phillips, Bob.	HOW CAN I BE SURE: A PRE-MARRIAGE INVENTORY.
Van Pelt, Nancy.	THE COMPLEAT COURTSHIP WORKBOOK, units 7 and 8.
Wright, H. Norman, and Wes Roberts.	BEFORE YOU SAY I DO: STUDY MANUAL.

Even if you have to
shorten your honeymoon a couple of days,
plan several very special treats
that you can remember and treasure
all your lives.

Chapter at a Glance

I. **Planning the Honeymoon**
   A. Should immediately follow the wedding
   B. Should last one to two weeks
   C. Plan a budget and then spend it
   D. Make it leisurely
   E. Get away from family and friends
   F. Include mutually enjoyable activities
   G. Total isolation is not ideal
   H. Should encourage spiritual growth

Everything You Always Wanted to Know About Honeymoons but Were Afraid to Ask

After the weeks of preparation, the round of showers, parties, presents, the wedding itself, and the reception line during which you have been kissed, squeezed, and patted until you feel like a sponge, you will be exhausted! At this point you will look forward to getting away from it all and being alone together to enjoy your honeymoon.

Whereas the wedding is a very public affair, the honeymoon is strictly private. It will provide your first real chance to be alone as a married couple. Nothing should divert your attention from each other while it dawns on you that you are really married at last.

The honeymoon provides a period of adjustment and transition from singleness to wedded life. According to popular thought, it is supposed to be a time of perfect bliss. In reality it can be one of the most strenuous periods of life. No matter how much you love each other or how great your excitement as you look forward to your honeymoon, it will take careful planning in order for it to be successful. Here are some pointers:

The honeymoon must follow the wedding immediately. It is an experience that must happen now or never. Whereas it is not absolutely necessary (but certainly preferable) to take a honeymoon, to postpone it would defeat the purpose and spoil

---

II. **Sexual Intimacy Is Central**
   A. Shift in thinking
   B. Mutual pleasure

III. **Learn Before the Honeymoon**
   A. Doing what comes naturally
   B. Good reading

IV. **Do Kegel Exercises**
   A. Muscle control
   B. Increased sexual pleasure

V. **Listen to Taped Instruction**
   A. Many available
   B. Suggestions

VI. **Purchase Surgical Jelly**
   A. Use of
   B. Reason for

VII. **Plan for Complete Privacy**
   A. Distractions
   B. Set the proper mood

VIII. **Proceed Slowly and Lovingly**
   A. Be sensitive to each other
   B. Is orgasm possible the first night?

IX. **Mutual Stimulation**

its uniqueness. In order to savor the intimacy of the newly created married unit, the honeymoon must be taken at once.

The honeymoon trip should last at least one to two weeks if you can possibly afford the time and money. Most people manage to find a week, at least, with the average honeymoon running about nine days. For a couple to marry over the weekend, move into a new apartment, and return to regular duties by Monday morning is entirely impractical. It does not allow the time needed to bask in the joy of each other's love.

Plan your honeymoon budget, and then spend it joyfully. This is probably going to be the last time you will be this carefree. Even if you have to shorten your honeymoon a couple of days, plan several very special treats that you can remember and treasure all your lives.

Plan a leisurely honeymoon. The most unsuccessful honeymoon would be one in which a couple planned a week to travel across several States, cramming in enough activity and sightseeing to last for five years! Instead plan only a short trip for the first night, and have a special dinner together. During the excitement of your wedding day, you probably will eat little and your blood sugar level may reach an all-time low. A leisurely dinner together before returning to your room will calm your nerves and provide some much-needed nourishment.

The honeymoon should be enjoyed away from family and friends. Trying to honeymoon in the home of parents or relatives would hardly allow the complete freedom that a couple need to get to know each other as man and wife. Parents sometimes encourage a couple to stay one night with grandma and grandpa, and another with cousin Matilda, et cetera. They do this because the honeymoon destination is often published in a newspaper account of the wedding. It therefore becomes a means of social status, and parents often try to pressure young people into making a trip that is worthy of public notice. Forget it!

Honeymoon plans should include activities you both enjoy. If you want big-city life with fancy restaurants and nightlife, spend it that way. If you are both nature lovers and enjoy camping, hiking, and fishing, then find a country hideaway. The important consideration is a location that allows you to participate in activities you both enjoy and that gives you time to be yourselves and relax. Avoid locations and activities where there are schedules, rising bells, or heavy commitments.

Plan time and opportunity to be with other people when and if you feel like it. Prior to marriage all a couple can think about is being alone every moment. Experience has shown that isolated honeymoons are more than most couples can take. Many hotels and resorts cater to honeymooning couples by offering lengthy meal periods and a variety of social and physical activities from which a couple might choose. Being with others and participating in group activities often eliminates stress during the honeymoon. A couple need time alone, but they also need occasions to interact with others.

The honeymoon should include a time for spiritual growth and development. Take time for Bible study and prayer together. Begin the practice now and establish it as a regular habit in your family. Perhaps you have already formed such a habit, so that no awkwardness exists now. One excellent resource to read aloud together during the honeymoon is the book of Proverbs. Search out all verses dealing with communication for the emotional life. Another is the Song of Solomon with its beautiful descriptions of physical love.

Sexual Intimacy

Central to the honeymoon experience is sexual intimacy. Your first intercourse will represent the consummation of your marriage. The relaxed atmosphere of your honeymoon will allow you to indulge your sex desires freely and with flexibility. For many couples the honeymoon represents a peak in sexual activity.

Now is the time when you make the transition to accepting sexual intercourse as a part of your total life together. For some persons, especially for the bride, this involves a shift in their thinking from the restraints of chastity to uninhibited married sex. This may take a little time and a patient husband. An emotionally mature woman should be able to readjust her attitude of self-protection prior to marriage to one of enthusiastic sharing after marriage.

A thoughtful groom will attempt to give first consideration to the satisfaction of his new bride rather than rapidly attempting to satisfy his own desires. Any male who learns this early in marriage will find his own enjoyment greatly increased. He must think of sex as a mutually shared and enjoyed experience rather than only a self-oriented experience.

Several other ingredients are necessary for you to enjoy the sexual side of the honeymoon to the fullest.

Learn as much as you can before your honeymoon. A couple need to study the subject of sexual fulfillment seriously just prior to marriage. Doing what comes naturally after marriage just isn't enough preparation. The lovemaking experience is an art, and it is *learned*, not innate. It is unrealistic to assume that two totally inexperienced young persons can approach the marriage bed on their wedding night and achieve sexual satisfaction with little or no effort or even by hoping or praying for it.

It would be helpful for a couple to read Chapter 8, "Sexually Fulfill Your Mate," in

"Because they're too young to cross the street by themselves, we'll have to go with them on their honeymoon."

my book *To Have and to Hold.* Chapter 4, on "Sex Education" in Tim and Beverly LaHaye's book *The Act of Marriage* should be read prior to marriage, along with Herbert Miles' book *Sexual Understanding Before Marriage.* Both bride and groom should study this material separately before marriage and in more detail with discussion after marriage. *The Act of Marriage* should be read on the honeymoon or shortly after in its entirety, as well as Ed and Gaye Wheat's book *Intended for Pleasure.* I often recommend that couples read aloud *The Act of Marriage,* because this greatly increases communication and understanding between couples on sexual topics.

At least six weeks prior to the wedding the bride should begin practicing the Kegel exercises as outlined in To Have and to Hold, *pages* 158, 159. This program will teach her muscle control that will help increase her sexual feelings during lovemaking. It will also enable her to provide a means of pleasuring her husband beyond his fondest dreams. It will also assist the couple in learning to achieve simultaneous orgasm. The groom might also want to practice the Kegel exercises. Recent information shows that it might help in learning to control premature ejaculation.

Approximately two weeks before the date of the wedding each should listen to "The Compleat Marriage Tapes" *(numbers 8 and 9) and to Ed Wheat's tape titled "Sex Technique and Sex Problems in Marriage."* Many counselors and pastors make these tapes available. You can purchase them at a Christian bookstore. Since the most teachable time in marriage is the first six weeks after marriage, I highly recommend that you take these tapes along on your honeymoon and listen to them again when each has become aware of the specific needs of the other.

Purchase surgical jelly from the drugstore beforehand for use the first night or two. Most brides cannot provide sufficient natural vaginal lubrication during their honeymoon experience. The possibility of pain can be eliminated by having surgical jelly handy for use at the proper time. Once she learns to relax completely, her natural lubrication will take over. It is also wise to have a small towel nearby that can absorb the secretions left after intercourse.

Plan for complete privacy without interruption. This may not seem as important to the husband as it is to the new bride. Women are much more prone to be distracted by noises, lights, and sounds in the night. Take necessary precautions beforehand to ensure that you will not be accidentally interrupted. A thoughtful husband may even take time to see that such things as flowers, candles, music, and soft light are available to further romance his bride. A husband who treats his wife as someone very special will usually find her responding to his expressions of love.

Proceed slowly and lovingly. The couple must become very sensitive to each other's needs at this point. He may wish to take her clothes right off her body and get on with it at long last! However, she may have romantic notions about making a grand entrance in a filmy negligee purchased especially for this occasion. Another couple may wish to lovingly and lingeringly undress each other. If you can discuss your feelings and wishes beforehand, you will be able to work it out to each other's satisfaction.

Some experts recommend that couples do not attempt intercourse the first night. They suggest instead that a couple carefully experiment and lovingly explore each other's bodies, all the while expressing love for each other. This allows time for each to get to know and understand the wants and wishes of the other without feeling pushed into intercourse the first night. It may not sound like much fun, but it can be a great experience that can pay off later on.

Research indicates that nine out of ten brides do not experience orgasm during the first intercourse. Unless a couple is armed with this information, both may feel they have failed miserably! When it is understood that intercourse can be an immensely enjoyable experience even when she does not experience climax, it will take the pressure off performance and allow them both to savor the experience of intimacy that is so important to a woman.

Naturally, the couple will work toward achieving sexual satisfaction for both partners, but they must realize that in a large majority of cases it will take time, study, experimentation, and open communication before the new bride reaches her maximum level of sexual responsiveness.

Some experts recommend that in order to promote sexual learning and understanding, sometime during the honeymoon the couple should bring each other to orgasm by hand. This will provide an opportunity for each to understand the other's physiological functioning during lovemaking. Carry out this exercise in a lighted room, free from all interruption. Some may object to this practice. But remember, the new couple is beginning a lifetime commitment in which sexual relations will play a permanent and prominent role for as many as fifty or sixty years. The more they learn and understand about each other during the early months of marriage, the more pleasure they will derive from it in the years to come. Learning by doing increases the likelihood of a better sexual relationship.

Dr. Herbert Miles, a well-known sex authority, suggests that sexual adjustment occurs in three stages: first, manual orgasm; second, orgasm in intercourse; and third, orgasms together or close together in intercourse. This suggests, then, that it is unwise for couples to bypass the first two levels and skip on to the third stage. It is better to slow down and make sure you have the first two levels mastered.

In a survey conducted by Dr. Miles on the length of time needed by Christian couples for sexual adjustment, 78 percent reported adjusting within a week, 12 percent took two months, and 6 percent adjusted only after 30 months. After being married six months to a year, 96 percent of the women who had adjusted sexually experienced orgasm all or most of the time. During this same period 41 percent of the couples indicated that they experienced simultaneous orgasms all or most of the time, and 38 percent said they did some of the time.

This rate of adjustment is higher than the rate of adjustment in other studies conducted on non-Christian groups. Perhaps it gives further credence to the benefits of Christian living. All participants had received detailed premarital counseling and had two to four years of college education, factors that contribute to success. Ninety-one percent had "discussed frankly together personal attitudes and rather complete details about sex" one month before marriage.[1]

A successful sex life will not come automatically. It does not happen overnight. You should look on sexual intercourse as an experimental, explorative adventure that the two of you will take over the next few years. You can achieve degrees of success in your sex life just as you can achieve degrees of success in your communication. Constantly search for new ways of delighting each other as you bask in your mutual love.

---

[1] Herbert J. Miles, *Sexual Happiness in Marriage* (Grand Rapids: Zondervan, 1967), p. 77.

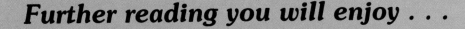

Further reading you will enjoy . . .

Miles, Herbert J.   SEXUAL UNDERSTANDING BEFORE MARRIAGE.
Van Pelt, Nancy.   TO HAVE AND TO HOLD, chapter 8.

After every wedding comes a marriage. Most couples find that within a few days after the honeymoon, the return to reality hits swift and deep.

Chapter at a Glance

And Now the Honeymoon Is Over— The First Year of Marriage

Harry and I met at church. He was in the Army, and I thought he was the most handsome man I'd ever seen, so my mother and I invited him home for dinner. Our family lived in a town that boasted Army, Navy, and Marine bases, and we were always prepared to do our patriotic duty! (My father used to mutter that he'd have to feed half of the armed services before he would get me married off.) On our first date Harry and I went to an air show, where we threw dimes onto glassware. We won a pair of green vases, which we jokingly said we would use in our house when we married and went as missionaries overseas.

As we dated, we fell more and more in love. Eventually Harry popped The Question, and wedding fever really set in. You would have thought I was bride-of-the-year! The wedding took place in the home of my parents. Even though it was a home wedding, it was lovely. My parents' house overlooked the bay, and it was picturesque and romantic. It was a perfect New Year's Day. Everyone shared in the holiday mood.

The organist struck the thrilling notes of the "Bridal Chorus" from *Lohengrin,* and on my father's arm I walked down the aisle that had been cleared through the one hundred chairs we had brought in to

---

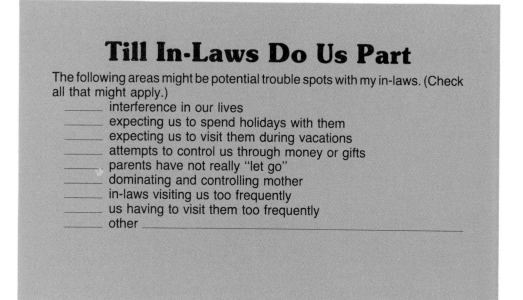

Till In-Laws Do Us Part

The following areas might be potential trouble spots with my in-laws. (Check all that might apply.)

_____ interference in our lives
_____ expecting us to spend holidays with them
_____ expecting us to visit them during vacations
_____ attempts to control us through money or gifts
_____ parents have not really "let go"
_____ dominating and controlling mother
_____ in-laws visiting us too frequently
_____ us having to visit them too frequently
_____ other _____

accommodate the guests. Although the beautiful little flower girl began to cry and would not scatter her rose petals or go up front, we had a storybook wedding. The ceremony was perfect. The setting was perfect. The day was perfect. And certainly two perfect persons were being united in love. But—after every wedding comes a marriage.

Reality Sets In

Most couples find that within a few days after the honeymoon, the turn to reality hits swift and deep. Yes, they feel elated over the excitement of settling into their first home, but they must also be prepared for the disillusionment that will surely follow—a letdown from the Cloud Nine of bliss, glamour, and all-absorbing interest they have had in each other. Thus originated the expression, "The honeymoon is over."

Probably the groom suffers from more severe symptoms of disillusionment than does the bride. Grooms tend to resent their loss of freedom, their new household obligations, and their financial worries. But brides feel let down as their new husbands begin to take them for granted. The masks that each may have worn prior to marriage

soon drop away. The put-ons gradually disappear, and the real self of moods and temper appears.

The first year is usually the rockiest in most marriages. In Old Testament times a newly married man could not be drafted into the army or given any other responsibilities during this adjustment period. For one full year he was free to stay at home with his wife. Imagine the luxury of one year to adjust to each other! I wonder what they did with their time after the novelty of the first three weeks wore off?

During the first twelve months, a couple must face the most problems but with the least experience. To be truthful, the future of the marriage depends on the adjustment that takes place during the first year. And the most teachable time of your marriage will be the first six weeks following the wedding. Gradually we learn that we must share our partner—that we cannot have 100 percent of his or her interest, affection, time, or attention. Employer, parents, friends, and relatives all will make certain demands.

Also during this disillusionment phase, the young bride may be shocked to find that her usually well-groomed husband wakes up with bad breath and a scratchy beard. He may find her habits of blanket-robbing and teeth-grinding real turnoffs. Other newlyweds are shocked to find out the hard way just how much time, effort, and money it takes to maintain a place to live. Whereas most couples are realistic enough to understand that maintaining a house takes time, they fail to recognize *how much time and effort* it takes to shop, cook, do the weekly wash, put clothes away, make beds, vacuum, dust, keep up with yard and car repairs, mop floors, take out garbage, clear clogged toilets, scour bathtubs, and scrub off caked-on grease.

Most likely you will encounter many more surprises than I have listed. What saves us from despair is that we all tend to daydream of happiness rather than drudgery. If we imagined all the routineness of marriage, none of us would ever marry! When it comes to marriage, we all err on the side of optimism. Hurrah for love!

The fact that 26.5 percent of all divorces are granted to couples married two years or less and that 51.3 percent of divorces occur before five years of marriage proves that disillusionment sets in early, hard, and fast. Since most couples live separately for a number of months prior to the filing and hearing of the case, it is reasonable to assume that many couples run into big trouble during the very early stages of marriage and that the pattern of disharmony persists.

However, once you get a little experience under your belt, you will realize that your marriage will survive even if you have some disagreements. You will also learn that some arguments are inevitable. You can still be friends and lovers although you don't agree on every issue. You will learn, too, that even if you can't solve every problem you encounter it does not signal the end of your marriage. At this point you can become less anxious about annoyances that pop up and realize that this happens even in the best of relationships.

Each year you spend together will greatly increase your chances for remaining happily married. By the time you reach your fifth anniversary, the possibility of divorce will decrease year by year.

What Makes Couples Happy?

A Chinese proverb states that when a newly married couple retires to the bridal chamber, whichever one sits on the bed first will be dominated by the other for all the years of their marriage! This, of course, springs from superstition, but we can gleen a grain of truth from it. Marriage counselors recognize that patterns of behavior established during the early portion of a couple's life together will affect their later years. In most cases it can readily be stated that the future happiness of the marriage is decided during the first year of married life.

It is difficult to isolate the factors that make couples happy. But generally speaking, how you react to your mate and how your mate reacts to you will largely determine your happiness level. Specifically, your reactions to each other in three basic areas are the most important: (1) your expectations for the future, (2) your pattern of communication, and (3) how the two of you will make decisions and settle disagreements.

Your reactions in these three areas have developed out of your total life experience dating back to early childhood. They have been derived from your parents and other family members. The differences you will encounter in expectations, communication, and decision-making will underlie most of the conflicts you and your mate will have. These differences must be identified, understood, dealt with openly, and worked through if your relationship is to become all you want it to be.

Expectations. It is vitally important for you to clarify your expectations during the early weeks of marriage. How you will get along thereafter is determined by how well you have understood these expectations and agreed upon them in advance. When you and your mate agree, you can each build confidently for the future, one doing one job and the other doing another. In the end you will enjoy mutually satisfying results because of your joint efforts. But if you expect to build a rambling one-story home and your mate expects to build a massive two-story colonial mansion, you will soon recognize that you are working at cross-purposes. The result will not be a sound structure, and you will share no satisfaction in what you have been building.

The expectations you usually hold when you marry center on five basic areas: (1) how you want to be treated as a person; (2) your concept of how your mate wishes to be treated as a person; (3) what you believe your responsibilities and rights as a married person are; (4) what you perceive the responsibilities and rights of your partner are; and (5) what you expect from marriage in the long run.

Some young couples deny that they have such expectations. Or if they do hold such expectations, they believe they can quickly alter them to fit any situation that arises. But expectations cannot be changed quite that easily. They have accumulated over a lifetime. They have become an intimate part of you, and to change them would be an enormously difficult task. Your expectations are as much a part of you as breathing. Just as you are not usually aware of inhaling and exhaling, you probably do not realize how deeply your expectations for the future are embedded in you.

Although your expectations are deep-seated, they are not immovable. They can be altered or changed. Naturally, making these changes will be difficult. And the more changes that need to be made, the more difficult it will be. The marriage that requires the fewest changes in economic, social, personality, and religious needs is the most likely to succeed. The marriage requiring the most changes between persons of vastly different cultural backgrounds is the most likely to fail.

It only makes sense, then, to clarify all your expectations *prior to* marriage, discussing them openly and honestly. If they conflict, you will need to discover a process by which you can alter, accept, or discard them. The position that some often take at this point—There is only one way to do things: *my way*—must be dropped. You must come to the realization that there are several ways to accomplish any given task.

Obviously, the more clarification of expectations that takes place prior to marriage, the less clarification will be needed after marriage. However, it is unlikely that any couple—try as they may to anticipate all their unrealistic expectations and preconceived ideas about roles, marriage, children, finances, personality, sex, and the future—will be able to forsee them all. Many adjustments will still follow marriage. But this is what marriage is all about: taking two different family systems of thinking, feeling, and behaving, and striving to combine them into one harmonious relationship.

Communication. If you and your partner want to learn how to get along well with each other, you must develop a system of communication, so that each of you knows and understands how the other feels about each issue.

Since I have already written an entire chapter on "How to Communicate With Your Mate" (See *To Have and to Hold,* chapter 5) I will not go into detail on the various methods of communication. But every newly married couple should understand certain factors.

Ideally, husband and wife should be able to discuss every subject of interest or concern to them. But couples quickly learn that certain subjects create fear, anxiety, doubt, or anger. However, the fewer subjects you put outside the bounds of discussion, the fuller and more satisfying your communication will be. (I assume that you will not bring up certain topics at inappropriate times for discussion.) But if a large number of subjects cause a major war when brought up, your communication will prove less satisfying.

When emotions are brought out for discussion, they can be analyzed and dealt with for what they are—feelings. Feelings are not bad. They are transient in nature and should never be a reason for shame. Everyone has feelings. We wouldn't be human without them. The real question is: Are these feelings appropriate to express now? Only clear communication between husband and wife can answer that question.

Here are some guidelines to help you

express your feelings properly:

1. Speak without anger or hostility. Lower your voice level rather than raise it. Learn to develop a pleasant tone of voice.

2. Be clear and specific. Try to think as you speak, and state clearly what you mean. Speaking clearly and specifically solves the problem of "muddled communication."

3. Be positive. This means no faultfinding, blaming, judging, name-calling, and other negative behavior. Be more appreciative.

4. Be courteous and respectful of your mate's opinion. You can do this even when you don't agree. Be as concerned for your mate's opinion as you are for your own.

5. Be sensitive to the needs and feelings of your mate. If your mate hurts, you can understand that hurt and even hurt too. Tune into feelings of anxiety and need.

Now some guidelines to help you become a better listener:

1. Act interested in your partner. Act as if nothing else in the world matters except hearing your partner out. Maintain good

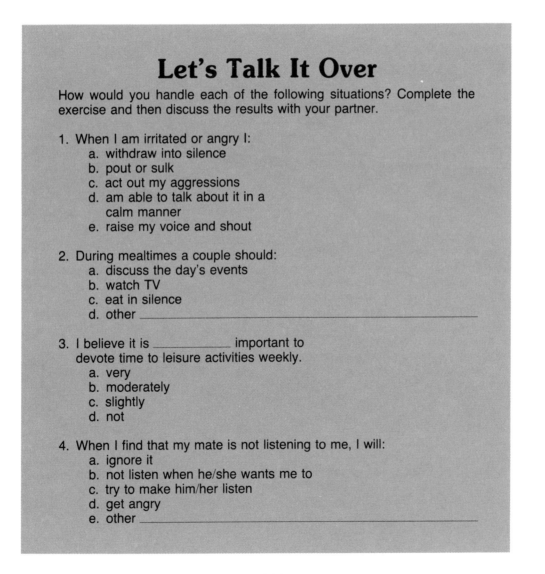

Let's Talk It Over

How would you handle each of the following situations? Complete the exercise and then discuss the results with your partner.

1. When I am irritated or angry I:
   a. withdraw into silence
   b. pout or sulk
   c. act out my aggressions
   d. am able to talk about it in a calm manner
   e. raise my voice and shout

2. During mealtimes a couple should:
   a. discuss the day's events
   b. watch TV
   c. eat in silence
   d. other _____

3. I believe it is _____ important to devote time to leisure activities weekly.
   a. very
   b. moderately
   c. slightly
   d. not

4. When I find that my mate is not listening to me, I will:
   a. ignore it
   b. not listen when he/she wants me to
   c. try to make him/her listen
   d. get angry
   e. other _____

eye contact, and respond with a smile or a nod of your head from time to time.

2. While listening use appropriate phrases to show agreement, interest, and understanding. Show your partner that you understand the ideas presented.

3. Ask well-phrased questions. This shows interest and encourages the speaker.

4. Listen a little longer. Just when you think you are through listening, listen thirty seconds longer.

A serious hindrance to developing good communication is that illuminated annoyance known as the television set. It is not my purpose to downgrade all television programming, but few people have the discipline necessary to select only the finest programs and then turn off the set. I highly recommend that all newly married couples refrain from getting a TV set during their first year of marriage. Television will rob you of many hours you could spend together, sharing and communicating with each other. When this happens, something is lost from your relationship. It is essential, then, that couples knit themselves together during the all-important first year to form an inseparable bond of intimacy through good communication.

Reaching Decisions and Settling Disagreements. Prior to marriage did you picture you and your mate bickering, arguing, or engaging in outright put-downs against each other? You may have seen your parents do this, but you probably told yourself that when you get married you would never do that to your mate. And the younger you are, the more likely you expect to manage every problem of daily life cheerfully and graciously. You believe that love can find a solution to every problem of life.

However, as you and your mate settle into the routine of married life during the first weeks and months of marriage, you will constantly have to make decisions concerning your daily routines, your roles, and your major goals. Every time you make a decision concerning one of these items, you are building the ability to make decisions for the future. You are also determining a future pattern for your marriage. In other words, when you encounter this decision again, it will not be necessary for you to proceed through the usual negotiations. You will tend to rely on the decision previously made.

One more question remains unanswered: How will the decision be reached? Will he reach a decision first and then try to win her to his way of thinking, or vice versa? Will she always have to give in to him? How much will winning and losing be emphasized as the decision is being reached?

Newlyweds are sometimes shocked to learn that it is absolutely basic to their relationship to air their feelings *aloud* as they come to a decision. Unless they each verbalize so they each can listen and begin to understand the other's point of view, they will never understand the underlying feelings about why they are disagreeing.

It is not the fact that you have disagreements that is important, *but the pattern you establish during the early weeks and months for handling them!* If each of you develops the habit of respectfully listening while your partner clarifies his point of view, and if you attempt to negotiate toward a compromise that will most closely meet the needs of both, you are well on your way to enjoying a need-meeting relationship.

Some points to remember in decision-making:

1. Be willing to discuss any problems. This includes every aspect of your relationship, whether it be large or small. Learn to express your feelings in a calm manner, with respect, and without offending the other.

2. Try to resolve differences without making one person "right" and the other "wrong." Few problems are absolutely black or white. Much might be said for your point of view, but just as much might also be said for your partner's perspective. Furthermore, if you are right, this automatically implies that your partner is wrong. Being right or wrong also means that there is no way out of an argument except to win or lose, and a real power struggle can ensue. Avoid an arbitrary stance on any issue.

3. Avoid angry outbursts. "Blowing your top" rarely produces positive results. Anger

almost always arises when we feel our self-worth is being threatened. Instead of giving way to angry feelings, how much better to recognize why you are angry and seek instead to discover why you feel you must defend yourself so strongly. And if you get an angry response from your mate, you can be sure that you have hurt his or her feelings or attacked his or her self-worth in some way. If you could reconstruct the conversation and analyze what you said that caused the hurt, you might be able to uncover hidden anxieties and concerns of which your partner may not even be aware.

Other factors need to be considered in decision-making. What are the real issues involved? If you differ on what to watch on TV, is it just a conflict over which show to watch or is a power struggle going on? How will your decision affect your basic goals? Even a couple who agree on basic goals may disagree on how to achieve them. Who will be most affected by the decision? If a wife feels that jogging is essential to her health and figure and wishes to rise early to do so but the husband resents being wakened and feels that his sleep is more important, it will be necessary to determine who is most affected by her jogging routine. Who has to live with the decision? If a couple plans to buy a new stove, it may come out of the husband's earnings, but usually it is the wife who must use it every day.

One final point. Regardless of how much you may disagree with your partner or how different your experience is, your mate's viewpoint will have some positive angles. The decision may have been achieved through sound reasoning or from a strictly emotional response, but you should not dismiss your mate's perspective from your mind. You need not agree with it, but you should seek, *with respect,* to understand why your partner feels that way about the matter.

You will want to establish a mutually satisfying method of constructively solving problems early in your relationship. In addition to these broad principles, several specific areas of potential conflict need discussion.

The In-law Crisis

In one study more than 500 university student couples in their first years of marriage ranked in-law relationships at the top of a list of difficult areas of adjustment. Comparison findings show that in-law disagreements affect the early years of marriage more than any other problem.

If the in-law crisis doesn't hit before the wedding, it is likely to reach its peak soon after. Parents have a hard time letting go of one whom they have cared for so long. One comedienne said, "When my daughter married, I made a vow that I'd let her live her own life, even if I had to show her how to do it."

Particularly during the early weeks and months of marriage, both sets of parents will be looking over the new addition to the family and judging that person by their own standards. But all studies show that the husband's mother will most likely pose the biggest problem. The husband's mother probably identifies more closely with the wife's role. Therefore, she is likely to be very critical of how another woman is performing a role that she has successfully filled for years. In some traditional societies, a son-in-law is not allowed to look his mother-in-law in the face or speak to her. Some cultures will not let the bride's mother attend the wedding. These people have learned the importance of keeping certain relatives at a distance.

1. Establish your own home after marriage. Do not live with your parents even temporarily. It is impossible to develop

213

"Do you believe in planned parenthood?" "Yup. Sure wish I could've planned mine."

intimacy in someone else's home, even if you have the whole upstairs to yourselves and even if they promise to leave you alone. Living with parents gives them the opportunity to behave as though you aren't grown up enough to know what's good for you. And you will feel restricted in many areas. Your sex life may be curtailed. He may be reluctant to show physical affection during the day, and she may be afraid of making noise at night. Intimacy cannot be developed under these circumstances.

2. Work at establishing a good relationship with your in-laws. In other words,

make friends with them. A new husband might send a bouquet of flowers to his mother-in-law on her birthday. A daughter-in-law would remember her new mother-in-law with a thoughtful gift on Mother's Day. On occasion, invite them to dinner or take them out to dinner. It might cost a little, but the rewards can be great. If you treat your in-laws like friends, you will find them treating you the same way.

3. Learn to accept your in-laws as they are. You might like to make a few changes in them, but they would probably like to make a few changes in you, too. Give them

214

time to find new interests in life and to adjust to you and the loss of their child.

Never, never, never . . .

discuss the faults of your mate with your parents.

quote your family or hold them up as models to your mate.

give advice to your in-laws unless they ask for it.

make a trip to your in-laws on your vacation.

threaten to (or actually do) "go home to Mama."

Treat your in-laws with the same consideration you show all your friends. When you visit them, make the visit short. If they give advice, do just as you would if your best friend gave you advice. Accept it graciously. If it is right for you, use it; if it isn't, ignore it.

Enter marriage with a positive attitude toward your in-laws. Look for the good in them rather than the bad. Determine to enjoy your new family. And remember: It takes at least two people to create an in-law problem. No one person is ever entirely to blame.

The Blessed (?) Event

Many couples expect to have children. Doesn't everyone? So they let nature take its course and give little thought to whether they should or should not become parents. Some couples want children in order to have a stake in the future. Others want children so they can relive their lives through them. Still others have a strong desire for self-perpetuation or feel that a home is not complete without children.

The truth is that the whole idea of having babies has been overromanticized. And this romantic picture is reinforced by relatives and friends who respond to the news of pregnancy with the same enthusiasm that they do news of a wedding. Many showers and gifts follow, but after the blessed event, most young people find themselves ill-prepared to cope with the demands of parenthood. In one study 83 percent of the couples reported "extensive" or "severe" crises in adjusting to the changes that occur with the arrival of the first child. The items

named most frequently were: loss of sleep, exhaustion, guilt at not being "better" parents, long hours, and a seven-day week in caring for a baby.

In addition, fathers complain about a decrease in sexual response from their wives, increased financial pressure, worry about a possible second pregnancy occurring too soon, and a general disenchantment with the reality of being a parent. Mothers noted that their homes were always a mess and the work never seemed to be done. They also worried about their figures. Both parents complained of feeling tied down. They missed the freedom and romance of the honeymoon stage of marriage.

But training children is listed as the biggest problem that parents face. Fathers tend to accuse mothers of pampering and spoiling the baby. Mothers complain that their husbands are too strict or harsh with the children and countermand what they say. It is now that all the differences in expectations become evident. Engaged couples are highly optimistic about their ability to cope with such matters. But when two young people enter marriage, each comes with a vast array of hearsay, little concrete information, and no practical experience.

Children are a joy, a "heritage of the Lord." Couples who want children and are emotionally and financially able to support them should be encouraged to have them. But it is important that they face the reality of parenthood. "Having a baby" sounds like such fun! But babies grow up to be challenging 2-year-olds, disrespectful 7-year-olds, sloppy 12-year-olds, and rebellious 15-year-olds.

The Family Plan

It is God's plan that the husband and wife have children, but He didn't make it so a couple *must* have children. Each couple needs to decide whether or not to bring children into the world. This is where "the family plan" comes in. Family planning simply means that a couple will choose the number of children they want, when they want them, and the intervals at which they want them. It means parenthood by choice, rather than by chance.

Some factors to consider include: (1) the length of time a newly wedded couple needs for adjustment to each other before assuming the responsibilities of parenthood (findings show that the presence of a child during the first two years of marriage doubles the likelihood of divorce); (2) the couple's ability to care adequately for the physical, emotional, and spiritual needs of each child brought into the world; (3) the wife's health (most women do not reach full biological development until about age 23, and the best time for motherhood is the five-year period following full biological maturity; also pregnancy before full maturity is full of risks: a high death rate among babies, high death rate among young mothers, spontaneous abortions, stillbirths, and toxemia); (4) the effect that the fear of pregnancy may have on the full enjoyment of the sex relationship.

Each couple will have to decide which

Can Two Live Cheaper Than One?

Questions about money form an important part of married life, since most activities revolve around it. The expectations you have on how money should be spent may differ widely from the expectations your partner has. Therefore the possibility for disagreement is great. Circle the response that most closely signifies your feelings in the following statements. Then compare your responses with your partner's.

1. I believe that after the birth of children the wife should _____ work outside the home.
    a. never
    b. sometimes
    c. always
    d. other _____

2. My attitude toward debt, credit cards, borrowing money, and time payments is:
    a. I like them and use them frequently.
    b. I use them only when necessary.
    c. I avoid them like the plague.
    d. They're OK as long as they don't control you.
    e. Other _____

3. The checkbook will be handled and balanced by:
    a. him
    b. her
    c. both

4. Living on a budget is _____ important.
    a. very
    b. moderately
    c. slightly
    d. not

method of contraception is best for them in order to plan and space pregnancies. There is no perfect method for every couple. Some couples change methods along with the circumstances in their lives.

In choosing a method you will want to consider its effectiveness, availability and cost, convenience, and your personal preferences. Any method a couple finds unpleasant, uncomfortable, or embarrassing will not be right for them.

Methods of birth control are listed here in order of their effectiveness (as listed by the Federal Food and Drug Administration). Also presented are the number of unplanned pregnancies among every 1,000 users.

The Pill. The Pill, when taken as directed, is the most effective contraceptive known. It is a powerful drug and should be taken only by prescription under medical supervision. When it is taken as prescribed, without omitting a single dose, there should be no more than one unplanned pregnancy per year in 1,000 women using the Pill. Because of its effectiveness and convenience, many physicians recommend the Pill for newlyweds. The bride should consult her family physician at least two months prior to the wedding and follow the advice given.

The Condom, With Cream or Foam. The condom, when used alone, fails at the rate of 26 pregnancies per 1,000 couples per year. But when combined with a contraceptive cream or foam, the rate is less than 10 per 1,000 women per year. The condom (or "rubber" as it is commonly called) is readily available without prescription, has no side effects, is easy to use, and places the responsibility for birth control on the husband rather than on the wife. The probability of pregnancy owing to a defective condom is less than one in 3 million chances.

Intrauterine Devices (IUDs). The rate of failure for the IUD is somewhere between 15 and 30 pregnancies per 1,000 women per year during the first year of use. The failure rate decreases thereafter. The IUD is a soft, flexible plastic loop or irregularly shaped disc that a physician inserts into the

cervical canal. The IUD should be checked about once a week by the user to be certain it is in its proper place. Some cramps, backache, heavier menstrual flow, or spotting between periods may result from the IUD, but 90 percent of the women who use it have no problems. It can easily be removed when pregnancy is desired.

The Diaphragm. The diaphragm is a strong, lightweight, flexible rubber cap that is inserted into the vagina to fit over the cervix like a dome-shaped lid. It prevents the sperm from entering the uterus but must be combined with a jelly, cream, or foam in order to be effective. It must also be fitted by a physician and inserted by the woman prior to intercourse. It should not be removed for at least six hours following intercourse. The failure rate is about 26 pregnancies per 1,000 users per year.

Vaginal Foams. Vaginal foam has been on the market for more than thirty years and allows about 26 pregnancies per 1,000 women. Foam products when placed in the vagina act on the sperm without harming the vaginal tissues. Foams, creams, and gels are available with an applicator that automatically measures the proper amount.

The Rhythm Method. The rhythm method is one of the oldest and least effective methods of birth control. It produces about 140 pregnancies per 1,000 women. The couple controls conception by abstaining from intercourse during the days just after ovulation. Ovulation most often occurs about the fourteenth day or two weeks prior to the beginning of the menstrual period for a woman with a regular twenty-eight-day cycle. However, because of the irregularity of many women's menstrual cycle, it is difficult to tell when ovulation occurs. To be on the safe side, it is recommended that other contraceptives be used one week before her period, during her period, and five days following her period.

Coitus Interruptus. If 1,000 couples used the coitus interruptus method, there would be 160 to 200 unplanned pregnancies during a year. With this method the male withdraws the penis from the vagina just prior to ejaculation. The semen is deposited outside the vagina rather than inside. Its disadvantages stem from the difficulty in controlling the time of ejaculation and the chance that sperm may seep from the penis prior to ejaculation. It also requires discipline and concentration in timing and therefore may decrease enjoyment for both husband and wife.

In addition to the previously mentioned methods, a woman may have her Fallopian tubes tied, both tubes removed, or the uterus and/or ovaries removed. Sterilization for the male—vasectomy—is also possible. This consists of blocking the ducts that lead from the testicles, where sperm are manufactured, to their point of exit. This is successful in 99 out of 100 cases and does not affect a man's sexual performance.

The aim of "the family plan," then, should be that each child should be joyfully wanted by responsible parents. Responsible parenthood cannot be achieved by "doing what comes naturally" or even by doing what your parents did. Each couple should attend a parenting class (preferably a Compleat Parent Workshop!) and read a book on the subject (preferably *Train Up a Child* by Review and Herald Publishing Association, 1984) prior to having children.

Whether you plan it that way or not, it is possible that when you marry you may have a baby within the first year. Are you ready to accept a baby if it should come— regardless of the plan you have? Do you have the discipline and maturity that caring for an infant requires?

Where Did All the Money Go?

Does there always seem to be too much month left at the end of your money? Money matters will play an important part in your married life. The way we use money signifies many things. Newlyweds may wish to tell their friends and relatives that they have a successful marriage. They believe the best way to do this is to show a well-furnished apartment in a good section of town. They may try to appear well-dressed and able to afford all the luxuries necessary to enjoy life.

But no young couple just starting out in life can afford all the articles that are advertised so alluringly—labor-saving appliances, high-powered cars, expensive furniture, television sets, stereo equipment, clothing, vacations, and so on. Therefore every young couple must choose the things that are most important to them. Because so much is offered and because your expectations of how money should be spent may differ widely, the possibility for disagreement is great.

Almost all couples who work out a successful financial agreement find that they must compromise in order to achieve a good working relationship in the area of finances. Both husband and wife should have responsibilities in handling the finances, but separate ones. Each must have an area of responsibility and be clear about what to do. A wife who is put on an allowance by her husband is being treated like a child. A husband who turns his paycheck over to his wife and expects her to handle everything has never grown up.

The division of responsibility that I consider to be the most effective and which I recommend particularly to newlyweds is to divide the financial decision-making into three parts.

First, there is the overall policy, which includes an agreement on financial goals for the future of the family. In this, both of you will participate equally. You will decide what you want six months from now, a year from now, five years from now. It also will include what you will need to do in order to achieve these goals.

You will have to agree on whose goals are most important. In other words, which comes first—the washing machine or the stereo? This is not as difficult as it might seem at first glance. It will not result in the disagreements you might imagine if—and it is a big *if*—you both try to reduce your selfishness and attempt to be a bit more giving and understanding.

Second, there are the day-to-day expenses—groceries, gasoline, and the dozen-and-one purchases that go into running a household. Such expenses should be built into an overall budget. A budget should be an avenue whereby you will plan together how your money will be spent. A budget will not in itself solve every problem of finances. It will still take wise buying practices, as well as wise planning.

Third, there are decisions that need to be made in order to implement long-range goals—for instance, how to save for furniture while financing a car. If you both try to tackle this one, it will probably bog down in endless discussions and conflicts. A plan of saving for long-range goals can be handled by either one who possesses the ability. Often it falls on the husband—not because he has any "right" to do this, but because many men have a better long-range view.

When a wife feels that she alone is stuck with planning vacations, setting up a budget, saving for college educations, selecting insurance programs, worrying about retirement funds, she begins to lose respect for a partner who is no longer an equal partner. A wife appreciates it when her husband takes the initiative in discussing financial planning of all kinds and clues her in. This makes her feel equal and prepared should anything happen to him.

When both partners assume their responsibilities, it should not be regarded as a masculine or feminine right. Each should attempt to serve the interests of the family unit, not just his or her own personal interests. Unless a couple can divide the responsibility for money management successfully, they will probably continue to jockey for first place in a power struggle. Control is at the heart of most marital squabbles over money, and control is just another word for selfishness. Therefore,

there needs to be one more rule.

Examine your own motives. Take a long, critical look at them before you react to disagreements over money. You may find that your motives are not too sensible. Recognize also that your expectations as to how money should be spent reflects your childhood programming, your insecurities, and your own interests. All of these probably differ from your mate's. You can learn to accept these differences and live with them without conflict. It's all up to you.

The Last Word

Can you be absolutely sure of a happy marriage? No, but if you have followed the suggestions in this book and have carefully studied the principles outlined in *To Have and to Hold* (published by Southern Publishing Association/Review and Herald Publishing Association, 1980), it will better your chances. I would like to end this book with four suggestions that could make the difference.

Make an absolute commitment to your marriage. Although right now you are positive you are marrying the right person, there is still some risk involved. However carefully you have checked out the other person, there are still things you do not know yet about your partner, about yourself, and about marriage. But the odds for a successful marriage will be heavily in your favor if, when you are married, you make an absolute commitment to yourself and to your mate for a permanent relationship.

Couples shift in and out of marriage today much like shoppers in a revolving door. But a firm commitment to each other and to the sacred vows that you have exchanged will keep you from following the path others are taking.

You have settled this in your mind through an uncompromising decision. When you are in the heat of an argument, you will not threaten divorce. Rather you will focus on solving problems, not extinguishing the marriage.

If serious trouble develops, seek help immediately. Although I do not wish to encourage young couples to run to a marriage counselor *every* time they have a misunderstanding, couples should seek help when they hit serious trouble. A couple should work together by themselves in overcoming difficulties *as long as they are*

satisfied they are making some progress. However, if despair begins to creep into their attitudes toward each other, it is time for outside help.

Howard F. Maxson, a licensed marriage-and-family counselor and personal friend of mine, recently told me: "For thirty-some years I have been a hospital chaplain and a part-time marriage counselor. For thirty-some years I have had a burden common to both roles. How often I have stood at the bedside of a patient painfully dying with cancer and thought: Oh, if only he had done something about the symptoms when they first appeared! How often I have sat with a couple painfully suffering from a dying marriage and thought: Oh, if only they had done something about the symptoms when they first appeared! A healthy marriage, like a healthy body, requires effort and learning to keep it so, a willingness to get periodic checkups, such as attending a Compleat Marriage Seminar, and a willingness to seek help when symptoms of marital illness appear."

Stay interested in each other—date your mate. Do not allow the routineness of life to swallow up your marriage. This isn't always easy to do when the responsibilities of life come at you faster than you can handle them. But in the midst of balancing the budget, raising a family, running a home, and earning a living, reserve some special occasions just for the two of you.

One couple I know go out once a week on what they call their "date night." They can't afford to go to a restaurant every week, but on these occasions she prepares a simple but festive dinner. He comes home and showers and dresses up. She wears a long dress of something slinky and feminine. It is the dressing up part of their date that makes it special. They dim the lights and dine by candlelight. Any talk about problems at work, leaky faucets, overdue bills, tires for the car, or whatever, is strictly forbidden.

Have Bible study and prayer together every day. Harry and I experienced numerous problems in our early married years. Even though we were not teenagers, we were young, naive, and unlearned in the disciplines of married life. We tried to work out our problems on our own, but we weren't doing too well.

Harry was training for, and finally entered, the ministry during this period of time when we were "rocking" along. We went to church faithfully, had family worship with the children, and did all the good things Christians are supposed to do. But things got no better. Had it not been for our faith at this point we could have thrown it all away, figuring that what we had together wasn't worth saving, that it might be better to go our separate ways and not torment each other any longer.

But the faith that we had been raised in as children held us and would not let us go. It became a stabilizing factor. Had it not been for our faith when the going got rough, we would have scrapped our marriage. Today we are stronger than ever in the Lord's love and in our love for each other, which has helped us to work through our difficulties.

You will get out of your marriage what you put into it. The problems you face together will not undermine your love *if* you develop an understanding kind of love for each other. But great as your potential is for having a happy marriage, you cannot achieve it without effort. A successful marriage requires courage, determination, humbleness, and, perhaps most of all, a vision of marriage as the most satisfying of all human relationships.

Where, then, does a successful marriage begin? Not at the wedding! Rather, it begins somewhere in an unending circle of living and giving and growing daily into the will of God for our lives. Welcome to the winner's circle!

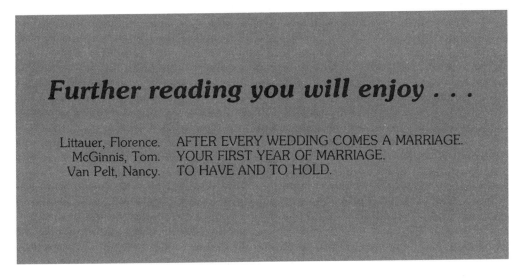

Further reading you will enjoy . . .

Littauer, Florence. AFTER EVERY WEDDING COMES A MARRIAGE.
McGinnis, Tom. YOUR FIRST YEAR OF MARRIAGE.
Van Pelt, Nancy. TO HAVE AND TO HOLD.

WELCOME TO

THE
LAST WORD
Courtship
is not the goal.
It is the living and giving,
the daily growing
into the will of God for
your life,
that makes for a winner,
my beloved friend.

THE WINNER'S CIRCLE

Family enrichment courses based on the concepts of—
We've Only Just Begun
To Have and to Hold
Train Up a Child
are available.

Thousands of persons have read these books and have awakened to the new possibilities in family living. There are several ways of taking advantage of this exceptional educational experience—right in your own area.

Courses are offered through churches, colleges, adult education centers, parent-teacher organizations, and special interest groups around the country and internationally. Seminars can also be arranged for conventions. Private home classes are available, as well as audiocassette tapes and a home study course for your convenience. Request more information from the publisher.

Bibliography

Avery, Curtis E., and Theodore B. Johannis, Jr. *Love and Marriage.* New York: Harcourt Brace Jovanovich, Inc.:1971.

Blood, Robert O. *Marriage,* 2d ed. New York: The Free Press, 1969.

Bowman, Henry A. *Marriage for Moderns,* 6th ed. New York: McGraw-Hill, 1970.

Burgess, Ernest W., and Paul Wallin. *Engagement and Marriage.* Chicago: J. B. Lippincott Co, 1953.

Butler, John. *Christian Ways to Date, Go Steady, and Break Up.* Cincinnati: Standard Publishing, 1978.

Cavan, Ruth, ed. *Marriage and Family in the Modern World.* New York: Thomas Y. Crowell Co., 1969.

Dobson, James. *What Wives Wish Their Husbands Knew About Women.* Wheaton, Ill.: Tyndale House Pub., 1975.

Duvall, Evelyn. *Why Wait Till Marriage?* New York: Association Press, 1968.

————. *Love and the Facts of Life.* New York: Association Press, 1963.

Fishbein, Morris, and Ernest W. Burgess, eds. *Successful Marriage.* Garden City: Doubleday, 1963.

Florio, Anthony. *Two to Get Ready.* Wheaton, Ill.: Victor, 1974.

Fryling, Robert and Alice. *A Handbook for Engaged Couples.* Downers Grove, Ill.: Inter-Varsity Press, 1977.

Guitar, Mary Anne, ed. *The Young Marriage.* Garden City, New York: Doubleday, 1968.

Hass, Aaron. *Teenage Sexuality.* New York: Macmillan Publishing Company, Inc., 1979.

Kelley, Robert K. *Courtship, Marriage, and the Family,* 2d ed. New York: Harcourt Brace Jovanovich, 1974.

Kent, Dan and Barbara. *About This Thing Called Dating.* Nashville: Convention Press, 1979.

Kirby, Scott. *Dating.* Grand Rapids: Baker Book House, 1979.

LaHaye, Tim and Beverly. *The Act of Marriage.* Grand Rapids: Zondervan, 1976.

Landers, Ann. *Ann Landers Talks to Teen-agers About Sex.* Greenwich, Conn.: Fawcett Publications, 1963,

Landis, Judson T., and Mary G. *Building a Successful Marriage,* 7th ed. Englewood Cliffs, New Jersey: Prentice Hall, 1977.

Landis, Paul H. *Making the Most of Marriage,* 3d ed. New York: Appleton-Century-Crofts, 1965.

Loeb, Robert H. *His and Hers: Dating Manners.* New York: Association Press, 1970.

Mace, David R. *The Christian Response to the Sexual Revolution.* Nashville: Abingdon Press, 1970.

————. *Getting Ready for Marriage.* Nashville: Abingdon Press, 1972.

————. *Success in Marriage.* Nashville: Abingdon, 1980.

Mazat, Alberta. *That Friday in Eden.* Mountain View, California: Pacific Press, 1981.

McDowell, Josh, and Paul Lewis. *Givers, Takers, and Other Kinds of Lovers.* Wheaton, Ill.: Tyndale House Pub., 1980.

McGinnis, Tom. *A Girl's Guide to Dating and Going Steady.* Garden City, New York: Doubleday, 1968.

————. *Your First Year of Marriage.* Garden City, New York: Doubleday, 1967.

Miles, Herbert J. *The Dating Game.* Grand Rapids: Zondervan, 1975.

————. *Sexual Happiness in Marriage.* Grand Rapids: Zondervan, 1967.

————. *Sexual Understanding Before Marriage.* Grand Rapids: Zondervan, 1971.

Naismith, Grace. *Private and Personal.* New York: David McKay Co., Inc., 1966.

Netherton, H. Eugene. *Boy Meets Girl.* 1035 Park Blvd., West Sacramento, California, 1975.

Nida, Clarence. *Before You Marry—For Men Only.* Chicago: Moody, 1977.

Petersen, J. Allan. *Two Become One.* Wheaton, Ill.: Tyndale House Pub., 1973.

Phillips, Bob. *How Can I Be Sure?: A Pre-marriage Inventory.* Irvin, California: Harvest House, 1978.

Roberts, Wes, and H. Norman Wright. *Before You Say "I Do."* Irvin, California: Harvest House, 1978.

Saxton, Lloyd. *The Individual, Marriage, and the Family,* 2d ed. Belmont, California: Wadsworth Pub. Co., 1972.

Shedd, Charlie W. *Letters to Karen.* New York: Avon, 1965.

————. *Letters to Philip.* Old Tappen, New Jersey: Fleming H. Revell, 1968.

————. *The Stork Is Dead.* Waco, Texas: Word Books, 1968.

Short, Ray E. *Sex, Love, or Infatuation: How Can I Really Know?* Minneapolis: Augsburg, 1978.

Stafford, Tim. *A Love Story.* Grand Rapids: Zondervan, 1977.

Trobisch, Walter. *I Loved a Girl.* New York: Harper and Row, 1975.

Van Pelt, Nancy L. *The Compleat Marriage.* Nashville: Southern Publishing, 1979.

————. *The Compleat Parent.* Nashville: Southern Publishing, 1976.

Wheat, Ed and Gaye. *Intended for Pleasure.* Old Tappen, New Jersey: Fleming H. Revell, 1977.

————. *Improving Your Self-Image.* Irvin, California: Harvest House, 1977.

Wright, Norman. *Premarital Counseling.* Chicago: Moody Press, 1977.

Wright, Norman, and Marvin Inmon. *Dating, Waiting, and Choosing a Mate.* Irvin, California: Harvest House, 1978.

Wright, Rusty, and Linda Raney Wright. *Dynamic Sex.* San Bernardino, California: Here's Life Publishers, 1979.

Art and Photo Credits

Illustrations
Tim Adams: 16, 24, 40, 70, 84, 102, 128, 154, 176, 198, 206.

Ronald Hester: 18, 21, 26, 31, 35, 45, 47, 50, 53, 54, 59, 62, 74, 78, 80, 86, 92, 94, 105, 106, 110, 113, 116, 121, 122, 130, 133, 136, 138, 142, 144, 148, 159, 163, 166, 178, 181, 184, 191, 192, 213, 219, 220, 223.

Photography
Four by Five: Front Cover, Back Cover, Endsheets, 68-69, 82-83, 126-127, 152-153.
Comstock: Back Cover.
David B. Sherwin: 22-23, 174-175, 204-205.
Meylan Thoresen: Front Cover, 100-101, 196-197.
Tom Radcliffe: 14-15, 38-39.

Scoring Instructions

Self-esteem evaluation from page 28.
TO OBTAIN YOUR SELF-ESTEEM INDEX: Add the individual scores of all EVEN NUMBERED statements. From this total subtract the sum of all ODD NUMBERED statements. This net score is your current self-esteem index, or SEI. The possible range of one's self-esteem index is from −75 to +75. Yours will fall somewhere in between. Do not be concerned with your SEI no matter how low, or even negative. Remember your self-esteem simply is what it is, the automatic product of your heritage and total life experience; and thus nothing to be ashamed or embarrassed about. It is important, however, that you be honest with yourself in order to obtain as valid a score as possible. For this score is a beginning reference point in gauging your progress in building self-esteem. Also remember, that no matter how low your present SEI may be, you can bring it up to any desired value by conscientious effort.

How good are you at making friends? from page 43.
Total the point value of each number circled. 50-60 points scored: You have friends because you show yourself as a friend to others. You are reliable, gracious, and unselfish—all marks of a good friend. 35-49 points scored: You are blessed with friends, but some are sticking with you in spite of yourself. Hold on to the friends you have and try to make one new friend each year. 20-34 points scored: You find yourself unable to make or hold friendships. Examine your life carefully, make necessary changes and you will find yourself worthy at last of knowing what it means to be a friend and have a friend.